City of Love and Revolution

City of Love

LAWRENCE ARONSEN

and Revolution

VANCOUVER IN THE SIXTIES

Vancouver
New Star Books
2010

New Star Books Ltd.
107 – 3477 Commercial Street
Vancouver, BC V5N 4E8   CANADA

1517 – 1574 Gulf Road
Point Roberts, WA 98281   USA

www.NewStarBooks.com
info@NewStarBooks.com

Copyright Lawrence Aronsen 2010. All rights reserved. No part of this work may be reproduced, stored in a retrieval system or transmitted, in any form or by any means, without the prior written consent of the publisher or a licence from the Canadian Copyright Licensing Agency (Access Copyright).

Publication of this work is made possible by grants from the Canada Council, the Department of Canadian Heritage, the Province of British Columbia, and the British Columbia Arts Council.

Cover illustration by Bob Masse
Cover design by Mutasis.com
Printed on 100% post-consumer recyled paper
Printed and bound in Canada by Gauvin Press
First printing, October 2010

LIBRARY AND ARCHIVES CANADA CATALOGUING IN PUBLICATION

Aronsen, Lawrence Robert
  City of love and revolution : Vancouver in the sixties / Lawrence Aronsen.

Includes bibliographical references.
ISBN 978-1-55420-048-1

  1. Vancouver (B.C.) — Social conditions — 20th century. 2. Vancouver (B.C.) — History — 20th century. 3. Vancouver (B.C.) — Social life and customs — 20th century. 4. Nineteen sixties. I. Title.
FC3847.4.A76 2010   971.1'3304   C2010-901741-2

CONTENTS

	vii	Acknowledgments
	3	Introduction: Images of a Hipper Era
Chapter 1	11	Hippies And Their Discontents
Chapter 2	33	Liberating Higher Education
Chapter 3	51	'The Sodom of the North'
Chapter 4	79	Getting Higher
Chapter 5	107	Taking It to the Streets
Chapter 6	135	'Peaceniks' and Protest
	167	Conclusion: Who Owns Sixties Vancouver?
	175	Notes
	191	Bibliography
	193	Index

ACKNOWLEDGMENTS

Several individuals and institutions provided invaluable assistance during the preparation of this book. Special Collections at UBC gave me access to the Vancouver Vietnam Action Committee document collection and the *Georgia Straight* picture collection. Special thanks are due to Weiyan Yan and to Ken Hildebrand of UBC Special Collections. The Vancouver Public Library was especially helpful with its extensive clippings files and newspaper indexes. The Faculty of Arts, University of Alberta, generously awarded a research grant for picture reproductions.

Several people contributed over a three-year period of research and writing, and the following deserve particular mention. Ken Lester, former Yippie activist and editor of the *Yellow Journal*, kindly have me access to his massive collection of sixties documents as well as his own memories and insights.

David Mills and Jeremy Rossiter, colleagues at the University of Alberta, patiently guided me along the well-travelled road from the Beatles to acid rock. John Thompson at Duke University provided insightful comments on the sexual revolution. The editors of *West Coast Line* published three chapters in draft form, and granted permission for their republication here. Michael Barnholden, managing editor of *West Coast Line*, supplied many pictures that appeared with the chapters in their original form. Two of the articles were co-authored with Julian Benedict, a fastidious researcher who possesses an insatiable curiosity about the sixties. John Tanner, the popular disc jockey of the eera, added his own particular insights. The generosity of poster artist Bob Masse, who created the cover and who let me reproduce three of his posters in these pages, is much appreciated.

Sheldon Goldfarb of the UBC Alma Mater Society opened the archives of *The Ubyssey* to me. Neil Douglas provided background information about the music scene.

Many thanks to the other photographers and artists who so graciously granted permission for their work to appear in these pages, especially Cory Portnuff, on behalf of his father Colin Portnuff; Murray Skuce; Martha Holmes, on behalf of Rand Holmes; Archie Miller; Neil Watson; and Rex Weyler. One of the great strokes of luck was tracking down Vladimir Keremidschieff to his current home in Sydney, Australia. Vlad, as he was known in his days as a photographer for the *Georgia Straight*, provided not only a wealth of great photographs, beautifully scanned, but thanks to his impeccably preserved negatives and records, much useful information about the pictures, and the times. Without Rick McGrath's fascinating website, rickmcgrath.com, we would not have found Vlad. Sandra Boutilier and Carolyn Soltau were helpful guides to the archival holdings of the *Vancouver Sun* and *Province*. Thanks too to Sean Griffin, for access to the *Fisherman* Publication Society archives, and to Dan Keeton, for access to the *Pacific Tribune* archives.

Audrey McClellan provided clear and concise editing, and helped steer the manuscript around an unexpected detour. Christina Cooke gave the book a careful proofread, and Stefania Alexandru, in the course of preparing the index, prevented a few other errors from creeping in. Elizabeth Dean also found time in her busy schedule to catch some pesky grammatical gremlins. Rolf Maurer's eye for the images in their historical context dramatically improved the picture layout.

In the end, I assume responsibility for any idiosyncrasies and indiscretions that may appear.

To my friends Margaret and Julian

The new cultural landscape: Vancouver longhair on a Fairview Slopes rooftop, circa 1970–71. COLIN PORTNUFF PHOTO / GEORGIA STRAIGHT COLLECTION, UBC SPECIAL COLLECTIONS

INTRODUCTION

Images Of A Hipper Era

From his vantage point at CFUN radio station on Fourth and Cypress, "Long John" Tanner, a popular Vancouver disc jockey of the late 1960s and 1970s, witnessed the origins of what was later described as the "hippie capital of Canada."[1] In 1966, teenage boomers from all backgrounds began "hanging out" in the "hip" neighbourhood of Kitsilano. By the summer of 1967 the area had established its counterculture reputation, and hundreds of "outsiders" visited Fourth Avenue just "to drive up and down to see the hippies." According to Tanner, what made Vancouver so memorable was the heady mix of American draft dodgers, drugs, and music flowing up from San Francisco, remnants of the 1950s beat community, and the thousands of receptive fifteen- to twenty-five-year-olds: "It was just a zoo."[2]

As an impressionable undergraduate at the University of British Columbia and a resident of Burnaby and New Westminster, I fondly recall the scene described by John Tanner. At the time, my purely sensual appetites could be whetted by hanging out in certain dens of hallucinogenic iniquity on West Fourth Avenue. In contrast, the free-spirited community activists inhabiting the eastside Commercial Drive neighbourhood held a certain moral and intellectual attraction for a restless Anglican still in touch with working-class reality. But my brief flirtation with the Campus Left Action Movement, a Maoist sect, was a rather undemanding revolutionary posture, at least in the context of the upheavals of the twentieth century. On occasion, I and like-minded youthful comrades played tennis in New Westminster's Queen's Park and socialized afterwards in

City of Love and Revolution

'Jolly' John Tanner, replete with mod hairdo and boots, poses in a studio at CFUN. Tanner was one of the star DJs and CFUN was the city's leading radio station during the rock'n'roll era until it was eclipsed by CKLG-FM in 1968. COURTESY JOHN TANNER

the rumpus room of the popular and youth-friendly "Cocke house," the home of Yvonne Cocke and Dennis Cocke, long-time CCF/NDP stalwarts.[3] It was there that we discovered the joys of integrating drugs, sex, and rock'n'roll with the progressive politics of the day. In effect, we were making what the American Yippie Abbie Hoffman would famously advertise as "a revolution for the hell of it."[4]

The most memorable historical markers for many Vancouverites of boomer-era vintage are the 1964 Beatles concert at Empire Stadium, the 1967 "summer of love," and the 1971 Gastown riot. As the music and words of the Beatles' "I Want to Hold Your Hand" and the Rolling Stones' "Street Fighting Man" spilled into the streets, Vancouver became a city of love and revolution. (I use the shorthand term "the Sixties" to refer to a period in history between, roughly, John F. Kennedy's assassination on November 22, 1963, to — again, roughly — April 30, 1975, when the United States abandoned its embassy in Saigon, marking the official end to the Vietnam War.)

Even today, the music conjures up impressions of the past, and the city presents us with many other subtle reminders of this distant world. On Robson Street, now the epicentre of mass consumer culture, Banana Republic (at least in the summer of 2008) offers the fashionable young man a purple shirt sporting a paisley design. Farther up the street, the display window of Le Chateau, in an effort to catch the eye of the culturally adventurous teenage girl, features a white top with a peasant motif, a reminder of an earlier age and a return to earthy innocence. Bell-bottom pants have reappeared in at least two fashion cycles since they dominated the scene in the sixties. All along Robson, the revolutionary icon Che Guevara is seen on T-shirts, coffee mugs, even Taco Bell burrito wraps.

Two blocks over on Georgia Street, a sign alerts those entering Vancouver from the Stanley Park causeway that they are in a nuclear weapons free zone. This sign is a reminder of Vancouver's active peace movement, which dates back to the 1950s.

Where the action was. Labels, which overlay current map of the city, show some of the late 1960s hotspots. SIMON FRASER UNIVERSITY PHOTOGRAPHY STUDIO

Images Of A Hipper Era

Across the street is a pleasant, grassy area planted with flower beds, which in 1971 was the site of a confrontational counterculture experiment, Four Seasons Park. Few people today are aware how close the parkland came to being privatized and redeveloped as a massive hotel and residential complex.

Heading up Georgia Street to Seymour and Richards, you enter the nightclub district. Here, baby boomers got high and, if they were lucky, paired up while listening to interpretations of the latest rock from London or San Francisco. The Penthouse nightclub on Richards was the location of an interesting early experiment in the sexual revolution, offering "girls with benefits," while the popular gay bar Celebrities, on Davie Street, was once the Retinal Circus, the venue for the latest acid rock music and bands from San Francisco.

. Next on the 1960s walking tour is Gastown. Throughout this area are the city's oldest buildings, and it has been home to colourful people from the beginning, as exemplified by its namesake, "Gassy Jack."[5] This was the setting for Vancouver's most explosive cultural confrontation, the 1971 Gastown riot. A Stan Douglas mural that hangs inside the main foyer of the nearby Woodward's condominium and commercial complex offers the observant walker a reminder of these events.

Moving to the east side, you arrive on Commercial Drive. Long an ethnic Italian neighbourhood, during the 1960s it became a centre for underground activities, and "the Drive" still retains some of the flavour of its radical past. As you walk by the site of the recently shut-down Da Kine marijuana café on Commercial Drive, you approach the Britannia Community Centre with its walls festooned with fading anti-Iraq War graffiti. A few blocks away, on Clark Drive, you can attend a movie about the Cuban revolution at the Centre for Socialist Education. And in spite of recent renovations to its façade, the Vancouver East Cultural Centre on Venables Street is still recognizable as the building

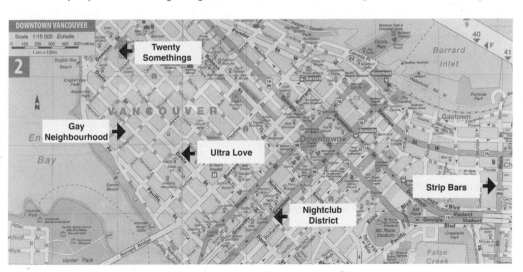

that housed a unique but long-forgotten cultural and educational experiment, Vancouver Free University.

It was in Kitsilano, however, that the hippies reached critical mass and left an indelible imprint on the music and business scenes. The Overtime, now the Russian Community Centre at Fourth and Arbutus, was famous for its light shows and acid rock concerts. What has endured, in name and place, is the Naam Restaurant. Now over forty years old, the Naam highlights two of the lasting themes of the sixties: the consumption of organic foods and a concern for "living gently on the Earth." Similarly, although the abundant organic food stores and yoga centres are more recent additions to the neighbourhood, they remind you that these products and services were first popular in Kitsilano during those years. Since 2005, local merchants have organized an annual Hippie Daze festival in recognition of Fourth Avenue's counterculture past.[6]

Counterculture figures such as Joachim Foikis, the Town Fool, were the city's contribution to the street version of comedy of the absurd. Equally infamous was the mayor of the day, Tom Campbell, generally identified as the face of the traditional conservative lifestyle. Representing the views of the "old left" was outspoken alderman Harry Rankin. In the end, many in the counterculture remained skeptical of all politics, even the "high-minded" politics of the progressive left.

Vancouver's new media, particularly

the underground newspaper, the *Georgia Straight*, confirmed Marshall McLuhan's pronouncement that the medium was the message. The *Straight*, published then as now by the indefatigable Dan McLeod, became the primary local means of communicating the ideas of the counterculture. Initially these ideas were borrowed from the United States, often via the Liberation News Service, which provided news and views from distant cities for the *Straight*'s pages. By the early 1970s the paper had developed its own Vancouver identity and, remarkably, has survived more than forty years to become a mainstream weekly news and

Kitsilano's annual Hippie Daze event celebrates and exploits the hippie roots of the local neighbourhood's business culture. **MARGARET STEFANOWICZ PHOTO**

A contemporary reminder of Vancouver's anti-war activism near Stanley Park JULIAN BENEDICT PHOTO

entertainment publication.

The *Straight* opened its first issue with a story about the Diggers' experimental commune in San Francisco's Haight–Ashbury district, an example of the influence Californian culture had on the Vancouver scene. The paper pessimistically concluded that Vancouver was repeating the pattern of "police harassment" of "the young and hip" that had plagued Haight–Ashbury.[7] In the next few years the *Straight* paid close attention not only to the latest drugs and music from the Bay Area, but also to the American counterculture's methods of surviving in the face of "creeping old fogeyism."[8]

No other city matched San Francisco's allure for Vancouver's young people. But if local youth were interested in drugs, sex, and rock'n'roll south of the border, not everything American was so appreciated. A certain degree of anxiety prevailed, a result of the Cold War and, in particular, the Cuban Missile Crisis of 1962. Later in the decade, several anti-Vietnam war protests erupted in response to that misguided Asian initiative. The decline of acid rock in the late 1960s and the US Sierra Club's lack of leadership when nuclear weapons were tested in Alaska marked the end of the cultural "special relationship."

City of Love and Revolution

As the 1970s dawned, Vancouver was developing its own, more locally based identity, unique but shaped by the tumultuous events and society-changing experiments of the 1960s. The 1960s in Vancouver were not unique because of the style of dress, music, or variety of drugs enjoyed by hippies, Yippies, and other youth, but because of Vancouver's focus on environmentalism, Native rights, and neighbourhood-based political reform. The city's reaction to the '60s was also different, less confrontational and ideologically driven, especially at the level of municipal government, as we shall see in the first chapter.

A return to a state of nature: Young Vancouver woman enjoying the moment during Vancouver's extended summer of love.
PHOTOGRAPHER UNKNOWN / GEORGIA STRAIGHT COLLECTION, UBC SPECIAL COLLECTIONS.

CHAPTER 1

Hippies and Their Discontents

Cultural Conflict in Vancouver, 1965-1970

The first widely publicized image of the emerging American counterculture appeared in *Newsweek* following San Francisco's January 1967 Human Be-In held in Golden Gate Park.[1] Only two months later, a "Celebration of Easter" by "the people of the rainforest" was held in Stanley Park, marking the beginning of Vancouver's chapter in the history of the counterculture.[2] A mural of the 1971 Gastown Riot, recently commissioned for the new Woodwards condominium and commercial complex, captures for modern memory a clash of cultures not unlike what was happening across the United States. But a closer look at the historical record before 1970 suggests that while there was often significant tension between the counterculture and the mainstream, the relationship was far more complex. Vancouver, in effect, extended the expiration date for the idealism of an alternative lifestyle beyond the disillusionment that was sweeping across the Bay Area in the fall of 1967.

San Francisco and the origins of American hippie

The prevailing image of the sixties counterculture is the shaggy-haired, colourfully dressed hippie indulging in some combination of mind-expanding drugs and indiscriminate sex, fortified by the electronic distortions of acid rock. On the surface this behaviour was not remarkable, but as historian James Ferrell notes, it did in fact pose a larger challenge to the prevailing myths and values in society: the work ethic, repressive sexuality, mainstream religion, technocratic scientism, and the capitalist system itself.[3]

Viewed in the larger historical context,

the *zeitgeist* of the counterculture directly confronted the enduring ideas of the eighteenth-century Enlightenment, which form the basis of industrialized liberal democracies. If the Enlightenment stressed the possibility of reason through intellectual discipline, the counterculture embraced feeling as a guide. Where the Enlightenment posited private property and the marketplace as the basis of the economy, the communal Diggers of San Francisco proclaimed "property is the enemy — burn it, destroy it, give it away."[4] And if the Enlightenment underscored the importance of science and technology in the formation of a modern urban environment, the hippies looked instead to nature and the simplicity of a pre-industrial lifestyle. In the end, the counterculture promoted such ideals as peace, love, community, and, as one wit concluded, "freedom from serious employment."[5]

The rise of hippiedom is a uniquely American phenomenon that in various guises spread to other westernized countries and occasionally appeared in the Far East. Vancouver in particular quickly embraced the Aquarian enthusiasms sweeping the streets of San Francisco, to the extent that the political border almost seemed to disappear. Signs of an unusual cultural revolt first appeared in the Haight–Ashbury district bordering on Golden Gate Park in 1965. Why San Francisco became the centre of action at that particular time can be attributed to its equable climate, the availability of cheap food and housing, the proximity

A Garden of Edenic invitation to Vancouver's first Easter Be-In, Stanley Park, in 1967. GEORGIA STRAIGHT COLLECTION, UBC SPECIAL COLLECTIONS

to liberal universities and parkland, and the presence of thousands of baby boomers in search of a generational identity. By 1967 an estimated 15,000 hippies were living in the "Hashbury."

San Francisco also had an established tradition of "hipness" centred around City Lights bookstore in the North Beach neighbourhood. It was there that beat writers like Allen Ginsberg and Jack Kerouac gathered to reflect on 1950s bourgeois America. The beats held closely to a refined aesthetic sensibility based on modern jazz, postmodernist art, and existentialist philosophy. Their public demeanour was bohemian — black berets, turtleneck sweaters, and sandals — and their sexual impulses were basically libertine. Although relatively few in number, the beats exercised a disproportionate influence on the rising generation of baby boomers.

Hippies were the next stage in the postwar revolt against mainstream culture. Baby boomers initially borrowed from the beat lifestyle but quickly moved on to establish their own identity. Overall, the hippie lifestyle was less cerebral, brooding, and introspective. Instead, hippies enthusiastically defined themselves as idealistic and optimistic, and they were inclined to express themselves colourfully through their cloth-

Hippies and Their Discontents

ing and the psychedelic remodelling of their houses in and around Haight–Ashbury. In short, the hippie lifestyle centred on the arousal of the visual, the aural, the libidinal, and the spiritual. Recent research indicates that in 1965, when hippies were limited in number, they embodied environmental values and communal ideals.[6] The Diggers of Haight–Ashbury are perhaps the best example of selfless communitarianism through their provision of free housing, concerts, and a "free" store for food and clothing.

This experiment, considered unusual by the revolutionary standards of the twentieth century, received an inordinate amount of coverage in the media. *Life* and *Look* magazines sent teams of reporters, and the national television networks covered the main counterculture events, most notably the 1967 Be-Ins in Golden Gate Park.[7] It was around this time that the term "hippie" came into common use. The increasing media coverage and the popularity of rock songs like "(If You're Going To) San Francisco" by Scott McKenzie, which promoted the scene, brought thousands more young people into the neighbourhood, causing untold health problems and violent crime. The hippie ideal was quickly disappearing and what took its place were runaway teenagers, the emotionally disturbed, and a variety of petty thieves and drug dealers. A less charitable view of hippies began to appear in the media, and they were consequently characterized as dirty, lazy, morally perverse, and devoid of values. By the fall of 1967, there was a notable exodus of hippies out of the Bay Area. Some moved north to Oregon, Washington, and across the border to Vancouver.[8]

The calm before the storm

Throughout the early 1960s, writer Alice Munro recalls, Vancouver had a rather stodgy and repressive middle-class culture that valued consumerism and economic growth over artistic accomplishment.[9] In 1965, Greater Vancouver's population was 894,000, its annual growth rate was just over 6 percent, and it was at the centre of an expanding provincial economy. Television culture and an abundance of automobiles and consumer durables meant it was not unlike many other prosperous North American cities.[10] Most Vancouverites accepted uncritically the material prosperity offered by a capitalist economy. In the early 1960s, the only cultural resistance came from a colourful but almost invisible beatnik community living in low-cost West End housing, frequenting lower Robson Street coffee houses, such as the International Café, and taking their libations at the Sylvia Hotel on Beach Avenue. Given their small numbers, the beats did not pose a serious challenge to the city's prevailing middle-class value system. Moreover, the baby boomers were too young at the time to appreciate beat poet Allen Ginsberg's warning that their parents were about to sacrifice them to a soul-destroying consumer Moloch.[11]

Flower children dancing at Sunset Beach near English Bay. Kitsilano is seen across the water in the background SHARKIE PHOTO / GEORGIA STRAIGHT COLLECTION, UBC SPECIAL COLLECTIONS

The only alternative to the political status quo was offered by the small but well organized Communist Party of BC. In contrast to the beats, these political radicals were more concerned with the redistribution of wealth to the lower classes than the alienation brought about by consumer-driven society. Writing in the *Pacific Tribune*, Ray Murphy, the national secretary of the Young Communist League, argued that the baby boomers could play an important role as soldiers in the class struggle aimed at overcoming

Hippies and Their Discontents

social and economic injustice. For boomers about to "turn on, tune in, and drop out," Murphy's message was a tedious reminder that life's only purpose was to expand the economy and convert the masses into middle-class consumers.[12]

Neither Munro, the beats, nor the Communist Party could predict how the cultural or political agenda of Vancouver's youth would unfold. It was civic authorities who first saw the wave of the future, noting an

'You remember this poster?' an ad in the short-lived around Kitsilano asked. 'It was done for around Kitsilano by a friendly local artist, who happened to be starving and needed the money. He has since starved, and doesn't need the money now, so we've decided to give the remaining few away.' ARTIST UNKNOWN / COLLECTION OF THE AUTHOR

unusual migration of people coming into the west-side community of Kitsilano in the summer of 1965.[13] According to local newspaper reports, a group of what appeared to be unemployed students, travellers, and runaways from various parts of the city started to congregate in that neighbourhood. These transients joined the small beat community, forced to move out of the West End by upscale high-rise construction and rent increases. Consequently, this diverse group of young people came to form the largest visible component at the beginning of Vancouver's hippie movement.[14]

Who were Vancouver's hippies?

There were five distinct categories of hippies in and around Vancouver. First, there were the "in your face" malcontents, the so-called angries, described as fierce-looking and expressing a strong anti-establishment mindset. Many of the social outcasts informed by the fashionable cultural criticism of the day were dropouts from Vancouver Community College and the University of British Columbia. The second category was referred to as the "freaks and heads." These unusual young people were distinguished by their habitual use of drugs — especially LSD and Methedrine (otherwise known as speed). The third group,

the cynical beats, or beatniks, were slightly older than the angries or the freaks and included those who had moved from the West End earlier in the 1960s. The fourth category included the economically minded "hip capitalists" who were involved in the operation of music stores, rock venues, and a variety of small businesses with a unique counterculture clientele.[15]

The most memorable and perhaps most easily accepted were the "love hippies," who composed the largest group of longhairs in the city. Living on their own without any visible means of support, these otherworldly dropouts had a strong pacifist tendency, believing that "love could conquer all."[16] They did not, however, offer a clear manifesto for bringing about social change. Instead of philosophizing about the ideal life, they preferred urban communal housing organized around the idea of the extended family. Most love hippies believed that the way to attain a higher level of spirituality was to reject material values. This alternative approach was best described by a local reporter who observed that love hippies were "gentle, thoughtful and intelligent young people, practicing a sort of economic passive resistance."[17]

The total number of people who ultimately

'Old Left' Vancouver City Alderman Harry Rankin listens to a voice from the counterculture, bicyclist Garth Clugston, on the steps in front of Vancouver City Hall.
MURRAY SKUCE PHOTO / GEORGIA STRAIGHT COLLECTION, UBC SPECIAL COLLECTIONS.

made up this community is open to debate. John Fisk, chief of the Vancouver Police Department, argued that there were only "150 full-time hippies" in the city during the late 1960s. Dan McLeod, publisher of the *Georgia Straight*, offered a much higher figure, estimating there were as many as thirty thousand in the city during the summer months. This higher figure included so-called weekend hippies, poseurs who adopted the appearance of the counterculture rebels, including love beads, headbands, and colourful clothing, but were not considered true believers.[18] It is more likely that there were approximately two to three thousand hippies permanently active in the city during those summers in the late sixties.[19] But it remained unclear to civic authorities exactly how many "really dangerous" hippies there were and how much influence they had. Thus, given the preponderance of pacifist-minded love hippies and weekend fellow travellers, city authorities reacted cautiously to the challenge presented by this cultural avant-garde.

Why turn on, tune in, and drop out?

At the most general level, some city officials, such as progressive alderman Harry Rankin, saw the emergence of hippies as a reflection of the existing economic system, which was too competitive, too consumer oriented, and too aggressive.[20] Sociologist Daniel Bell has elaborated on this point, suggesting that societies driven by industrial capitalism had become overly efficient and productive, resulting in too much leisure time for youth. In short, the Protestant work ethic, which had served society so well during earlier stages of industrialization, was now being replaced by an undisciplined youth culture.[21]

There were also external factors — notably the relentless cultural pull along the west coast from the United States, made almost instantaneous by modern communications technology. The available evidence suggests that San Francisco, more than any other city, significantly influenced how the hippie scene unfolded in Vancouver. Images of the January 1967 Be-In at Golden Gate Park were broadcast across the border by the CBS affiliate in Bellingham as well as by other American stations in Seattle, and popular magazines, such as *Time* and *Newsweek*, which reported on American trends, were widely read in Vancouver. The presence of visiting American rock bands also confirmed that a cultural revolution was taking place south of the border. A new and unique hitchhiking craze, a cheap way for young men and women to take in the full spectrum of American culture, emerged. When young Vancouverites returned from their adventures, they told their friends about the virtues of an alternative lifestyle informed by the psychedelic "Age of Aquarius."[22]

What was remarkable, at least in the early stages, was the almost total replay of the Bay Area scene in Vancouver.[23] Like the

As churches lost their flocks, their basements became rehearsal spaces for new rock bands fashioning the psychedelic sound. PHOTOGRAPHER UNKNOWN / GEORGIA STRAIGHT COLLECTION, UBC ARCHIVES

hippies in Golden Gate Park, the locals flew kites, strummed electric guitars, and dreamily danced on the wet turf. They also parroted many of the same slogans popular in the American hippie movement, such as "Make love not war" and "Burn pot not people."[24] Pictures of Be-Ins in both cities suggested parallel visions of how the future would unfold, unimpeded by the national border.[25] The San Francisco inspiration was most evident in the choice of names of various hippie shops on Fourth Avenue, including the Psychedelic Shop, which was named after a similar alternative bookstore located in the Haight–Ashbury district.[26] And like San Francisco's counterculture, within which drug use was prominent, the dawn of Vancouver's hippie movement also featured drugs.

The dawning of Vancouver's 'Age of Aquarius'

The first indication that Vancouver was on the verge of a countercultural revolt came in January 1966 when a man was arrested near Kitsilano Beach while deliriously screaming that "he was God."[27] According to the police report, the man, probably experiencing an LSD high, "had a wild-eyed appearance and was completely devoid of reason."[28] In the past the city's drug scene

Hippies and Their Discontents

had been concentrated on East Hastings and Cordova streets; however, it was clear that a different and more unsettling hallucinogenic drug culture was taking hold on the west side.[29] In keeping with its celebration of San Francisco's scene, Vancouver's hippie drug culture largely preferred LSD and marijuana to harsher drugs, like the cocaine and heroin common to the East Hastings scene.[30] By the summer of 1966, established Kitsilano merchants started reporting the presence of grungy, drug-addled youth in the neighbourhood. Local businessman R.D. Keir noticed that younger elements of what he referred to as "the lunatic fringe" appeared to be moving into dilapidated housing around Fourth Avenue near Arbutus. These "oddly attired and fierce looking characters" seemed "a little amusing at first," wrote Keir, who had not seen such odd-looking creatures before. The vanguard of the psychedelic revolution had arrived.[31]

The explosive transformation of Kitsilano in early 1967 was fuelled in part by flower children fleeing San Francisco, bringing their psychedelic habits with them. These American hippies joined others already residing in and around the district.[32] Where individuals lived in the neighbourhood often indicated their involvement with drugs. Heavy drug users tended to inhabit the area north of Fourth Avenue, between Arbutus and Yew streets, known as "Chemical Row." The more recreational users or those favouring softer drugs — student dropouts, artists, and those with part-time jobs — tended to live on or just south of Fourth Avenue.[33] But the developing drug culture was only one part of the hippie scene.

Vancouver's longhairs wore unique clothing, adopted unkempt hairstyles, and grooved to folk and rock'n'roll music.[34] Women popularized the "peasant skirt" while both men and women sported tie-dyed T-shirts. Both sexes blurred gender lines with unisex clothing.[35] Kitsilano hippies also developed a lasting organic food tradition in the area and promoted the concept of vegetarianism. At the time of the 1967 "summer of love" there were at least five hip-capitalist merchants on Fourth, including a vegetarian eatery called The Naam.[36]

Rebellious longhairs in the city also celebrated their culture by producing products, including alternative books, colourful posters, and psychedelic music, that spread hippie ideals.[37] Be-Ins were a major venue for public displays of the culture. One band that frequently contributed its talents at such events was the Seeds of Time. Other rock groups that were popular on the local scene included Papa Bear's Medicine Show, The Collectors (predecessor to the band Chilliwack), and Mother Tucker's Yellow Duck. The connoisseurs of hippie music were not averse to the American soul sound or rhythm and blues, but they favoured the more experimental San Francisco acid rock. Hippie music, primarily folk and acid rock, was the acoustic glue that held the culture together. Curiously, although Vancouver groups adopted the American psychedelic sound, they preferred the way British bands interpreted it. Locally, the United Empire Loyalists provided a live source for the British sound.[38] Besides listening to this new sound at Be-Ins, the cultural avant-garde also congregated at Kitsilano music establishments, notably the LSD-inspired Afterthought on Fourth Avenue.

Sexuality was another issue on the fault line between mainstream and hippie culture. Whereas the mainstream saw sex as a private activity occurring inside the home, hippies often chose to display their sexuality in much more public ways. One successful

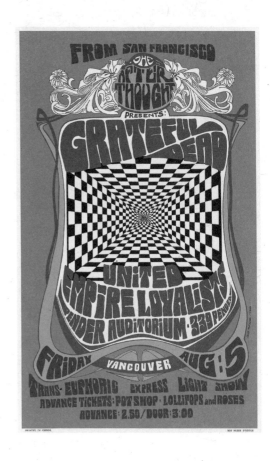

example of this was the conversion of Wreck Beach into a nudist enclave. Less successful was an attempt to promote nudity at the popular family bathing area on Jericho Beach. Local hipsters even tried to rename Fourth Avenue "Love Street," a nickname that found its way into the names of local businesses.[39]

The hippies' celebration of sexuality is reflected in the personals section of the *Georgia Straight*, Vancouver's new underground newspaper, but it was usually a celebration by males on their own terms. As one male writer stipulated in a September 1967 personal ad in the *Straight*, his ideal "chick" would be "intelligent, good looking, and docile."[40] In accordance with this 1960s *Playboy* mentality, nude photos in the *Straight* often focused on women's bodies.[41]

Throughout 1967, Vancouver's "straight" citizens viewed the emerging hippie culture with a mixture of curiosity and mild apprehension. They perceived the counterculture avant-garde as a movement driven by irrational impulses and preoccupied with engaging in spontaneous events.[42] However, a local CBC television reporter interviewing Kitsilano hippies confirmed that there was at least a core group of activists who were committed to organizing and coordinating Be-Ins and other festivities.[43] The *Georgia Straight* acted as a media clearing house and, together with local rock bands, was actively involved in advertising and promoting upcoming events.[44]

Vancouver's hippie event to remember came in the spring of 1968 when six thousand people attended a widely advertised Be-In at Stanley Park.[45] It was an idyllic "back to the garden" moment that anticipated the Woodstock Festival the following year. Although not memorable for its original music or the presence of cultural gurus, the event highlighted Vancouver's contribution to the counterculture: minimal policing with no inter-racial violence, biker gang bullying, or life-threatening LSD overdoses. (Although West End residents did express dissatisfaction over traffic jams on Denman and Beach Avenue.[46]) Even though the dark side of the hippie revolt, rooted in drugs and sex, posed a cultural threat to Vancouver's mainstream society, the movement itself never experienced the levels of violence and inner turmoil seen in the Haight.

Vancouver's initial response: Conservative but not reactionary

If Vancouver's establishment accepted the softer side of the counterculture — long hair, colourful clothing, communal living, and loud music — it drew the line at more overt sexual displays and rampant drug use. Drug use was viewed as the most dangerous part

Bob Masse designed this poster for a Grateful Dead concert in Vancouver. Masse was one of a group of San Francisco graphic artists who developed the 'psychedelic' style. He brought it with him when he moved to Vancouver in 1969. COURTESY BOB MASSE

of Vancouver's developing hippie scene — especially given that hippies appeared to be publicly flaunting their psychedelic lifestyle.[47]

Mayor "Tom Terrific" Campbell led the fight against hippies in Vancouver. Campbell was first elected to city council as an alderman in 1961, and in 1966 he became the youngest mayor of Vancouver to that time. He was a successful real estate developer and drew his support from working-class voters, small-business owners, and middle-class homeowners on the west side.[48] Originally elected as a cost-cutter and critic of bureaucratic red tape at City Hall, Campbell was perhaps best known for advocating the construction of a freeway through Vancouver's historic Chinatown, and the demolition of the old Carnegie library — the city's museum at the time, and today the building that houses Carnegie Community Centre.[49]

Campbell's first mayoral campaign in 1966 made no mention of hippies, but within a few months of the election they began to appear on his political radar. Even so, the mayor appeared to be concerned about the drug problem only when it had spread to the respectable middle-class neighbourhoods on the west side. He rarely discussed the longstanding drug problem in the seamier east side neighbourhoods. But as Kitsilano's drug scene became an issue, Campbell vigorously supported the efforts of local health and welfare officials and the Vancouver Police Department (VPD) to contain the problem.[50] He framed it in

Developer Tom Campbell stepped into the mayor's chair in 1966, just as the 1960s were about to hit Vancouver with full force. VLAD PHOTO / GEORGIA STRAIGHT COLLECTION, UBC SPECIAL COLLECTIONS

apocalyptic terms, saying in one interview, "I think society is entitled to use everything that is available to it in order to stamp out this cancerous growth that is invading society."[51] Such views inspired numerous hippie caricatures of the mayor in the years that followed.

The Vancouver School Board launched one of the first public education programs aimed at detecting drugs and educating youth about them. Medical health officers were sent to local schools to warn young people about substance abuse — particularly the dangers of LSD.[52] In an open letter to Vancouverites, medical health officer Dr. J.L. Gayton warned what could happen to impressionable teenagers abusing the hallucinogenic. Citing a frequent side effect — the inability to judge the dimension of surrounding physical space, the doctor warned: "A person on the fourth storey of a building may believe he is two feet from the ground and jump to his death."[53] The document also outlined the legal implications of getting caught. Gayton concluded by arguing that drugs would likely undermine the existing social order, stating that "illicit use of drugs tends to drive young people into groups separated from the rest of society." Underground newspapers mocked such

education, encouraging people to drop out, and publishing photographs that encouraged drug use among youth.

One Children's Aid Society worker warned that the city was facing "a grave social problem" as runaways were being "taken in" by the hippies and at risk of becoming "involved in sexual immorality."[54] Given the social worker's belief that teenage girls were likely to engage in sex if they took drugs, hippies quickly became the primary target of these authorities.

The VPD set up the second front in the war on psychedelic drugs. Enforcement measures included greater reliance on specially trained drug dogs, chosen for their ability to detect the scent of marijuana.[55] Uniformed officers, trained to identify the smell of marijuana, continued to confront hippies, and undercover officers were schooled in the language of the drug culture so they could move about freely in the Kitsilano underground. The police response would prove to be the most aggressive component in the cultural confrontation. During a sixteen-month period from 1967 to 1968, VPD officers working with the Royal Canadian Mounted Police conducted six major drug raids.[56] In contrast to the arbitrary imposition of law and order in the Haight, however, the Canadian police were reminded to exercise due process and use minimal force when making arrests.[57]

The mainstream media initially expressed curiosity and ambivalence towards hippies. The *Vancouver Sun* eventually hired a full-time reporter sympathetic to the emerging underground culture (Bob Hunter, who was later involved with Greenpeace), while the *Province*, equally solicitous, asked its readers "Are hippies good or bad?"[58] Reporters commented on minor issues regarding loitering and property rights throughout the spring and summer of 1967 but avoided sweeping negative generalizations.[59] Their approach could ultimately be seen as promoting education and understanding over confrontation.

Established Kitsilano merchants did not initially view hippies as a danger to the community, although as early as February 1967 one concerned property owner, infuriated by the appearance of pro-marijuana posters in the storefront window of a hippie business, had urged the mayor to take "the strongest action possible ... NOW in an attempt to prevent Vancouver's Kitsilano district ... from becoming a second Toronto's Yorkville, or San Francisco's North Beach."[60] Harold Kidd, a spokesperson for the Kitsilano Ratepayers' Association, was more sanguine, observing in April 1967 that there were minor issues concerning the maintenance of hippie businesses, but he added, "I don't have any problems with them."[61] Within the span of a few weeks, however, shop owners were sounding the alarm bells. The Kitsilano Chamber of Commerce wrote the mayor in May to warn that hippies were posing a threat to the health and safety of others: "Due to their lack of cleanliness they have brought many contagious afflictions into our community."[62] Anti-hippie pamphlets also circulated, effectively stereotyping the counterculture as "the other."

The negative reaction to hippies grew during the summer months of 1967, some of it coming from unexpected sources. Newspapers reported the emergence of greaser gangs in Kitsilano, who were found hurling insults at "long hairs," while UBC undergraduates, cruising Fourth Avenue in their Chevrolet Impala convertibles, "subjected" hippie girls "to obscene remarks and propositions."[63] These incidents make it clear that the animosity was not only coming from Campbell and the local police as "upper class frat boys" aligned with "lumpen-greaser" elements in a larger cultural rejection of hippies for their own reasons.

Complaints from Kitsilano merchants prompted the VPD to step up its investiga-

tions of hippies. One detailed police report from August 1967 identified certain hippie businesses as the source of the counterculture threat, and as a result several hippie merchants were targeted, including the Psychedelic Shop, Phase 4 Coffee House, Rags and Riches, and the Horizon Book Store.[64] VPD Chief Constable R.M. Booth singled out the Afterthought dance hall on Fourth, locally known for its resplendent psychedelic light shows and reverberation sound system. Booth observed that many patrons of the hall seemed to be high on drugs, noting, "On the dance floor proper, numerous persons appeared to be in a trance-like condition and two persons had to be shaken to arouse them." There was also a problem with underage youth entering the premises, "obviously under the influence of something."[65]

Ultimately, the police recognized that drug raids and educational campaigns were stopgap measures. In their view, hippie culture spawned social problems that were not necessarily violations of the law. As Patrol Superintendent T. Dixon noted in a candid report on the Kitsilano scene: "Much of what is offensive about the hippies is not against the law no matter how offensive their hairstyles, styles of dress, and living habits may be to more stable sections of the community." He added a measured conclusion that shifted responsibility to other authorities: "I cannot offer, nor can I suggest a solution to the problem."[66] It was clear that the hippie predicament required a more comprehensive solution at the political level.

The progressive response: Moderating the confrontation

The city's reaction to the counterculture was moderated by the balance of political forces on council. Tom Campbell had been elected with a slim majority in 1966, which forced him to adopt a more cautious political approach than he might otherwise have done.[67] The three most prominent moderates on council through 1967 were Harry Rankin, Edward Sweeney, and Marianne Linnell. On 15 August 1967 they were all appointed to "a special hippie committee of council," which was to investigate the underlying causes of the counterculture and offer some solutions to the problem. Their report, released in October 1967, recommended more employment and housing assistance. Although city council eventually approved additional funding for hippies, the mayor voted against the recommendation.[68]

The special committee was reestablished early in 1968 after Kitsilano merchants again protested to the mayor and council about "long haired vagabonds."[69] A Kitsilano Chamber of Commerce letter stated: "We

Having served its purpose, this hitchhiker's sign is consigned to the trash next to a bed at the Beattie Street Armory in this September, 1970 photo. The armory, at the west end of the Burrard Bridge, was hastily converted into a shelter for the flower children arriving every day in the city. **VLADIMIR KEREMIDSCHIEFF PHOTO**

are not accustomed to having dirty, filthy, creatures of this nature on our streets . . . we were also informed by anxious parents of what was happening to their teen age children . . . they were losing control of them, particularly through their free-love practices."[70] By March 1968, the Kitsilano Ratepayers' Association was also writing to Ronald Basford, the Member of Parliament for Vancouver-Burrard, pointing out that established retail businesses in the area had seen profits drop by 60 percent due to the hippie influx.[71]

According to Aldermen Linnell, Sweeney, and Rankin, the solution was to expand existing social programs.[72] On the issue of law enforcement, they argued that hippies must be given equal treatment under the law. The committee also recognized that the hippie problem was largely a seasonal issue, with hundreds of young people coming into the city during the summer months and congregating at Kitsilano and Jericho beaches. The reconstituted hippie committee recommended the council continue to support the Greater Vancouver Youth Communication Centre — otherwise known as Cool-Aid. This agency, established in 1967 with funds provided by the United and Anglican churches, coordinated various youth programs, including daily feed-ins around the city. Many Vancouver hippies found temporary shelter, as well as access to basic healthcare, at the Cool-Aid house, located at 1822 West Seventh Avenue.

This house and its location became a source of controversy. When it was suggested that the city purchase the house from the Cool-Aid society in 1968, conservative members of council and Kitsilano merchants were incensed. "Sending hippies to Cool-Aid is like sending alcohol to a drunk to be rehabilitated," argued Harold Kidd, president of the Kitsilano Ratepayers' Association.[73] From Kidd's perspective, the progressives were not solving the cultural conflict — they were exacerbating it. In one particularly anxious 1968 interview, Kidd suggested that hippies represented a culture driven by animalistic impulses: "We suffered through a summer of heartbreak and horror as the element swarmed in to create a nuisance, disregarding law and order, living more like animals than humans, disregarding and disrupting business, bringing LSD, marijuana, heroin and other illegal drugs in our community."[74]

In spite of opposition, progressives on council continued to lobby for funds to provide social assistance for hippies. Even Mayor Campbell's approach to the hippie problem can be characterized as vacillation rather than continuous confrontation.[75] Perhaps most controversial were his repeated attempts to shut down Vancouver's hippie newspaper, the *Georgia Straight*. Yet he did approve a Mother's Day Be-In "in his honour" on the grounds of City Hall in May 1968. At that time Campbell said, "I may not approve of hippies but they are entitled to the same rights as any other group."[76] This conciliatory approach did not last long. In

Cool-Aid House at 1822 West 7th Avenue in Kitsilano, August 1968. Cool-Aid provided short-term care for hippies. BRIAN KENT PHOTO / VANCOUVER SUN.

the months leading up to the December 1968 civic election, Campbell resumed his war with Vancouver's hippies.

The hippie legacy

By 1970 the hippie phenomenon was beginning to change and fragment. Several factors explain this shift. The weakening Canadian economy and the realization that they had young families to support pushed many hippies to refocus their priorities. At the same time, the continued gentrification of Kitsilano forced many hippies to move on. Unable to afford the expensive urban lifestyle, they moved to more attractive rural communities on the Gulf Islands or along the Sunshine Coast. Mainstream culture increasingly adopted certain aspects of the hippie lifestyle — especially fashion — thereby undermining its anti-establishment *raison d'être*. The so-called angry hippies, meanwhile, had become disillusioned with hippie pacifism and gravitated towards the more politically minded Yippies. Other emerging avant-garde movements, such as women's liberation, environmentalism, gay rights, and Hare Krishna, offered equally appealing, but more narrowly based, opportunities for counterculture enthusiasts to advocate for progressive social change and defy the mainstream.[77]

Internal factors also contributed to the changing hippie scene. The hippie lifestyle itself was not sustainable: malnutrition and ill-health, as well as bad drug trips, prompted many to reconsider the direction of their lives.[78] The spread of hepatitis via infected needles took its toll, as did exposure to the elements and unsanitary toilet facilities. Although their popular image suggested that hippies were licentious and sexually adventurous, there is little to suggest that their activities were as unfettered as imagined.

By 1970, moreover, the fault lines between hip-capitalism and mainstream hippies had become more apparent. For example, the popular local band The Collectors were heavily criticized within the hippie community for not donating enough of their concert earnings to support local communal projects.[79] Even the hippies sensed all was not well in the movement. After the 1969 Stanley Park Be-In, Muz Murray, a local dropout, lamented the decline: "Whatever happened to the magic of psychedelic summers past when we could walk out in the streets and know that anyone with hair and timeless garb was one of ourselves in the evolving Brotherhood of the Spirit?"[80] Hippies identified the worsening drug scene as the key factor underlying their decline. In a letter to the *Georgia Straight* in 1969, one hippie

The **Georgia Straight***'s Dan McLeod, right, presents reader-contest winner Ed McCallum with his 'Donny' prize in front of the* **Straight***'s original Powell Street storefront. MacLeod and the* **Straight** *were particular* bêtes noir *of 'Tom Terrific', and a constant flashpoint in the conflict between 'straight' Vancouver and the hippies.* SHARKIE PHOTO / GEORGIA STRAIGHT COLLECTION, UBC SPECIAL COLLECTIONS

City of Love and Revolution

observed that "Fourth has been dying miserably for months and with the exceptions of a few beautiful individuals and Cool-Aid holding it together spiritually it was merely a terminus for burnt out heads."[81]

The divide between mainstream and hippie culture from 1965 to 1970 has been misunderstood in both the past and the present. At the time, Mayor Campbell occasionally exaggerated the threat that hippies posed to society, not unlike the Red scare tactics of American politicians in an earlier era. Alderman Harry Rankin, for his part, could never reconcile his Marxist views with a hippie culture that wanted to change its perception of reality rather than reconstruct the political economy.[82]

The passage of time has highlighted the paradox of Vancouver's cultural conflict in an increasingly commercialized age. The annual Hippie Daze festival, a summer event sponsored by Kitsilano merchants, appropriates 1960s counterculture in an effort to advance their own commercial interests.[83] But the hippie legacy in Vancouver is far greater than what has been neatly packaged by Kitsilano merchants. Certain aspects, including an admiration for eastern mysticism and traditions (expressed in the current enthusiasm for yoga, massage therapy, and alternative medicine), remain indelibly imprinted on the collective consciousness of Vancouver. Moreover, the interest in vegetarianism and organic food, and an

Couple at the Strawberry Mountain Fair, May 1970 long weekend. It was the era of the outdoor music festival; Strawberry Mountain would be our Woodstock.
VLADIMIR KEREMIDSCHIEFF PHOTO

appreciation for the environment, can also be linked to the 1960s counterculture.

Historians assume that the Gastown Riot of 1971 was the logical continuation of the confrontation between hippies and Vancouver's mainstream during the late 1960s. In fact, it marked a significant departure from the fairly benign relationship between hippies and Vancouver's mainstream. The city's hippies, especially the "peace and love" variety, remained largely apolitical, and few were mobilized to play a significant role in the 1971 mêlée. Vancouver's 1960s counterculture was preoccupied with the pursuit of peace, spirituality, transcendental sexuality, and recreational drug use.

This is in direct contrast to the chaos and violence of the San Francisco scene where, by the end of 1967 alone, the Haight district reported "17 murders, 100 rapes, and 3000 burglaries."[84] Indeed, the local drug scene had become dominated by criminal elements peddling impure and unsafe psychedelics. That fall, Charles Manson, recently released from prison, descended on the Haight and cast his spell on those looking for "something to believe in."[85] Another source of violence in San Francisco was inter-racial, with "roving gangs of blacks" entering the Haight to attack hippies for sport and pleasure.[86] In a desperate act of defence, these children of the new age sought the protection of the local biker gangs, more often than not the infamous Hell's Angels. Vancouver hippies were never drawn into the abyss of nihilism and violence of the San Francisco scene.[87] At worst they were subjected to the taunts from "frat boys" and "greasers," but they continued to enjoy police protection.

Vancouver's authorities took a fundamentally different approach to dealing with hippies than did the city of San Francisco. From 1967 onward, Vancouver hippies received at least some government support at the federal, provincial, and municipal level. By 1969, Cool-Aid alone was counselling more than 1,200 local youth each month, as well as providing services ranging from legal advice to food, clothing, and housing to over 12,800 visitors.[88] Local churches continued to respond to the hippie problem too, offering temporary housing and food. Even the UBC student society assisted local hippies.[89] In the end, when confronted with a fundamentally different worldview, Vancouverites remained cautiously conservative but not implacably intolerant.

Funky student carrying a copy of Playboy *points to the sensual component of the VFU curriculum.* BOB MASSE POSTER / KEN LESTER COLLECTION

CHAPTER 2

Liberating Higher Education

The Vancouver Free University, 1969–74

Aristotle's philosophy, creative dancing, Gestalt encounter groups, Vancouver politics, tennis, erotic poetry—whatever your interest, if you know it well, come share it with others who share your zeal.

VANCOUVER FREE UNIVERSITY CALENDAR, 1970

The east side of Vancouver in the 1960s was a completely different cultural landscape than that of the Kitsilano avant-garde. Economically and socially, it was a traditional working-class community and was particularly attractive to the first wave of Portuguese and Italian immigrants after the Second World War. By the early 1970s there was some spillover of hippies as they moved out of the increasingly expensive Kits area. Also noticeable at that time was the presence of university and college students from Simon Fraser University and the Langara campus of Vancouver Community College, who brought with them a certain activist mindset. Those who had recently graduated with liberal arts degrees but sought a position no farther up the career chain than Canada Post union activist contributed a radical class-conscious flavour to the progressive political stew. Given the availability of cheap housing, single women with children, including some lesbians, also began to appear in limited numbers.

The political character, described historically as "mellow ethnic," was usually on the social democratic left, but it began to change with the inflow of younger people.[1] Commercial Drive, the street that bisects the Grandview–Woodlands neighbourhood of East Vancouver, became a favourite habitat for anarchists, Marxist–Leninists, and assorted drug activists. Popularly known as "the Drive," the area contained a large stock of public housing, and soon, ethnic and vegetarian restaurants, alternative businesses, and public displays of drug usage. Graffiti was the popular form of protest, mostly attention-grabbing "kill your rapist" admonitions. Local writer Bruce Serafin noted that these public utterances had all the quality of "romantic brutalism" without offering any specific agenda to make things better in the neighbourhood.[2]

At the end of 1969, Vancouver Free University (VFU) set up operations on Venables Street, two blocks east of the Drive. At the time it was seen as a rather quixotic cultural experiment that added a certain charm to the eastside neighbourhood. Viewed in the larger historical context, Vancouver's short-lived "Free U" was essentially a transitional institution connecting the neighbourhood's ethnic traditions to the new advancing counterculture and feminist politics of the 1970s. VFU was also part of a larger alternative cultural phenomenon that swept North America from the mid-1960s to the early 1970s. The advocates of this cosmic new order envisioned a way of life outside the control of bourgeois society, a life based on free clinics, free churches, free schools, and collectives of lawyers, auto mechanics, filmmakers, and gardeners.[3] Located in this ethnically diffuse and predominantly working-class neighbourhood, VFU offered its students a radically independent learning environment without tuition or arbitrary

Eastside setting for Vancouver Free University, a one-time United Church, the later Vancouver East Cultural Centre, shown here circa 2007.

bureaucratic regulations. In short, VFU was designed to "liberate not alienate."[4]

For historians of the 1960s cultural rebellion, VFU provides a case study of how a radical experiment in American higher education was recontextualized at the local level in Canada by labour and feminist activists. If American free universities were initially preoccupied with larger issues related to race and imperialism, VFU was a "movement for itself," designed to provide vocational training for the working poor, address the social and economic problems of women and the family, and create a forum for Vancouver's counterculture in its quest for spiritual development. But while local factors determined the curriculum, the organizational evolution of the Free U was linked to the 1960s American concept of "participatory democracy" — the idea that students should be involved in policy making while also ensuring that the institution remained non-bureaucratic and decentralized. The story of VFU, then, can only be understood by tracing its philosophical origins in the American free university movement.

The idea of the free university in the United States, 1962–65

Beginning in 1965, the first wave of nearly fifty free universities appeared across the

United States.[5] These counter-institutions rejected the excessive restrictions of postwar higher education. Their genesis can be traced back to the social democratic student politics at the University of Michigan in 1960, when campus activists established Students for a Democratic Society (SDS), a national student organization that in 1962 produced a manifesto known as the Port Huron Statement.[6] The statement offered both a philosophical perspective on the purpose of higher education and a practical blueprint showing how to make large bureaucratic institutions more accountable.

For this younger generation of American New Left radicals, it was students, not the organized labour movement, who assumed the historical mandate to reform society. Thus the modern university, which was seen as too impersonal, hierarchical, and detached from the problems facing American society, was singled out for criticism and reorganization.[7] The first objective was to expose the university's ties to the corporate world and the military-industrial complex, and then redirect the education "process towards peace, civil rights, and labor struggles."[8] The next step was to import the concept of participatory democracy into established institutions. Tom Hayden, a prominent member of the SDS and primary writer of the Port Huron Statement, later recalled that this idea was the most enduring legacy of the manifesto.[9] He believed that democratizing the decision-making processes at universities would not only break their corporate and military ties but would also make students' involvement in schooling more meaningful, helping them overcome their "loneliness, estrangement, and isolation."[10] To achieve this, he argued that students should be allowed to provide input on matters including course content, the hiring of professors, and the requirements of their degrees. In effect, the universities should be like SDS itself, "open, experimental, and decentralized."[11]

It was not until 1964, in the midst of the civil rights movement in the South, that SDSers considered the possibility of cre-

ating educational institutions outside the mainstream. In that year, over three hundred university students from the North participated in voter registration drives in the South and also worked to establish free schools for African Americans in Mississippi.[12] What came to be known as the Mississippi Freedom Schools, a series of separate educational institutions located in churches, basements, and community halls, aimed to teach African Americans about their own history in an attempt to enhance their self-confidence and help with voter education as well as political organizing.[13] Prominent white student participants in the movement later returned to their home universities in the North to champion educational reform.[14]

When these civil rights activists began classes at Berkeley in 1964, their attention shifted to the issue of free speech on university campuses. One troublesome legacy of the McCarthy era on the Berkeley campus was a regulation that disallowed political action groups from recruiting and organizing members on campus. This restriction on freedom of assembly sparked a confrontation when the university administration banned a pro-communist group from operating on the periphery of the campus in the fall of 1964, prompting a massive student demonstration. In response, local police arrested some eight hundred students, thus setting the stage for the Berkeley Free Speech movement. In early 1965 the fight escalated as students started organizing "teach-ins" critical of the Vietnam War—these large public gatherings were held on and off campus by professors and anti-war activists. In the summer of 1965, when an SDS newsletter proposed the idea of a permanent alternative off-campus institution, the free university was born.[15]

The two most prominent counter-universities established in late 1965 were in Berkeley and New York City.[16] At both schools the majority of students were activists from mainstream universities. The Free University of Berkeley (FUB) initially enrolled approximately 750 students and offered more than twenty-four classes focusing largely on radical leftist political ideologies and the consequences of American imperialism.[17] Some of the more popular courses included A Marxist Analysis of the Week's News, Psychology for the Left, and The History of Black Exploitation.[18] Efforts to expose the "condition of our lives" reflected the anti-capitalist ideological agenda of the instructors, and these views came to dominate the curriculum at FUB over the next two years.[19]

The Free University of New York (FUNY), like FUB, was conceived in a spontaneous burst of leftist enthusiasm. The director "and janitor" of FUNY was Dr. Alan Krebs, a former sociology professor from Adelphi University, who lost his academic appoint-

Under the gaze of Uncle Sam, a student discusses registering for VFU courses. PHOTOGRAPHER UNKNOWN / GEORGIA STRAIGHT COLLECTION, UBC SPECIAL COLLECTIONS

ment after visiting Cuba in 1964.[20] He joined a group of instructors from Adelphi and other schools who had been fired for their political convictions. Some of the more controversial classes at FUNY highlighted the themes of fascism and racism, raising the consciousness of students who enrolled for Black Ghetto Radicalism and Malcolm X or Germany Then, America Now: A Study of Fascist Trends.[21] According to one local newspaper article from 1966, over half of the school's forty-three courses had an overtly socialist perspective that was critical of the United States. The theoretical framework providing the basis for a radical critique was rigorously explored in Imperialism: A Marxist-Leninist View or Marxism and American Decadence.[22] The influence of the counterculture was limited to one course on new-age mysticism, taught by an instructor who lectured in a Batman cape.[23]

After FUNY was criticized as a "commie-tool" by one New York newspaper, the city

VFU's library was stocked with books that were largely donated, and loans were on an honour system. **PHOTOGRAPHER UNKNOWN / GEORGIA STRAIGHT COLLECTION, UBC SPECIAL COLLECTIONS**

government attempted to have the school evicted from its headquarters.[24] This came on the heels of Mrs. Krebs' participation in an armed bank robbery, which prompted her dutiful spouse to reconsider his revolutionary enthusiasms. Krebs eventually found a more comfortable station in life, pursuing a career in radio repair.[25] FUNY closed its doors shortly thereafter, in 1966.

Despite some American baby boomers' initial enthusiasm for free universities, the movement entered the first of a series of boom-and-bust cycles in 1967–68, mainly because of the excessive number of politically oriented courses taught by overbearing and, at times, humourless instructors who tended to alienate rather than educate their students. Other issues included a chronic lack of funding, poor organization, and the growing support for reform within mainstream universities.[26] But the most important factor was the youth movement's growing preoccupation with countercultural delights: drugs, sex, and rock'n'roll. As the American movement declined, however, the limited but nonetheless vibrant Canadian free university phenomenon began to develop.

Hand-drawn ad for VFU that appeared in the Yellow Journal. **KEN LESTER COLLECTION**

Liberating Higher Education

The origins of Vancouver Free University

Although younger Canadians were less willing to embrace all aspects of the American cultural revolution, the counter-university phenomenon had some appeal north of the border. Canada's first and most notable experiment in this area came in 1968, with the creation of Rochdale College in Toronto, Ontario. Located in an eighteen-storey building in the downtown core, the school was supposed to represent the very best in innovative education — a student-run, cooperative-living environment independent of formal ties to the educational establishment.[27] Rochdale, however, quickly descended into an abyss of drugs and violence that was closely monitored by the national media. Far less attention was paid to Canada's West Coast contribution to the counter-university movement, Vancouver's "Free U."[28]

John and Margaret Baillie, two local residents who helped found Vancouver Free University (VFU), were particularly impressed with Rochdale's efforts to provide alternative forms of education to dropouts and the working poor. The Baillies decided it was time Vancouver had its own counter-university. The fledgling school started operating out of a neighbourhood kitchen in Kitsilano, but given the obvious space limitations, the enterprising couple soon sought to relocate. They found an ideal spot, and also solved their chronic funding problems, when they forged a partnership with Vancouver Inner City Service Project (VISP), a social agency established to coordinate programs for young people in the city. The Baillies convinced VISP to give VFU rent-free status in a deconsecrated United Church at 1895 Venables Street in Grandview–Woodlands, in addition to other forms of assistance.[29]

VFU officially opened its new headquarters in the fall of 1969, offering students a radically independent learning environment "free" of tuition, competitive grading, and traditional teacher-student power relations. The facility also included a free in-house library of donated books, which were borrowed on the honour system. In keeping with the prevailing anti-bureaucratic mindset of the times, VFU was content to appoint only a few coordinators to answer student inquiries and receive a token registration fee of five dollars.[30]

In contrast to established universities, VFU did not restrict what its volunteer teachers taught, as long as they attracted enough interested students. Most instructors did not have any professional credentials and ranged in age from early twenties to mid-sixties. Classes were usually taught at the homes of instructors; this kept class schedules flexible while also creating a more relaxed and informal environment. Initially, the Free U advertised its course offerings in the city's underground press, including the *Yellow Journal*, and local student papers, such as *The Peak* (SFU) and *The Ubyssey* (UBC). Its first calendar, published in late 1969, featured some twenty-two courses organized on a trimester basis.[31] By early 1970, the mainstream press recognized VFU as a major cultural phenomenon, attracting

an estimated six hundred registered students each semester.[32]

VFU's offerings: From radical politics to vocational training

The Ballies (and city officials) initially envisioned VFU as a practical vocational training institution that would integrate youth into mainstream society. They did not anticipate the counterculture's influence on the curriculum, and it soon became clear that the demands of the counterculture would prevail. Apprenticeship courses in journalism, for example, prepared students to set up underground newspapers rather than helping them get a job at the *Vancouver Sun*. Similarly, a course on print-making did not lead students to permanent employment at an advertising company but taught them how to design psychedelic posters, which soon decorated the hippie enclave of Kitsilano. This culturally subversive training did not preclude students' learning about capitalism as envisioned by Adam Smith; the school even offered a course explaining how to play the stock market.[33]

Although a large number of students were drawn to VFU's avant-garde offerings, what distinguished the Free U from Toronto's Rochdale College or counter-universities elsewhere was the limited number of radi-

The 'Free U' movement was the last expression of Rousseauian naturalism. PHOTOGRAPHER UNKNOWN / GEORGIA STRAIGHT COLLECTION, UBC SPECIAL COLLECTIONS

cal political courses.[34] For one thing, topics such as the Theory and Practice of Anarchy or Libertarian Socialism were already being studied in seminars at SFU and UBC. A second factor was that many radical left-wing activists in the city were unwilling to teach at VFU. Only one of the professors dismissed as a result of the PSA (Political Science, Anthropology, Sociology) Department controversy at SFU ended up briefly teaching at the eastside school.[35] Indeed, students' repeated calls for courses on the history of the Communist Party and guerilla warfare were left unanswered. Charlie Boylan, a spokesperson for the BC chapter of the splinter Communist Party of Canada (Marxist–Leninist) at the time, rejected the idea that students entering institutions of higher learning would ever form a revolutionary base to transform society, dismissing them as petty-bourgeois theorists "who exaggerated and distorted conclusions about the role of the university in promoting social change."[36] Even the mainstream labour unions, wary of the counterculture atmosphere at VFU, declined invitations to teach at the school.[37] Finally, racism and the Vietnam War, the subjects of courses at FUNY and FUB, were less pressing in the minds of most Vancouverites. As a result, VFU was more libertarian than American counter-universities and reflected different political priorities.

Free U students were not as concerned with contemporary American politics, but they were interested in drugs, sex, and

City of Love and Revolution

rock'n'roll. These themes were popularized in American movies, such as the motorcycle adventure *Easy Rider*, and were reexamined in Free U classes that combined vocational training with American counterculture enthusiasms. One of the school's most popular workshops, on motorcycle repair, advanced the libertarian idea that leading a motorcycle lifestyle was a transcendant imperative if one wished to achieve a higher level of individual freedom. Moreover, the motorcycle itself had a certain aesthetic appeal. According to the instructor, "a motorcycle is not 400 pounds of honed steel — it's a musical instrument . . . and a dancing instrument."[38]

Class instruction was non-hierarchical; for the most part, students and teachers saw the learning process in egalitarian terms. Even the most non-academic course offerings had a distinctly progressive message. As Mark Marcinkiewicz, formerly a VFU fencing instructor, explained, "Everyone was equal. The instructor was not revered as the

Hippies and their 'tiny tots' hanging out at a modern playground near VFU. Child rearing was to become a central component in the VFU course offerings. PHOTOGRAPHER UNKNOWN / GEORGIA STRAIGHT COLLECTION, UBC SPECIAL COLLECTIONS

sole authority figure or font of all knowledge. Much of this group learning was focused on what we might now call praxis (the point at which theory is turned into practice) ... the practical application of eastern philosophical thought in every action, in every movement."[39] This informal, people-centred pedagogical approach stood in contrast to the bureaucratic practices of the mainstream universities in the city.

The increasing interest in environmentalism and sustainable communities or communes, meanwhile, was reflected in various courses. Jim Bohlen, one of the founders of Greenpeace, taught dome-building workshops that emphasized the alternative architectural style of Buckminster Fuller. Bohlen's idea was that the mass production of geodesic domes was linked to the growing environmental movement, which sought to use more energy-efficient materials while also pioneering a collective lifestyle. Classes on basic beekeeping renewed a 1960s enthusiasm for the idea that humans should work in harmony with nature as opposed to exploiting it.[40] By the end of 1970, courses on these and other counterculture topics were in far more demand than those on radical politics.

New-age spirituality, yoga, and counterculture sex

Also in demand were courses on eastern mysticism, Sufism, the Zoroastrian roots of Judaism, and Islamic calligraphy. Vancouver's counterculture adventurers who wished to explore and enhance their spirituality were finding that traditional Christianity, with its claim to be the only route to personal salvation and its doctrine of a heavenly afterlife, was no longer meaningful. Equally unsatisfactory, in their view, was capitalism's preoccupation with soulless consumerism.[41] They turned instead to the "exotic" foreign cultures of East Asia, India, and the Middle East and to what the *Georgia Straight* described as "freak interest" topics, such as sensory awareness, Zen and Eckankar (the ancient science of soul travel), all of which offered alternative ways to reach a state of Nirvana.[42]

Gaining insights into foreign religions and cultures in and of themselves was not enough. Students believed they could attain inner peace only by developing the concept of "body as temple." This focus on the metaphysical self, as opposed to a narcissistic preoccupation with the body, brought with it a new interest in lifestyle courses, including yoga and tai chi, which combined fitness with spirituality.

The Free U also offered a totally different approach to discussing sex and sexuality. At the time, rudimentary sex education

City of Love and Revolution

Historical irony: Page from VFU calendar draws parallel with 19th century capitalists on the move. KEN LESTER COLLECTION

classes had been introduced in mainstream high schools, but they were highly clinical in nature, emphasizing the importance of cleanliness and protecting against unwanted pregnancy, and the need to practise abstinence before marriage. This traditionalist mindset did not meet the needs of sixties youth.[43] Instead, the course outline for Creative Lovemaking stressed openness in discussing all aspects of sex — there were, according to one of the instructors, Lynn Stenning, "no limit[s]."[44] The popular class was organized into sections of twenty participants, divided into singles and couples, and dozens of prospective students were turned away because of a lack of space. Stenning indicated that "the classes ran the gamut of everything from wife swapping to [the] sexual positions of the Kama-sutra." And the course outline reminded participants that the instructors "will act as hosts and guides of the course, but it will be an 'everybody contribute' thing."[45] As former VFU coordinator Roger Mattiussi recalled, willing but sheepish participants almost always registered by phone to maintain their anonymity. The instructors, meanwhile, were virtually never seen on site but called in occasionally to confirm the number of registered students.

Creative Lovemaking generated widespread attention in the mainstream press. One *Vancouver Sun* editorial from 1971 observed that, "because the course is described as primarily a discussion class, one must assume that secondarily it is quite another cup of tea," and concluded, "lovemaking, alas and alac, is not free, never has been free, and never will be free, whether creative or derivative, ask the teacher."[46] The editorial was not far off the mark. Other VFU instructors appeared to be aware of the course's questionable objectives, including one teacher who commented in a local paper that "some people abuse the intent of the course by using it as a contact place for wife-swapping parties."[47]

In contrast to popular sex magazines such as *Playboy*, which offered readers the prospect of immediate gratification, workshops on sexual technique were described as teaching students how to attain a higher state of inner spirituality through intimate relations. This approach was highlighted in Sexual Aesthetics, which borrowed from the wisdom of the east, specifically the philosophy of the Kama Sutra and Tantric yoga, to offer "a positive look at human phantasy [sic] and the human body,"[48] and, more practically, to enhance the orgasm in an effort to transcend the ego. A seminar entitled Life Energy examined the theories of German eroticist Wilhelm Reich.[49] Central to his thinking was the idea that sexual repression was at the root of individual and collective neurosis.

Equally important were seminars exploring how love-making could transcend bilateral relationships and open up a communal world. A course on Group Marriage drew on the work of anthropologist Margaret Mead to examine the possibility that monogamy was passé and was not "the last product of the process of evolution."[50] Challenging the notion that sex was a private activity took the concept of communalism to another level.

Other classes covered more mystical and other-worldly topics, including witchcraft. One such course rejected the prevailing notion that sorcery was designed to promote evil in the world. Astrology seminars, meanwhile, explored how the alignment of Venus and Neptune was linked to the state of love and peace in the world. Some astrology classes were even more specialized, such as one that involved creating natal charts for pregnant women. Still another popular counterculture fringe theme was "Magick." Differing from traditional "stage magic," this form of the occult suggested that human will could manipulate physical objects.[51] These subjects challenged the traditionally conservative Catholic mores of the Commercial Drive neighbourhood without producing any notable tension or cultural conflict.

Shifting the focus: Tiny Tots Together

After three years of counterculture consciousness-raising, VFU reached a dramatic

Front page of the final VFU course calendar suggests a higher philosophical imperative. **KEN LESTER COLLECTION**

City of Love and Revolution

turning point in 1972. Its headquarters moved to a new location at 1111 Commercial Drive, and the course offerings began to shift as well. Initially controversial aspects of drugs, sex, and rock'n'roll were increasingly being absorbed into the cultural mainstream. The counterculture was also fragmenting: prominent subgroups were emerging, including the environmental movement, the gay rights movement, and the women's movement.

Many women in Vancouver were becoming more independent, forming groups that sought to advance political change on their own terms. Betty Friedan's bestseller *The Feminine Mystique* reached a large audience throughout the city. It clearly explained that the malaise afflicting modern women, which until then "had no name," was a consequence of patriarchal oppression. The solution was simple and obvious: women had to be able to establish careers independent of men. As a result, feminist newspapers around the city, and other non-mainstream media outlets, began running articles about such issues as daycare and

Prime Minister Trudeau, a Roman Catholic, meets with members of the Women's Caucus at the Bayshore Inn, June 14, 1970 to discuss abortion issues. Feminism had been gaining strength throughout the decade, influenced by bestsellers like Betty Friedan's The Feminine Mystique, *and made itself felt especially in issues touching on childrearing and education.* VLADIMIR KEREMIDSCHIEFF PHOTO

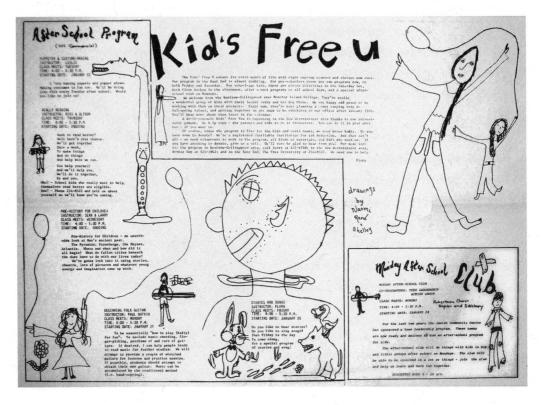

Liberating Higher Education

vocational training for women.⁵²

This shift had a significant impact on the curriculum at the Free U. As early as 1972, VFU calendars listed a growing number of classes detailing the historical oppression of women throughout the world. Women's workshops, such as one on Bhakti yoga, sought to provide solutions to gender inequality by stressing "the use of Yoga in heroin rehabilitation."⁵³ Vocational training also became more gender exclusive. One class, The Women's Video Workshop, which offered opportunities for media networking, was taught by women and open only to women students.⁵⁴

The Free U's constituency was transforming the course content at the same time as British Columbia's political landscape was shifting to the social democratic left. The election of the provincial New Democratic Party in 1972 brought with it a new emphasis on innovation in education. The new education minister, Eileen Dailly, appointed John Bremer to chair a commission on education. Bremer had been informed by the free university movement in the United States and even chose to teach courses at a counter-institution in Philadelphia, Pennsylvania. His rise and subsequent conflicts with the NDP government in British Columbia did not prevent him leaving his mark on education reform. Under the NDP, the system was modernized and diversified, and support was offered for community-based alternative learning methods.⁵⁵

This political shift complemented the

This poster for VFU's Tiny Tots childcare program mirrors modernist painter Joan Miro. KEN LESTER COLLECTION

growing demand for government support of VFU programs that met the needs of women. Targeted funding was instrumental in the creation of the Kid's Free U program, which ran a variety of after-school activities for children. One was the Tiny Tots Together daycare program, which quickly became so successful that over thirty volunteers were needed to run it.[56]

The licentious individualism of the counterculture was simply not in keeping with the changing conditions at the Free U. By 1973, most courses at VFU were related to the needs of women and children. At the same time, the provincial government's ongoing educational reform emphasized the integration of schools with new community centres. Several volunteer staff from VFU accepted salaried positions at local school boards, the UBC Faculty of Education, and the growing number of recreational facilities being built around Vancouver.[57] The school may have closed its doors in 1974, but its spirit lived on in many dynamic new programs established by the Vancouver School Board and the city's community and recreational facilities, such as Britannia Centre. Ironically, the Free U disappeared as it reached its peak enrolment of over three thousand students.[58]

Conclusion

The short history of VFU was determined by a series of factors unique to Vancouver during the late 1960s and early 1970s. In contrast to Rochdale, the Vancouver Free U exhibited a libertarian spirit that was grounded in the community values of the

VFU offered childcare activities for Tiny Tots while their mothers studied. Betty Friedan's influence is evident in VFU's determination not to let children be a barrier to their mothers' education. KEN LESTER COLLECTION

Commercial Drive neighbourhood, which was never overcome by biker-gang violence and drugs.[59] Moreover, VFU's counterculture courses embraced the softer side of the 1960s rebellion — the search for more meaningful sexual experience and a place to explore one's spirituality. The Vietnam War and racism were minor concerns to VFU students; consequently, the school never embraced the radical political nihilism associated with many American free universities. Rejecting an extreme American political agenda, VFU students and instructors tended to adopt a moderate social democratic reformist mindset.

From the beginning, the school established strong roots in the eastside Commercial Drive area, which was populated by young families and, increasingly, single women with children. These groups formed the core of VFU, and because they did not have a larger political agenda, they quickly accepted the NDP government's emphasis on community centres and school board programs. As a result, the "tiny tots agenda" of VFU carried over into the Britannia Community Centre, one of the first integrated school and community centre projects in Canada. The founders of VFU never anticipated that what was once on the fringes of society would so quickly become part of the progressive mainstream.

SEX IN THE STREETS!!

WE DARE TO SHOW "DOING IT" RIGHT ON THE FRONT PAGE!!!

A REVOLUTIONARY "FIRST!"

CHAPTER 3

'The Sodom of the North'

Vancouver's Sexual Revolution, 1961–74

In the fall of 1961, a Vancouver librarian, concerned about the growing legal controversy in the United States over Henry Miller's *Tropic of Cancer*, contacted customs authorities for clarification about the book's status in Canada. The next day the RCMP raided the downtown branch of the public library and two local bookstores and confiscated all copies of Miller's book.[1] Rather than marking a return to the puritanical restraints of the 1950s, however, this arbitrary act of censorship reflected the last gasp of those restraints and moved Vancouver one step closer to the rousing mass sensuality associated with the 1960s sexual revolution. Over the course of the next decade the baby boomers redefined sexuality as a consumer preference, an element of an academic discourse, or a new countercultural lifestyle.

In contrast to their parents' generation, which was steeped in the history of the Depression and the Second World War, the youthful boomers were not inclined to defer their gratification. They were especially unwilling to allow traditional values to block exploration of their sexual impulses. For guidance on the road to liberation they preferred the example of California — depicted in the drawing by popular American cartoonist Robert Crumb that the *Georgia Straight* chose for its cover in 1971 — to that of the rest of Canada. Their elders noted this north-south axis of sexuality with some apprehension. A decade after the suppression of *Tropic of Cancer*, Vancouver

The public outing of sex was a constant theme of the Georgia Straight. R. CRUMB / GEORGIA STRAIGHT COLLECTION, UBC SPECIAL COLLECTIONS

Sun columnist Alex McGillivray warned that Vancouver was "in danger of becoming the Sodom of the north just as San Francisco almost became the Sodom of the South."[2] There was abundant evidence that an erotic genie had been unleashed on Vancouver. Alex Comfort's *The Joy of Sex* was a local bestseller, go-go clubs with topless dancers appeared downtown, and sex shops thrived on Davie Street. Young men seeking condoms no longer had to brave the stare of a pharmacist; a quarter in one of the ubiquitous condom dispensers let them avoid the embarrassment.

Few historians have considered the historical patterns of sexual behaviour in Canada,[3] and Vancouver's 1960s reputation as the home of a colourful countercultural experiment suggests it is the place to begin such an enquiry. The city also offers a case study of the influence of American ideas (specifically California's "culture of sensuality") and popular culture in Canada. Finally, an examination of Canada's west coast Lotus Land sheds light on the clash of intergenerational cultural ideologies and the expansion of a market society.[4] At least three groups in Vancouver advocated and (presumably) participated in these changes — the academic community at the University of British Columbia (UBC), the young adults of the post-war generation who were working and socializing in the downtown core, and the counterculture media. His-

THE GOOD OL' DAYS THAT PRECEEDED THE ONSLAUGHT OF PSYCHEDELIC SEX; WHEN PEOPLE ACTUALLY MOVED TO THE MUSIC.

torians who study shifting attitudes about human sexuality have traditionally looked at memoirs, private letters, censorship laws, and the sale of erotic literature. I draw on these sources as well as medical reports, public statements from health authorities, articles in the mainstream press and underground media, and interviews.[5]

The sexual revolution in America

Doug Owram, a leading chronicler of Canada's baby boom generation, argues that although Canada was more socially conservative than the United States, the rapid spread of mass culture was narrowing the differences between the two countries.[6] To understand the situation in Vancouver, one must therefore look at events that were unfolding south of the border, aided by the analytical framework developed by American historians and social scientists who have studied the sexual behaviours and attitudes of the 1960s.

Sexual behaviour can be measured in terms of the quantity of sex or the quality, which might include an aesthetic component, exploring multiple zones of the body (and understanding how these zones affected sexual arousal), or experimenting with polysexuality.[7] Historians have detected changes in qualitative sex dating

What the sexual revolution swept away: 1950s teenagers innocently dancing 'cheek to cheek', in a montage from the Georgia Straight. GEORGIA STRAIGHT COLLECTION, UBC SPECIAL COLLECTIONS

back to the Second World War, but it was an increase in the rate of activity (quantitative sex) that was most notable. Men and women, who led largely separate lives during the war, paired up after the conflict ended and, within the context of marriage, recorded the highest levels of intimate behaviour and reproduction in the twentieth century. Moreover, recent research by Allan Petigny suggests that the rate of pre-marital sexual activity was also on the increase long before the so-called sexual revolution. When measured in terms of the rate of copulation, sexual behaviour in the 1960s can be considered more evolutionary than revolutionary.[8]

What really changed were public attitudes. Young people rejected sexual absolutes and displayed a new behavioural relativism when it came to how, when, and why people engaged in intimate relations. There was also a new openness about discussing sex, which stood in contrast to the privacy, reticence, and self-control of what has been described as the "cold war Puritanism" of their elders.[9] Historians explain this particular form of Puritanism as a consequence of the socially conformist movement that gripped America in response to the threat of international communism. The advent of television in the 1950s provided a mass media to popularize this neo-Victorian mindset. The bedrooms of the postwar families in many of that decade's sitcoms, for example, offered the viewer a sanitized spectacle of separated twin beds with each

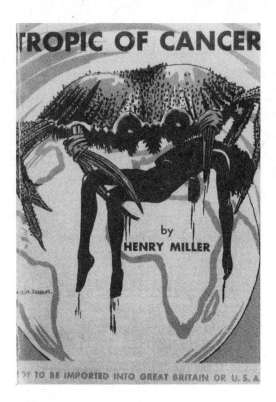

The cover of the continental European edition of Henry Miller's Tropic of Cancer *suggests a darker side of sexual intimacy.*

partner suitably clad in matching flannel pajamas.[10] Intimacy was rarely depicted, and while the pleasurable aspects of intimate relations were acknowledged, the purpose of sex was procreation.[11]

This "quiet conservatism" of the boomer parents' generation was quickly replaced by a willingness to publicly reveal one's personal fantasies regarding masturbation, extramarital sex, and homosexuality. Historians have noted that the conservative mindset was first challenged in New York and San Francisco in the 1950s by the beat fringe, whose licentious behaviour was appropriated by the counterculture in the 1960s. Discussions of sexuality also entered the public domain through the relentless eroticization of mass consumer culture and the "chattering" of the academic community. Academics, hippies, and the devotees of pleasurable consumerism each had their own ideas about the meaning and purpose of human sexuality, and brought into the open a discussion of what had been private in the 1950s bedroom.[12]

Academics on American campuses explained sexual behaviour using theories and hypotheses that drew on modern advances in psychology, sociology, and medical science. Reason and scientific inquiry prevailed, and traditional views were considered either irrational or simply irrelevant to contemporary reality.[13] In a survey of American campuses, one historian detected a preoccupation with exposing the systems of "ideological and structural" control rooted in Victorian epistemology.[14]

Mass culture was occasionally affected by the latest thinking on university campuses, but more overpowering forces had a decisive influence. The central characteristic of post-industrial capitalist society was materialism, the continuous expansion of the consumer lifestyle. Consumers chose products that made them feel good, which ineluctably led them to adopt lifestyles that made them feel even better. In this context, recreational drugs and freer sex were new consumer commodities.[15] The commoditization of sex, in particular, unleashed primal forces that marked the dawning of what one historian has described as America's "Culture of Narcissism."[16]

One of the most popular examples of the new mass eroticism, the "*Playboy* philosophy", took the form of the bestselling monthly magazine and local Playboy Clubs. *Playboy* introduced the public to the idea that sex was a form of consumerism in which the value of one's life was measured by the number and quality of orgasmic experiences. Academics debate whether *Playboy* was evolutionary or revolutionary, but all agree that the hedonistic lifestyle advocated by the magazine detached sex from love and procreation and from accompanying Christian guilt.[17]

The *Playboy* lifestyle was little more than a male preoccupation with reducing sex to a consumer function, and if its adherents considered women's needs at all, it was only to calculate how they might increase their own gratification in return. These men were ambivalent about the emergence of women as independent sexual entities with their own agenda, which began in the early 1960s, shortly after the mass marketing and distribution of the birth control pill in 1961 and the appearance of Helen Gurley Brown's *Sex and the Single Girl*, which became a national bestseller.[18] This risqué treatise, and the articles that later appeared in *Cosmopolitan* under Brown's editorship, challenged the prevailing "cold war Puritanism" and offered women a seemingly unconventional, but liberated lifestyle.[19] Thanks to technology (the pill) and the removal of Christian guilt, they could enjoy unencumbered sex outside the traditional institution of marriage. Brown's infamous catchphrase "Good girls go to heaven, bad girls go everywhere" became the prevailing wisdom of the upwardly mobile urban female.[20] Going beyond *Playboy*, Brown made the case that sex could also be used to enhance one's options in the career marketplace.

Helen Gurley Brown's proto-feminist manifesto was a North America-wide bestseller which left its mark on Vancouver too.

City of Love and Revolution

The Georgia Straight's *frankness* around sexuality brought heavy-handed policy scrutiny. Here, police seize materials during a 1968 raid on its Gastown offices. PHOTOGRAPHER UNKNOWN / GEORGIA STRAIGHT COLLECTION, UBC SPECIAL COLLECTIONS

Playboy and Cosmopolitan viewed sexuality as simply another consumer preference, albeit a particularly personal and erotic one. In contrast, the hippie counterculture sought to create an entirely new meaning for the sexual experience. To hippies, sex was not an act of consumption but a form of communication, an expression of love or a new form of religion. But it was a vaguely defined religion devoid of an organized church and a coherent theology. One author explained that it was "love of nature, love of life, love of oneself, and love of love."[21] Literature on the subject suggests that sex in the hippie community was neither more frequent nor more experimental than in mainstream society.[22] What was different was the attitude toward sex — it was openly discussed and practised and sometimes communally shared. Everything was considered natural, and hippies believed one should never be embarrassed about engaging in the most intimate acts. In the end, they thought the purpose of the erotic life was to restrain the overpowering ego and create a communal experience based on the union of many bodies, which one Freudian skeptic described as "polymorphous perversity."[23] For those inclined to look for a larger historical purpose, the works of Herbert Marcuse provided some insight. The German émigré philosopher, a popular guru for cultural progressives, suggested that a sexual revolution had to occur before the arrival of the socialist nirvana, primarily to prevent the rise of a Stalinist tyranny.[24]

All Quiet on the Sexual Front: Vancouver 1961–64

The sexual scene in Vancouver before the upheavals of the mid-1960s was comparable to that of any other North American city. For the most part, intimate behaviour was contained within the family and infrequently mentioned in the press. The *Georgia Straight* found amusing the unadventurous teenage "petting parties" in the family rumpus room, always within reach of parental authority. Gay males remained hidden, only indulging their impulses late at night in a West End after-hours club near English Bay.[25] The beats, few in number, practised a licentious lifestyle but drew little attention. Until the reforms introduced by Justice Minister Pierre Trudeau in 1968, gay sex and the public sale of birth control products were illegal. Condoms were purchased discreetly by going to the back of the local drugstore and tapping on the counter with a quarter between one's fingers. Recognizing the significance of this unusual gesture, the clerk quickly produced a brown bag with the appropriate goods.[26] In the television age before *Oprah*, controversial subjects were carefully vetted. The CBC, featuring such adult entertainment as *Don Messer's Jubilee*, remained as uncontroversial as the family programming on American networks.

Occasionally newspapers alerted readers to life in their city's erotic zones, which generally took the form of street prostitution and a few strip bars in east Vancouver. With the suppression of the street trade in the 1950s, prostitutes began to organize call girl operations, working out of cafés, dance halls, and beer parlours. Stories about several prominent court cases involving call girls made it into the newspapers in the early 1960s.[27] More adventurous women began travelling to the booming construction sites across the interior of the province, tapping into new, disease-ridden constituencies. Upon returning to the city, these "camp followers" posed a new problem for public health authorities. While the core of Vancouver prostitutes "stayed clean to stay in business," the increasing numbers of outside women were less conscious of personal hygiene and the problem of sexually transmitted diseases (STDs).[28]

In August 1964 the provincial health department released data for STDs, and a growing concern about the health problems associated with lascivious pursuits in the red-light district brought sex into the limelight in Vancouver. The Minister of Health acknowledged that although there was some difficulty in detecting all cases, the statistics nonetheless accurately reflected the situation in Vancouver. From 1960 to 1963 the rate of gonorrhea increased from 3,546 cases to 5,012, infectious syphilis rose from 56 to 280, and the STD rate rose to 310.5 per 100,000, the highest in Canada.[29] Government officials did not attribute these "alarming" health issues to any widespread

Starting in 1966, the 'restricted cougar' was used to flag films regarded by the BC Film Classification Board as too strong for immature palates.

changes in the behaviour of the public at large, but the "city of sin" image was reinforced by the fact that Vancouver already boasted Canada's highest per capita rate of drunks and drug users. The city was beginning to develop a unique moral identity, but not necessarily one to be advertised in the tourist brochures. The immediate response from local politicians and the clergy was to step up efforts to outlaw "smutty" books and "girly" magazines, and by the mid-1960s some higher-minded politicians and church authorities were promoting the idea that "moral looseness was bigger than cancer." They called for a campaign to impose a new moral code on wayward adults and the teenagers of the baby boom generation.[30] However, they found themselves fighting a rearguard action in the years ahead.

External influences also helped put sex on the public's radar. One of the best examples of the cross-border transfer of American mass eroticization was the local appearance of Playboy bunnies and the famous monthly

Concerts by the Beatles — here, their August 1964 show at Empire Stadium — were remarkable for the passions they unleashed among the band's young female fans. BILL CUNNINGHAM PHOTO / THE PROVINCE

centrefolds in *Playboy* magazine. Initially some parents expressed alarm at the availability of these images, and the magazine was relegated to the upper shelves of the adult section at news outlets. Its content was considered to be "soft-core porn," but official censors conceded the magazine had its literary merits and, more importantly, it encouraged "normal heterosexual behavior."[31]

At the time, Vancouver authorities did not realize that *Playboy* and its flamboyant publisher, Hugh Hefner, had a larger agenda: to exploit and profit from the sexual revolution. Hefner's conceit was to present *Playboy* as a men's literary magazine and then use it to incrementally push back the pornographic frontier. This subterfuge did not catch the attention of civic authorities until it was too late. Censorious alarm bells went off only after the appearance of the November 1967 issue of *Playboy*, which contained four pages of photographs from a stag movie showing men and women in compromising positions. Mayor Tom Campbell believed that issue of the magazine was vulgar, crude, and in bad taste, but he recognized that an attempt to pursue obscenity charges in the criminal courts could backfire.[32]

Still another influence was the overt representation of sexual themes in Hollywood movies. These were shown locally, albeit with some limitations. Movie distribution was controlled by the provincial government's censorship branch. Ray McDonald, the former petty officer in the

City of Love and Revolution

Canadian Navy who was appointed censor by the Social Credit administration, held the post from 1952 to his retirement in the late 1970s.[33] One of his major contributions was the introduction of a film classification system. The most controversial films were assigned a unique, designed-in-B.C. "restricted" logo. In the early to mid-1960s, Vancouver distributors tried to import the latest versions of the infamous "sexploitation" films from California, but customs officials moved quickly to stop this potential "violation of community standards." For those Vancouverites in search of more advanced visual arousal, a quick trip across the border to Blaine in Washington State was often the only alternative.[34]

The Turning Point, 1964

Vancouver's shift toward permissiveness unfolded against the backdrop of a culturally conservative province governed by the Social Credit Party, which relied for its majority on voters outside the city. Within Vancouver there were occasional reports of vigilante action to seize "girly" magazines, some parents wanted to restrict teenage dating, and occasional prudish noises wafted from church pulpits on Sunday mornings. But the city moved ahead of the rest of the province in the showing of restricted films, sales of controversial novels, and displays of public nudity, not to mention enjoying the delights of the downtown "meat markets."[35] In the end, there was little that traditional churches and the Social Credit provincial government could do to stop the erotic cultural advance.

The baby boomers entered puberty encouraged by the erotic messages of popular music and movies, and the omniscience of American mass culture. Adult society remained cautious except for some progressive-minded faculty at UBC and New Democratic Party (NDP) strategists who recognized the importance of wooing the boomer vote. More than any other mainstream political movement, the NDP understood the changing balance of cultural power and played the sexual modernist card in the decade leading up to its success in the 1972 election.[36]

The first legal step toward Vancouver's liberation was a redefinition of what was

Evidence of the American commodification of sex, this popular poster attracted the attention of UBC feminists.

'The Sodom of the North'

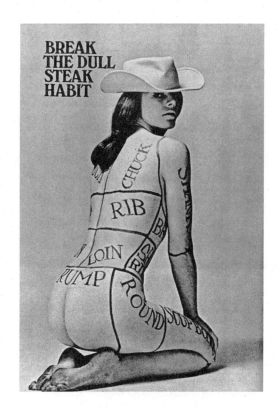

considered pornographic. By 1964, several previously banned novels had survived court challenges and appeared in stores across the city. In the spring of that year the NDP opposition took up the issue of movie censorship, arguing with some success that individuals were perfectly capable of deciding for themselves what was appropriate sexual content.[37] Later that summer the Beatles came to Vancouver, one of the stops on their first North American tour, and played before thousands of ecstatic teens at Empire Stadium. Love was in the air and sex was not far behind. For those Canadians who could not figure out "the times they are a-changin'," *Time* magazine appeared on Vancouver newsstands reminding them that the "second sexual revolution" was underway in the United States.[38]

The first condom dispensers appeared in the Student Union Building at UBC in the smmer of 1969. But acceptance of the new sexual mores took some time: the machines were still controversial in 1974, when this picture was taken to accompany a story in The Ubyssey. THE UBYSSEY, ALMA MATER SOCIETY ARCHIVES

The Academic Avant-Garde, 1965-69

In some respects "a revolution in thinking" about sexuality was already well advanced on the UBC campus by 1960. The university had always been in the avant-garde due to its modernist critique of traditional values. In the words of one observer, writing in the student newspaper, *The Ubyssey*, in 1955, students were exposed to "an overabundan[t] application of science to love (or sex — which might be the same thing),"[39] possibly a reference to the Kinsey reports on human sexual behaviour, which demonstrated that sexual behaviour could be studied scientifically and conclusions drawn about orientation and activity. Viewed in this context, sex was essentially a secular activity, not part of the sacred. It was also more about pleasure than procreation, and could take place outside a romantic relationship "as long as [the] people doing it [had] freely consented."[40]

What separated the environment at UBC from the experience students had in high school was explained to an incoming freshman class in 1965: "You must spend four hours a day drinking coffee with your friends and discussing Love, Philosophy, and Sex," unrestricted by parental authorities.[41] "Frosh" were informed that, in contrast to their censored school libraries, the main stacks of the university's library provided access to "books on free love, love before marriage, and contraception."[42] For those in pursuit of a higher aesthetic, the Free Love Society extended an invitation to discuss moments of human intimacy in the great classics of art, literature, and music.[43] For the less cerebral, several on-campus fraternities provided alcohol to willing co-eds at weekend parties that often became extended sleepovers.

It is not surprising that a certain degree of activism accompanied the critical perspective on campus. UBC students were well aware of the integration of co-ed dorms and liberal male/female visitation hours on American university campuses, and in 1965 they began pushing for a corresponding relaxation of rules on their own campus.[44] That same year the Demographic Society, acting on a conviction that scientific research trumped outdated cultural values, began distributing literature on birth control without the approval of the administration.[45] In the fall 1965 term, the university hospital began prescribing birth control pills in response to student demands. Unwilling to pose a legal challenge to existing federal government regulations banning the sale of contraception, university officials were care-

UBC engineering students ('Gears') were stereotyped as sexually primeval beasts. ARTIST UNKNOWN / THE UBYSSEY, ALMA MATER SOCIETY ARCHIVES

ful to point out that this was a health-related service extended only to married students.[46] Another initiative providing public access to birth control was the introduction of condom dispensers in the Student Union Building in the summer of 1969. The student society, informed about the latest technological advances, supported the sale of only the "safest and most satisfying micro-thin transparent prophylactics" on the market.[47]

Changes in public attitudes were most notable at the institutional level — specifically in the liberalization of the curriculum. In 1970, UBC offered a course on human sexuality that covered physiology, deviancy patterns, and cultural attitudes toward the subject. This science-based course became the most popular offering on campus, drawing nearly a thousand students.[48] With the legitimization of higher academic authority came a greater willingness to promote sex education, based on the content and structure of the UBC course, in public schools.[49]

There were, however, limits to what UBC's enlightened marketplace of ideas would tolerate. One of the most egregious displays of sex as a commodity, a poster depicting a nude woman as a piece of meat, with chalk butcher markings on her body, became a popular item for sale in the campus Thunderbird Shop.[50] This "Break the Dull Steak

Habit" poster, originally distributed in the United States, had previously attracted critical attention on campuses south of the border.[51] Editors at the *Ubyssey* recognized the local importance of the issue and acted quickly to oppose the presence of such a degrading object so close to home. In response to student demands, sales of the poster were discontinued almost as quickly as police authorities had removed *Tropic of Cancer* from bookstores in 1961.

By the late 1960s, UBC was the scene of a clash of sexual ideologies that broke down along faculty lines. Students and faculty in the arts and humanities tended to be more sexually open and egalitarian, while those in engineering and business (faculties that also had few female students)

retained a male-centred conceptualization of sexuality. The UBC engineers were particularly well known for their annual "Lady Godiva ride," in which they paraded a naked woman around the university on a horse. The engineers claimed this was a principled defence of nudist rights, but in the mind of the sexual avant-garde the ride confirmed the engineers' objectification of women and their indifference to women's autonomous sexual desires — in short, their sexism. In the words of one campus feminist, "They [engineers] seem to be sensually shallow and emotionally inhibited to an extreme."[52] Riding the wave of general university unrest, feminists at UBC picketed the ride and publicly questioned the engineers' "*Playboy*-minded" ethic, which reduced all women "to the position of commodities bought and sold on the market as any other commodity [was]."[53] The feminists campaigned against the ride, offering a philosophical critique of capitalism and gender discrimination and a scientific understanding of women's sexual needs. They pointed out that Masters and Johnson's research into human sexual response, notably the evidence they found supporting the primacy of the clitoral orgasm, meant women could enjoy sex as much as men and therefore had the right to do so.[54] Also popular among younger feminists were the new theories claiming that men had used sex for centuries as an instrument of power to relegate women to second-class status.[55]

The attitudes of faculty and students underwent a major shift in the 1960s, but in terms of behaviour, Dr. Robin Smith, director of Student Health Services in the 1980s, has argued that the idea a sexual revolution occurred at UBC during the 1960s is "largely a myth."[56] Based on student health records, he noted that, even before the widespread availability of the birth control pill, as many as 50 percent of female university students were having intercourse by the time they were twenty. Smith cited other factors that made it easier for students to give in to their desires, including the disappearance of the chaperone, the temptations posed by going steady, the accessibility of the automobile, and the disappearance of the double standard. Moreover, given the fact that by the early 1960s university women were delaying marriage until they were twenty-five or twenty-six, it was to be expected they would have some sexual activity during their early single years.[57]

Intimate liaisons downtown

The behaviour and attitudes of the downtown crowd were different from those at UBC. The rapidly expanding population of young adults, on their own for the first time and concentrated in the newly constructed high-rises throughout the West End, was particularly receptive to the messages of sexual commoditization in the American media.[58] Members of this twenty-something cohort were less concerned with the academic treatises of Masters and Johnson, Reich, Kinsey, and others and looked to *Playboy* and *Cosmopolitan* for their carnal knowledge. Hitchhiking to San Francisco, especially during 1967's Summer of Love, gave them a direct, personal experience with the counterculture.

The result was of some historical importance for the baby boomers' coming of age. As Danny Baceda, owner of a popular downtown club, succinctly observed, "The West End has done tremendous things to a man's sex life."[59] In many instances the

Oil Can Harry's, shown here in a June, 1966 photograph, run by a young local entrepreneur named Danny Baceda, became a popular downtown "meat market" as the first waves of the sexual revolution broke over Vancouver.
DAN SCOTT / VANCOUVER SUN

twenty-something male adopted a *Playboy* lifestyle, though one lacking the higher aesthetic aspirations; it was based instead on instant physical gratification and the attainment of status within his peer group. "I got lucky on the weekend and scored three times" was a typical view of the hormonally driven male cruising the downtown clubs.[60] These "proles on the prowl" were pleased with the cards history had dealt them, which

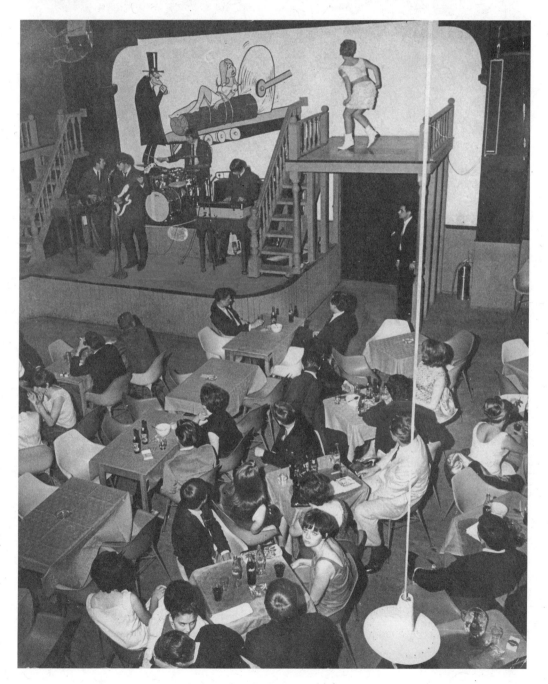

Masturbation – A Look Under the Sheets –
or Is That Spot On The Wall Really Snot?

meant sex was much more accessible than it had been for their parents in the 1940s and 1950s. Interviews with those who worked in or owned popular nightclubs confirmed that there was a measurable increase in the rate of sexual activity, at least for a period in the late 1960s.[61]

Young female urbanites expressed their views about the intimate life less crudely than their male counterparts, but those views were definitely different from the attitudes of their mother's generation. "What does a working girl think about sex?" Bonita Lee, a *Ubyssey* reporter, asked in a 1968 survey of the downtown scene.[62] She was able to discern a new attitude and, to some extent, a behavioural change. The 1960s working girl was "more sophisticated and more sexually knowledgeable than the working girl of your mother's generation."[63] Most working girls were quick to condemn promiscuity but at the same time were inclined to have "intimate relations" if there was at least some kind of emotional connection. There was evidence that the downtown girls were aware of *Cosmopolitan's* message to young women.[64] The single girl was less inclined to get married early and was not about to remain virginal. "Girls today," one doctor told Lee, "want sex and they have every right to it as a man does. They practice the right."[65] In short, there was a new attitude regarding losing one's virginity, a reduced fear of pregnancy, and, most importantly, an enthusiasm for enjoying sex on one's own terms.

Demystifying sex. Mickey Mouse and friends pleasuring themselves in Georgia Straight *cartoon.* ARTIST UNKNOWN / GEORGIA STRAIGHT COLLECTION, UBC SPECIAL COLLECTIONS

The mass distribution of the birth control pill was of some consequence for the downtown shop girls and the rising professional class. First legalized for sale in the United States in 1961, the pill was widely discussed in the American media, and news of its arrival spilled over into Canada. The effects were noticed within a few years. At the 1966 convention of the BC Medical Association, one doctor noted that a prescription for the pill was the number one request from women aged eighteen to forty.[66] There were, however, qualifications about just how revolutionary the pill was when it appeared on the scene. Doctors would only prescribe it to married women, or women who said they were married or engaged, so it was not always widely available. Bonita Lee interviewed one woman who pointed out that taking the pill "makes the inevitable a lot simpler, but if you are going to do it, you're going to do it."[67]

With or without the pill, the twenty-somethings in the downtown scene would meet at the grocery store or in the hallways of their singles apartment buildings, but the downtown nightclubs became the most popular way to get together. Frank Hook, a twenty-three-year-old local entrepreneur, first recognized the market opportunity provided by this "pairing up." In 1966 he opened what became one of Vancouver's best-known night spots, Oil Can Harry's. Given the high number of young women working downtown, the key was to create a comfortable and inviting club where they could be picked up without conveying the impression that they were in a pickup place.[68]

While downtown clubs offered opportunities for both sexes to pair up, prostitution was primarily a convenience for the male seeking gratification without the charm of conversation or the promise of commitment. Local historian Daniel Francis has described Vancouver's cyclic acceptance and rejection of the red-light district,[69] and an important chapter in this history involved two Italian brothers, Joe Phillliponi and Ross Filippone (Joe's name was misspelled by an immigration officer when he arrived in Canada in the 1920s).[70] They had been involved in the sex trade since the 1950s, allegedly running call girl operations out of their Diamond Cabs taxi business.[71] In the 1960s the brothers, astute observers of the contemporary scene in San Francisco, sensed a changing attitude in Vancouver that was establishing new sexual boundaries. They believed what the city needed was a social club that provided "girls with benefits." By 1965 the Philliponi club, appropriately named The Penthouse (a reference to *Playboy* publisher Hugh Hefner's description of the ideal lifestyle of a bachelor, whose home was a penthouse apartment), had become one of North America's premier strip bars. After obtaining a liquor licence in 1968, The

Penthouse opened its doors to prostitutes on an informal basis. On any given night as many as sixty women worked in the club, which provided a safe environment for them and a relatively hygienic venue for its male patrons.[72]

In 1964 a "topless" bar appeared in San Francisco, followed by a more controversial "bottomless" venue. Their popularity was noted by the Vancouver media. Striptease had been a feature in Vancouver nightclubs since the 1940s, but it wasn't until the late 1960s and early 1970s that total nudity clubs like Shanghai Junk, Café Kobenhavn, and the Zanzibar opened for business. They avoided public scrutiny by locating, along with the X-rated movie houses, on the edge of Chinatown, "adjacent to the area's historic skid road, Vancouver's first so-called slum district" (around Main and Hastings streets), which was "inhabited by waves of immigrants, unemployed poor, and mobile male laborers."[73] According to historian Becki Ross, these dens of iniquity "reproduced the classed and racialized divide that split the affluent West End from the impoverished East End."[74] This academic insight would have been of no interest to the clientele, however, who welcomed the shift to increasing nudity.

Ultimately, Vancouver's "bottomless" activity attracted only modest controversy, and the "birthday suit" dancers became the most vocal defenders of the right to nakedly exhibit themselves in the marketplace.[75] Curiously, the strongest negative reaction came from rival clubs that offered only topless stripping. The "total nudity" clubs had a competitive advantage, the "topless" owners claimed, but they were reluctant to match it because nudity violated city bylaws and they feared their clubs would be raided and they would be fined.[76] However, among the general public few concerns were raised

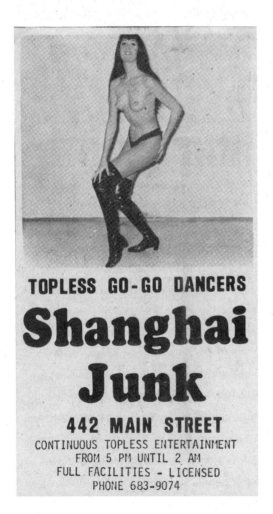

Going topless on Vancouver's eastside. This advertisement ran in the Georgia Straight *in 1970.* GEORGIA STRAIGHT COLLECTION, UBC SPECIAL COLLECTIONS

Indefatigable Georgia Straight *dealer and activist Korky Day combine two of his passions, the underground press and nudism, with the December 1970 issue of the paper. Note his button with its anti-drug message.* VLADIMIR KEREMIDSCHIEFF PHOTO

on moral grounds about the propriety of the clubs. *Playboy* and other magazines were seen as much more dangerous because they reached a wider audience.

Hippies, nudity, and communal free love

The counterculture scene blossoming in Vancouver by 1967 adopted a carnal worldview that was perceived to be an alternative to mindless consumer sex. Bob Cummings, writer of a popular column in the *Georgia Straight*, dismissed the *Playboy* philosophy as "obscene." "The idea that virility comes with the right brand of aftershave, a collection of jazz records, a sports car, and of course *Playboy* magazine" offended these moral authorities of the counterculture.[77] They claimed that what Vancouver really needed was a new erotic lifestyle that was artistic, authentic, and accepting of equality between men and women.

Yet the counterculture did not always meet the high expectations of its philosopher kings, frequently due to the behaviour of the seemingly humane and sensitive male, who had his own sexual agenda, often at the expense of women.[78] The story of one progressive-minded woman who sought an alternative lifestyle is instructive. After living in a communal house in Kitsilano for over a year, she came to have profound reservations. Men saw themselves as being "liberated," she wrote in a letter to the *Georgia Straight*, only by "manipulating other people on their backs ... well the times they are a-changing. Women are no longer content to be used and you're not going to get anywhere on anybody's back anymore."[79]

Proponents of a more humane social order borrowed loosely from psychological theorists for insight and philosophical rationalization. Earlier in the twentieth century, Sigmund Freud had posited that eros — the capacity for love rooted in the subconscious id — was overshadowed by the dominant ego. Norman O. Brown, a classical scholar who updated Freud for the 1960s *zeitgeist*, believed a revolution could be realized, at least in one's mind, by infusing the ego with more of the loving and erotic impulses of the id.[80] One check on the unrestrained ego which proved popular among certain cultural adventurers was to expose one's naked body, with all its imperfections and shortcomings. This led to the promotion of public nudity, which met with resistance from city authorities. In an effort to avoid further controversy, the counterculture nudity movement found an ideal location at Wreck Beach, an isolated bathing area in the West Point Grey area. By the late 1960s the beach was attracting hundreds who enjoyed "losing one's sense of self" and returning to something "so completely natural."[81] Of course there were those who went only to witness the spectacle, and these interlopers attracted criticism. "I don't know why everyone's so down on voyeurs," said one non-participant. "After all, we're people too."[82]

Group marriage was another attempt to restrain the ego with the loving id, and it became the subject of a popular course at the Vancouver Free University. This practice of "intimate collectivism" first appeared in a Kitsilano hippie commune and was later adopted by communes farther up the Fraser Valley. Like many other experimental social forms sweeping Vancouver at the time, marital communalism was not indigenous to the west coast but was introduced by hippies moving up from northern California. One of the Kitsilano commune's oracles described group marriage as a simplified version of

Neil Watson opened Vancouver's first sex shop, Ultra Love, on Davie Street in 1971. The shop is still there, attesting to the demand for its offerings. NEIL WATSON PHOTO

Norman O. Brown's concept of restraining the ego: "There's more love going on and not so much ego." Another less-committed member of the commune acknowledged that he was not as interested in philosophy as he was into "feeling the sexual energy in living with other people."[83]

The cultural spillover from California, the erotic discourse at the Vancouver Free University, and the commentary of the *Georgia Straight*, which began publishing in 1967, provided the base on which a local countercultural lifestyle was built. The new sexuality was often cast as promoting "freedom and liberation" from outdated social values that arguably led to widespread alienation and occasional violence. *Georgia Straight* publisher Dan McLeod actively sought to affront mainstream Vancouver society, especially in the paper's editorials and cartoons. This "in your face" journalism not only entertained long-haired readers but also served as a reminder of the hypocritical moral stupor of mainstream society. Sometimes the "shocking" was presented with light-hearted humour, for example, in cartoons displaying animals indulging themselves.

Notwithstanding the *Straight*'s commitment to a higher counterculture aesthetic, sex also served a commercial function for the paper. The want ads, a significant gen-

erator of income in the early years, were replete with overtures considerably more offensive than anything from *Playboy*, as some counterculture males, unrestrained by custom or law, reached new levels of vulgarity and self-absorption. One progressive lothario advertised himself as "a notorious middle-age activist poet (who) wishes to meet pretty chick, 25-35 for . . ." Another ad offered to "stud women 18-35."[84] One woman working in the *Straight*'s want ads section indignantly pointed out, "This man will never get a response. No woman thinks of herself in these animal terms. This man should get a milking machine or a dog."[85] After "heated discussions" with the women staffers, the *Straight*'s male editors agreed not to run "egregiously sexist" ads and to tone down the cartoons.[86] The *Straight*'s owners also agreed to run a special series on women's issues, including sexuality.[87]

But it was not the ads that provoked city authorities into launching legal action against the *Straight*. In its first year of publication the paper tested the boundary of what was considered legitimate free speech in Vancouver. Several stories offered by the paper as so-called news aroused suspicion, and in the fall of 1967 the city sought to close the paper down on the grounds that it violated community standards. By 1969 the paper faced as many as twelve obscenity charges in response to its risqué pieces, including a risible article on Cynthia Plaster Caster, known for her casts of rock star genitals.[88] As the 1960s came to an end, the counterculture's sexual alternative was challenged by a growing number of problems from within in addition to certain external legal restraints.

Commercialized sex and the shift to 'total body sex'

The 1960s counterculture was, at best, a fleeting historical event. "By the spring of 1970," according to Ron Verzuh, there were

City of Love and Revolution

A well equipped bedroom for the modern lover included a waterbed and a panoply of sex toys: a shop display at Ultra Love.
NEIL WATSON PHOTO

clear signs that the hippie moment "was but a millisecond."[89] The sexual revolution the hippies envisioned did not expand to the larger public. Instead, what prevailed as Vancouver marched into the 1970s was a form of commodified sex for males, the carnal enthusiasms of newly liberated women, and the nocturnal desires of the rising gay minority. In the years ahead, all groups shared an interest in exploring oral, anal, and any other erotic zones of the body, described by historian Edward Shorter as the shift to "total body sexuality."[90] Serving this new market were the expanding erotic business outlets on Davie and Granville streets in the downtown core.

Vancouver's first sex shop, Ultra Love, opened on Davie Street in 1972 and initially targeted a conventional middle-class, middle-aged clientele. The owner, Neil Watson, was a dynamic young entrepreneur who did not see himself pioneering a sexual revolution in Vancouver. Instead he recognized the expansion of the lucrative sex business in the United States and believed there were new market opportunities on the west coast. Within a year the business was thriving. Watson later recalled that there was an unexpectedly high demand by women and the gay community for "special needs" toys.[91]

Canada's largest homosexual community, estimated to number about ten thousand in the early 1970s, was concentrated around Davie Street, extending down towards English Bay.[92] Although the Canadian government had repealed restrictive anti-gay legislation in 1968, this did not alleviate the stigma of social ostracism. Inspired by a series of protests south of the border in New York (particularly in response to the police raid on the Stonewall Inn, a gay bar, in June 1969), Los Angeles, and Chicago, members of Vancouver's "alternative lifestyle" movement sought to engage each other in public the same way heterosexuals did. In the spring of 1971, a Gay Liberation Front was formed and almost immediately organized the first "gay kiss-in" at the Castle Pub on Granville.[93]

Gay preferences in toys reflected Professor Shorter's point about the contemporary shift to "total body sex," and Neil Watson recalled that their fetishes were addressed by German products, especially those made with latex and rubber. There were particular demands for toys to service genital stimulation (cock rings) and anal explorations (butt plugs). But anal play devices were often held up by Canadian customs officials, who had little appreciation for the historical significance of the dawning age of total body sex.[94]

Watson estimated that over a third of the visitors to his Davie Street store were women who, with a new awareness of their erotic desires, expressed an unexpected curiosity about the latest technologies. The Kama Sutra line of products, in particular lotions and oils, were in high demand. The move towards oral sex was addressed by scented vaginal lubricants. Some women explored the market for toys to enhance the bedroom act with their partners. But mechanical stimulators were the most popular item as well as being "the biggest attraction to shoplifters."[95]

There was another dimension to women's interest in the mechanically erotic. The liberated woman's expectation of acceptable male behaviour led to inevitable disappointments when it came to finding lasting relationships. At least one woman wanted "to do away with men and love" after an affair that failed miserably. "Men can be pricks," this despairing creature cried out in a pique of frustration. Her solution: "why not take the penis without the man?"[96] The wares of the sex toy industry provided a convenient solution to her problem.

The most conventional consumers of erotic toys were males, forty to fifty, some committed to a bachelor lifestyle. For these "solitary travellers," the course that offered the fewest emotional complications was finding a substitute for the female body. The most popular item for this group was the

Erotic drawing in the Straight *illustrates both the influence — by way of San Francisco — of Victorian artist Aubrey Beardsley, and the centrality of male desire in the hippie version of the sexual revolution.* JANET WOLFE STANLEY / GEORGIA STRAIGHT COLLECTION, UBC SPECIAL COLLECTIONS

inflatable doll outfitted with masturbatory orifices. By the mid 1970s these men had broadened their interests to latex and rubber undergarments, cock rings, and stimulating lubricants.[97]

Several activist groups, including the early gay liberation organization GATE, shared space with VFU. PHOTOGRAPHER UNKNOWN / GEORGIA STRAIGHT COLLECTION, UBC SPECIAL COLLECTIONS

Conclusion

The dawning of Vancouver's age of eroticism confirms what historian Mary Beth Norton found in her study of the United States: there were multiple sexual revolutions in the 1960s, each with its own appeal and limitations.[98] On the UBC campus, external authority (the administration) initially imposed restrictions on the pill and sexual activity in the dorms but quickly gave way to student demands for change. Campus authority after 1966 almost always overlooked the use of birth control and the practice of qualitative sex (cunnilingus and fellatio).[99] In its place, internal constituencies (the feminist movement) actively imposed new restrictions, particularly on the sale of pornography and the "uncivil" behaviour of the engineers.

Outside the university there were fewer internal and external constraints. The downtown core was populated with hormonally charged younger males, gays, and the first generation of "sex in the city" women. Interacting within a set geographic space, these groups provided the most dynamic base for the changes sweeping Vancouver. If biology drove their search for carnal knowledge, information on how to exercise that knowledge came from America, transmitted through movies, television, print media, and pilgrimages to California. Vancouver society columnist Jack Wasserman believed that the city's urban scene was most influenced by the California example. "In its own quiet way," Wasserman observed, "Vancouver has become the San Francisco of the north, with more toplessness, bottomlessness, and assorted variations of full disclosure, than any other city in the country."[100] Clearly 1960s Vancouver added a sensuous component to its west coast identity.

For the less adventurous, Wasserman pointed to the growing popularity of the "American style" pickup club. In the early 1960s there were fewer than a dozen nightspots, but by 1974 there were thirty-one major clubs, nine of which provided striptease or nude dance shows. Many of the other mainstream clubs in the downtown core were considered "Los Angeles-style meat markets." Club owners borrowed ideas about what sold from California, but they came up with their own erotically charged names, such as The Body Shop and The Pink Pussycat.[101] At the time, this aspect of American culture was viewed as an opportunity for liberation rather than a new form of US domination.

The available evidence suggests that

younger males were most receptive to American-style mass eroticism. Especially appealing was women's participation in the mass commoditization of sex. One reporter described this "easy going *Playboy* sex" as "good clean fun ... a prank engaged in by fresh young girls who go to bed with the same eager but passionless enthusiasm that they eat pizza, play volleyball or dance the frug."[102] But as was the case with the UBC scene, a small but vocal group of feminists occasionally raised questions about the limits of casual sex. According to *Woman Can*, successor to the feminist newspaper *The Pedestal*, the new Playboy mentality altered the "hidden meaning of 'no' — translated, it now means either sexual immaturity and conservatism, or a symptom of being a cold, castrating bitch."[103]

If downtown sex was essentially an extension of the American commoditization of the erotic, the counterculture viewed sexuality as an important conditioning mechanism in building a new social order. Members tried to create a more loving, less ego-ridden society, but their pursuit of a collectivist nirvana quickly dissipated in the face of the 1970s culture of narcissism, stymied by possessive human nature generally and male incivility in particular. What was left of the vision was co-opted by the mainstream. The Wreck Beach scene was quickly populated by poseurs, adventurers, and professors of sociology doing field research. The mainstream also adopted its own version of communal marriage, including wife swapping and group sex parties. The Vancouver counterculture sexual experience suggests that historians may have exaggerated its unique importance to the 1960s legacy in North America.[104]

Vancouver's upheavals during this decade confirm the influence of the California scene: the shift towards qualitative sex and, for a brief period, an increase in quantitative sex. But changing attitudes and the emergence of a new sexual *zeitgeist* were the most enduring legacy. On the surface these attitudes seemed to be open, progressive, and liberating, but there was an inability, especially among twenty-something males, to see beyond the siren song of sensuality.

That there might be casualties on the road to mass eroticism was not apparent at the time. While the city always had relatively high STD rates for adults, the counterculture was generally unaware that the same high rates were now appearing within its own teenage cohort. All was not well in the gay neighbourhood either. Newspapers sensationalized accounts of pimps from Quebec procuring underage boys for ten-dollar sessions in the Davie Street bath houses. As in the political revolutions of the twentieth century, the first casualties of the sexual revolution were its children.[105]

On another level, the downtown crowd exhibited a lack of awareness of the other side of liberation. Local religious authorities were quick to point out that this 'freedom' only made the boomers slaves to their libidinal drives; it didn't offer them the possibility of attaining a higher spiritual union.[106] The talking heads at UBC were not reticent about publishing, speaking out, or generally exposing the myths and bourgeois conceptions surrounding human sexuality. But higher intellectual authority failed to see that in the aftermath of relentless exposure, sex became less mysterious, and according to one contemporary critic looking back on the era, "mystery can be titillating."[107] The irony is that while public attitudes of the 1960s may have been revolutionary, when the lights were out the behaviour of the 1950s may have been every bit as interesting.

CHAPTER 4

Getting Higher

Drugs and Music in Vancouver, 1961–73

In the summer of 1961, Vancouver's drug-free and socially unconcerned teenagers could be found enjoying a day at English Bay, listening to American "boy meets girl" pop melodies on their transistor radios. When the message of folk informed rock music a few years later, baby-boom teenagers discovered a new *zeitgeist* embracing peaceful times, brotherhood, solidarity, and collective fulfillment. By 1965 some rock musicians recognized the dawning of a new age, one preoccupied with reaching a state of nirvana by altering one's inner consciousness, often with the assistance of mind-expanding drugs. Over the course of what has been described as the "age of psychedelic rock," 1965 to 1968, Vancouver's teenagers did not simply enjoy the "loud and heavy" amplified electronic beat of the musicians on stage; they also tuned in to the spiritual rhythms of the universe.[1]

San Francisco was the incubator for a fusion of contemporary rock with the popular drugs of the hippie counterculture. The most publicized event associated with the start of the new era was the January 1966 Trips Festival, held in the Longshoremen's Hall near the Haight–Ashbury district.[2] Those in the hall listened to distorted cadences supercharged by megawatt speakers set against pulsating strobe lights and moving images projected on the walls. Drugs not only inspired the writing and performance of this music; they were also consumed by what Tom Wolfe described

The hedonism of the sexual revolution was never far from the surface of the music and festival scene. **VLAD PHOTO / GEORGIA STRAIGHT COLLECTION, UBC SPECIAL COLLECTIONS**

as the "wound-up wired-up teeny freaks" in attendance.[3]

News of this unusual event spread quickly to Vancouver.[4] That summer, local organizers brought the San Francisco electronic circus to the city, an event remembered as Canada's first mass psychedelic "happening." The following year Mayor Tom Campbell received news that a second Trips Festival was planned for Vancouver. Alarmed by the advancing psychedelic frontier, the recently elected mayor led an initiative to stop this "grotesque spectacle" from reappearing in the city. (It took place in nearby Richmond instead.)[5]

Campbell acknowledged listening to, and enjoying, the 1950s rock of Elvis Presley, but in his opinion the music of the psychedelic era was a "major menace to society," a decadent American experiment in licentious individualism that was leading Canadian youth astray.[6] What really disturbed the mayor was the willingness of young boomers to become slaves to "irrational impulses" and risk permanent damage to their minds. He feared they would cease to be productive members of society and might ultimately become wards of the state. Yet within the undifferentiated northward flow of American entertainment, one form of popular music crossed the border just as easily as any other. If Canadians were listening to Elvis, they were listening to San Francisco acid rock as well, and while governments could impose economic barriers such as tariffs and investment restrictions, the flow of American mass culture was not so easily controlled.[7]

After some initial resistance, local radio stations enthusiastically promoted the San Francisco sound. The underground press reprinted American Liberation News Service articles, and American underground cartoons entertained Vancouver's youthful adventurers. Canadian cartoons frequently had an American connection too, as when Zipp Almasy, cartoonist for the *Georgia Straight*, depicted the Jefferson Airplane's use of Lewis Carroll imagery in their best-selling song "White Rabbit." In short, California was the psychedelic Nirvana Vancouver's youth tried to attain.

The psychedelic revolution comes to America

In the twentieth century, drugs have played a prominent role in the American "pursuit of happiness." Nonetheless, individuals didn't always have the legal right to decide what drugs could be consumed and in what quantity. The first two decades of the century, in particular, marked a turning point for legislative anti-drug activism, highlighted by the Harrison Narcotics Act of 1914, which criminalized the sale and use of heroin and cocaine in the United States. Shortly after

One pill makes you larger: The White Rabbit comes to Vancouver. This drawing appeared in the August 11, 1967 issue of the Georgia Straight. PETER ALMASY / GEORGIA STRAIGHT COLLECTION, UBC SPECIAL COLLECTIONS

Getting Higher

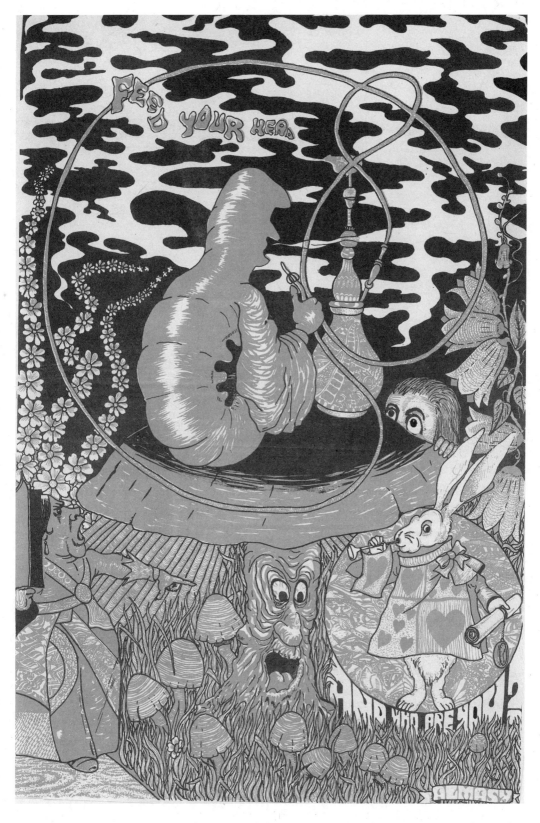

the end of the First World War, the sale and consumption of alcohol was also banned, and in 1937 legislation was passed outlawing marijuana.[8]

During the Second World War, the consciousness that you could be dead tomorrow tended to temper views on illegal drug consumption. Shortly after the war ended, underground communities of beat musicians and poets in New York and San Francisco increasingly began enjoying their drugs of choice: marijuana, peyote, and psilocybin — "magic mushrooms." And as social critics have often pointed out, the middle-class had its own legally sanctioned drugs for travelling the road to happiness. For example, in 1964 alone, 123 million prescriptions were written for tranquilizers and sedatives, and an estimated 24 million doses of amphetamines were consumed.[9]

By the mid-1960s the baby boom offspring of the middle-class, in search of their own chemical identity, were less inclined to go down the conventional upper/downer road. New drugs of choice were consumed, and the most controversial and revolutionary was lysergic acid diethylamide, otherwise known as LSD. This drug was discovered and synthesized in 1938 as a respiratory stimulant by Albert Hofmann, a scientist working for the Swiss pharmaceutical company Sandoz. A few years later, Hofmann was accidentally exposed to LSD and later recalled, "[It felt like] a demon had invaded me, had taken possession of my body, mind and soul."[10] Psychiatrists later recognized that there were some beneficial aspects to LSD, particularly the drug's usefulness in treating schizophrenia and other mental illnesses. In the early 1950s

Hollywood Hospital in New Westminster, shown here shortly before its 1975 demolition, was the site of experiments with LSD in the 1960s. ARCHIE MILLER/ OUR FORGOTTEN PAST

the CIA also began conducting LSD tests, sometimes on unsuspecting subjects, in the cause of advancing national security.[11]

The CIA experiments coincided with the psychic explorations of English novelist Aldous Huxley, who began taking mescaline in 1953. Huxley, famous for his dystopian novel *Brave New World*, moved from England to California to explore larger spiritual questions. Unlike the CIA, he was more interested in self-discovery than national security. He subscribed to a theory that the human brain and nervous system was essentially a screening mechanism that allowed in only the information needed for one's immediate survival. Through his use of mescaline and later LSD, Huxley concluded that the screening process could be reduced, allowing for an authentic mystical or religious experience.[12] However, he cautioned that experimentation with psychedelic drugs should only be undertaken by the philosophically and scientifically trained, people who were able to take reliable notes and conduct rigorous tests.[13]

As the 1960s unfolded, other chemical adventurers, such as the controversial Harvard psychologist Timothy Leary, suggested that LSD was the most effective catalyst for creating a mass-based religious movement, allowing the initiated to "groove to the music of God's great song."[14] Leary's only qualifier was that the drug should be taken responsibly, preferably with other experienced mind travellers. Ideally, if the population in general and government officials in particular turned on, a harmonious world order would emerge and social justice would prevail. Although Leary believed he was a visionary, the guru of the acid experience never established much of a following. Ken Kesey, the popular California writer, dismissed him as too elitist, publicity minded, and opportunistic.[15]

What ultimately prevailed was a psychedelic movement that was less concerned about a higher purpose than with attaining a momentary high divorced from any conventional theological or philosophical considerations. Kesey was first introduced to LSD in the early 1960s through a Stanford university testing program.[16] He later recalled having "a communion with the universe" and shortly thereafter began writing his LSD-inspired novel *One Flew Over the Cuckoo's Nest*.[17] Kesey's close circle of friends, who came to be known as the Merry Pranksters, adopted the drug as part of their daily lifestyle and saw themselves as a "head-based" movement going beyond the older and demographically limited beat community. To facilitate such a mass movement intent on "getting high," a cheap supply of LSD was necessary. This problem was shortly resolved by the generosity of Stanley Owsley, a dropout chemist who set up an underground lab that produced an estimated 10 million "hits" of acid in

1965–66.

Kesey recognized that the most effective way to expand the appeal of LSD was to harness it to the next wave in the rock'n'roll rebellion. In the words of the writer Chester Anderson, rock music was perfectly suited to the task because "it engages the entire sensorium...with no interference from the intellect."[18] Thus the style of music known as the San Francisco sound or acid rock, the musical preference of the Age of Aquarius, presented a dramatic departure in form.[19] In contrast to the "brief, concise, verse-chorus-verse patterns" of 1950s rock, the San Francisco sound was characterized by a movement "toward more free-form, fluid song structures."[20] As for the musical performance itself, there was a degree of improvisation on stage, an assortment of electric instruments was played, often in extended instrumental solos. The music offered dissonant tones without harmonization or ultimate resolution. The folk-inspired lyrics, which were less memorable than the instrumentation, explored drug-induced fantasies and mind-altering techniques.[21]

One drug-inspired Bay-area band, the Grateful Dead, particularly attracted the attention of Kesey. In the fall of 1965 the Dead participated in a series of informal gatherings around San Francisco known as the Acid Tests, which culminated in the main event, the famous Trips Festival, early the next year. Kesey explained the purpose of creating an acid-based mass movement to some Hells Angels visiting his La Honda, California, retreat: "You break people's bones, I break people's heads."[22] According to the Grateful Dead's leader, Jerry Garcia, the acid-inspired music encouraged a nihilistic impulse to tear down the old order. "Everybody would be high and flashing and going through insane changes," during which "everything would be demolished."[23] This made the somewhat conventional challenges to bourgeois society posed by the pelvic gyrations of Elvis Presley passé during the 1960s.

The San Francisco sound, rooted in the liberalized drug culture of the bohemian community, produced another popular "head band," the Jefferson Airplane, which was celebrated for lead singer Grace Slick's rendition of "White Rabbit," an innovative if indulgent celebration of an acid trip. Los Angeles produced its own musical psychedelia, essentially an edgier electronic sound without the overtones of folk. In April 1966 a Los Angeles band, the Byrds, released "Eight Miles High," considered the first psychedelic rock hit to make it onto the national charts.

Across the Atlantic the immensely popular Liverpool group the Beatles, inspired by the American awakening, discarded its earlier sound and "mop-top" image. In contrast to the music of the California bands, John Lennon's "Tomorrow Never Knows" suggested a sunnier, more whimsical and surreal approach to psychedelia. But the Beatles quickly moved beyond the San Francisco sound, most memorably in the hugely

The establishment warns of the consequences of recreational drug use. ARTIST UNKNOWN / GEORGIA STRAIGHT COLLECTION, UBC SPECIAL COLLECTIONS

City of Love and Revolution

The agriculture of the future takes root in the shell of the old. PHOTOGRAPHER UNKNOWN / GEORGIA STRAIGHT COLLECTION, UBC SPECIAL COLLECTIONS

popular album *Sgt. Pepper's Lonely Hearts Club Band*. Here the English band experimented with new audio splicing techniques, using a full range of classical instruments to produce what has been described as a "baroque pop sound." They then mixed in their own Indian-inspired mysticism accompanied by the use of esoteric instruments such as ragas and sitars.[24]

Within a few years the psychedelic mania, particularly the popularity of acid-inspired music, began to wane. In 1968, Bob Dylan's *John Wesley Harding* pointedly rejected acid rock, and the Beatles also shifted back to a more conventional rock form with songs like "Lady Madonna" and "Hey Bulldog," both recorded in February 1968. A disturbing reminder of the consequences of excessive experimentation with drugs came in 1970 with the sudden deaths of three prominent drug-using rock stars, Janis Joplin, Jim Morrison, and Jimi Hendrix.

The market's insatiable demand for novelty also prevailed, and the boomer generation began searching for new highs that went beyond the acid sound. The enduring appeal of suggestive sexual lyrics was demonstrated by the popularity of the Rolling Stones' "Let's Spend the Night Together" and "Brown Sugar." And with increasing disaffection over the Vietnam War, rock groups tapped into a renewed interest in anti-war themes. Despite the peace and love enthusiasm of John Lennon and Yoko Ono, darker clouds loomed on the horizon. After the Kent State shootings in the summer of 1970, Neil Young's poignant reminder of the tragedy, "Ohio," remained on the charts for months.

Drugs and Music in Vancouver, 1961–64

Reflecting the multifaceted influences that a Pacific coast seaport is exposed to, Vancouver had a seamy and exotic reputation for drugs. Historically, the illegal use of drugs was confined to the marginalized individuals living on the east side of the city, especially in the area around Hastings and

Columbia streets. The drugs of choice were heroin and morphine, while more upscale users preferred cocaine. Opium was available and was particularly attractive to members of the Asian community in nearby Chinatown. By the mid-1960s, Vancouver had the largest street addict population in Canada, totalling an estimated 3,000 to 3,500.[25] A typical member of this group was a white male, thirty to forty years old, who engaged in shoplifting and other petty crimes. Some pimps and other "ne'er-do-wells" were thrown into the mix. These men often came from broken homes or marriages, moved to impoverished neighbourhoods like the Downtown Eastside — better known then as Skid Road — and frequently got entangled in the drug scene. Heroin addiction was the most important issue discussed in the media, but there was never a public sense of urgency about resolving the problem. City officials were confident that the behaviour of the drug community, although not acceptable to society in general, would stabilize at a certain level and remain out of sight of the larger community.[26]

Laboratory-manufactured psychedelic drugs were uncommon in the early 1960s, although there are stories of magic mushrooms being imported from Mexico and reports of LSD treatments carried out between 1957 and 1975 at the Hollywood Sanatorium in nearby New Westminster.[27] Traditionally a centre for treating alcoholism and other mental illnesses, the sanatorium received a visit from an unusual American activist, Al Hubbard, known as the "Johnny Appleseed" of LSD. Shortly thereafter, the somewhat impressionable medical staff began using LSD in their treatment and recovery programs, and unconfirmed rumours suggest sanatorium officials shared clinical reports with the CIA.[28] The media paid little attention to the local patients, who included schizophrenics, prostitutes, and a disproportionate number of "drunken sherry party" wives from the British Properties in West Vancouver. After the US Congress passed legislation in October 1966 banning the use and sale of LSD,

Slightly higher in Canada: A 'Vansterdam' pioneer tokes up in the Georgia Straight *office.* PHOTOGRAPHER UNKNOWN / GEORGIA STRAIGHT COLLECTION, UBC SPECIAL COLLECTIONS

Crowd scene from Elvis Presley's Vancouver concert in 1957 — seven years before the Beatles' concert at the same venue. The Vancouver music scene would never be the same. **VANCOUVER SUN**

more Americans reportedly came to the New Westminster facility, including Hollywood celebrities, the son of the novelist Kurt Vonnegut (whose bestselling novels were emblematic of the time), and some prominent pioneers of the computer revolution.[29]

The drug of choice for the Vancouver mainstream, however, was alcohol. The law-abiding middle class also consumed vast quantities of prescription drugs, notably tranquilizers and amphetamines. Although there were no broad-based studies until 1970, it was estimated that one in three Vancouver adults were regular users of prescribed sedatives and stimulants.[30] Even coffee was identified as a problem. The young David Suzuki, at the time a rising star in the UBC genetics department, cited research that showed three or four daily cups of coffee did "150 times as much chromosome damage as one day of fallout during periods of nuclear testing."[31] This liberal use of "uppers and downers" undermined the credibility of mainstream critics who later condemned the chemical indulgences of the youthful baby boomers.

Marijuana and magic mushroom highs were associated with Vancouver's beats and the jazz community, but there is little evidence that the rock'n'roll rebellion of younger teenagers in the late 1950s involved the use of drugs. Glen Altschuler, a historian of modern popular culture, notes, "In several ways '50s rock'n'roll was less than its critics feared"; it exhibited "an ostensibly defiant pattern of gestures...and fantasies of youthful revolt," with some bouts of unruly alcohol consumption, but only minimal use of marijuana. If one was disaffected, it was often revealed more in the poutiness of "a rebel without a cause" than the angry rage of the Stones' "Street Fighting Man."[32]

In almost every instance, from the musical selections of local bands to the "top 40" ratings on radio stations, Vancouver's rock'n'roll scene followed trends in the United States. The most raucous rock event that "foreshadowed a generation gap wide as the Grand Canyon" was Elvis Presley's August 1957 appearance at Empire Stadium.[33] Red Robinson, a popular local disc jockey, acknowledged that he closely followed the American trendsetters, especially those in California, and promoted their songs in Vancouver.[34] According to a November 1961 CFUN chart, the number 1 song was the Pilots' patriotic salute "The Flying Blue Angels," a paean to American airpower. Close behind at number 4 was another American celebratory ballad, Johnny Burnette's "God, Country, and My Baby," while Elvis Presley's ode to Pacific romanticism, "Blue Hawaii," stood at number 3.[35]

During a brief lull in the appeal of American rock'n'roll in the early 1960s, local Van-

couver rock groups made an impact on the music scene. In 1962 the Vancouver Playboys were noted for their brass and electric guitar renditions. The Night Train Review appeared the next year and became popular for covers of American rock classics as well as some original tunes. In an era preceding human rights commissions and political correctness, a group improbably named Four Niggers And A Chink (the "Chink" was Tommy Chong of later Cheech and Chong fame) briefly rocked the community before changing its name to Bobby Taylor And The Vancouvers, and counting a young Jimi Hendrix among its members for a short time.[36] But the international musical tides were shifting and the appeal of local groups waned. In the summer of 1964 the British invasion hit Vancouver.

The Beatles craze swept the United States after the group appeared on the popular *Ed Sullivan Show* on broadcast TV in February 1964, and the foursome's popularity immediately soared in Vancouver. In effect, the American media prepared Canada for the British rock invasion. When the Beatles appeared at Vancouver's Empire Stadium in August 1964, between sixteen and seventeen thousand teens saw first-hand what their American cousins were swooning over: the spectacle of the British lads sporting mop-top hair and seductively harmonizing the Mersey sound. For the thousands of Vancouver's teenage girls seeing the Beatles for the first time, getting high was associated with the wakening of their sexual impulses. The seemingly innocent "Fab Four" provided an idealized vision of suit-

City of Love and Revolution

able opposite-sex partners. One observer has offered a gender-based interpretation, suggesting that young women were rigorously socialized to be prim and proper without expressing their own opinions, and that the primal screaming unleashed at a Beatles concert was a rare opportunity for them to act beyond the control of adult authority.[37]

Predictably, older middle-class adults tended to dismiss the event as a display of adolescent silliness and a loss of self-control, but interestingly, the BC Communist Party, the standard-bearers of a traditional political revolution, proposed the view that the Beatles offered a valuable lesson on the road to the socialist transformation of Vancouver society. In the party's Marxist interpretation, the Beatles represented the possibility of raising one's consciousness about class solidarity. One editorial writer in the *Pacific Tribune* was particularly impressed with the group's climb from their humble social origins in industrial Liverpool, offering it as an example of what could be achieved through working-class cohesion.[38]

What the Communist Party did not anticipate was how the Beatles would raise their own consciousness. Shortly after the Vancouver concert, they had a chance encounter with Bob Dylan and were exposed to the hallucinogenic world of folk-rock and jazz. Paul McCartney later reflected on the significance of their drug experimentation with Dylan. Up until that point, he recalled, "We'd been hard scotch and Coke men. It sort of changed everything that evening."[39]

The Beatles' discovery of consciousness-raising drugs did nothing to dampen this city's Beatlemania. This colourful Gastown record store took its name from the Four Mop Tops' post-acid, Peter Max-inflected album of the same name. PHOTOGRAPHER UNKNOWN / GEORGIA STRAIGHT COLLECTION, UBC SPECIAL COLLECTIONS

The Psychedelic Era Comes to Vancouver, 1965–67

For most baby boomers in Vancouver during the 1960s, getting high meant toking up on a marijuana joint or, for the more adventurous, tripping out on a tab of acid or a hit of mescaline. These drugs distinguished the baby boomers from their more restricted and seemingly unimaginative parents, most notably because their drugs of choice were either illegal or viewed with great suspicion. In Canada, marijuana became illegal in 1923; the law was so effective — or irrelevant — that there was only one recorded arrest for possession in the year 1965. The aura of social opprobrium that surrounded marijuana in the 1950s became part of its attraction a decade later.

Vancouver's interest in marijuana dates back to the late 1950s. The bohemian writer Peter Trower, who spent his early days working in the logging camps of British Columbia, recalled rumours of black porters on the Great Northern trains bringing supplies in from Seattle. In the early 1960s the availability of marijuana increased with the establishment of ties to Mexican suppliers. But Trower attributed the really "big explosion" of pot usage in the mid-1960s to the large number of American draft dodgers; some came to Vancouver while others went to the hinterland to grow cannabis in the Kootenays and the Gulf Islands, and pot came to form the basis of their new Canadian identity.[40]

Offering the possibility of spiritual enlightenment, LSD emerged as the most exotic of the psychedelic drugs appearing on the local scene. Applying Norman O. Brown's neo-Freudian analysis,[41] Dan McLeod of the *Georgia Straight* wrote that he believed an acid high weakened the ego and made it easier for individuals to overcome an innate feeling of "separateness or loneliness." Moreover, by reaching a higher state of consciousness, everybody could become a philosopher or a poet. McLeod came to share Timothy Leary's view that LSD was a religious experience and imagined "thousands of people in Vancouver using mind-expanding chemicals for the first time, to experience the God powers of all your senses."[42]

LSD first became popular among younger university students who had heard about the experiments in California. In the summer of 1965, Robert Smith, a promising UBC undergrad, decided not to return to classes that fall. Instead he and a small group of friends went south to Mexico, where they experimented with marijuana. Next stop on Smith's adventure was a visit to southern California; he stayed there for several months, enjoying the pot and acid parties that were becoming increasingly popular. When he returned to Vancouver in late 1965, according to one newspaper account, "He came home — but some LSD came with him."[43]

Throughout 1966, many other Robert Smiths would pursue their own California travels, returning home to tell exaggerated tales of their psychedelic experiences. That same year the American media gave Vancouverites enticing images of events in Golden Gate Park, the Trips Festival, and the antics of the Merry Pranksters. The works of Timothy Leary and Allen Ginsberg appeared in local bookstores and lent a certain literary and academic authority to the LSD lifestyle that resonated with impressionable teenagers and even some faculty members at UBC.[44]

In a survey of provincial drug use, the Narcotic Addiction Foundation concluded that use of LSD increased dramatically throughout 1966. Psychiatrists noted that fifty-two persons had suffered some disabling consequences from taking the drug; thirty-four involved ambulatory treatments, ten were hospital referrals, and eight were evaluations.[45] One reason for the growing popularity of LSD was that possession was not illegal, in contrast to the draconian laws pertaining to marijuana (until the mid-1960s, marijuana possession could net a seven-year jail sentence). Others pointed

at the excesses of American culture as an explanation. According to UBC psychologist Conrad Schwartz, much of the new popularity of drugs could be traced to Timothy Leary, "the high priest of the LSD cult." His "preaching" about a psychedelic religion had particular appeal to Vancouver's youth, who were unable to distinguish between theology and the wares of "a snake oil salesman...He has a lot to answer for from a moral point of view," noted the concerned doctor.[46] One distraught mother blamed the allure of the San Francisco drug lifestyle when her son returned home "a helpless crying vegetable."[47]

Local psychologists noted that the age cohort and sociological profile of the local LSD user basically followed the American precedent. LSD was not a drug of "the criminal population," stated Dr. A.M. Marcus of the Narcotics Addiction Foundation; rather, it was "a mind expansion drug which criminals are not interested in."[48] And it was not the Downtown Eastside underclass that became users, but the highly educated middle class. "College students, many of whom lead lonely isolated lives, are being seduced into using LSD or other psychedelic drugs by the promises of increased creativity," argued one Vancouver psychiatrist studying the topic.[49] In the 1966 fall term, fourteen UBC students were treated by university health services for LSD-related symptoms, and it was estimated there were over a hundred users overall on campus.[50]

University students getting high did not attract widespread public attention, but more alarming incidents off campus did. In December 1966, two LSD-related deaths were reported. One involved a youth who was "probably experiencing a distortion of his sense of space," according to the police report, and tragically miscalculated his leap off the Burrard Street bridge.[51] What really ignited an LSD-inspired wave of hysteria was a police report that thirty teenagers from four high schools on Vancouver's west side were regularly experimenting with the drug "for kicks."[52] The police believed the drug was being brought in from California and students were paying $12 a pill, which would typically be divided into four doses. One constable believed it was time for public authorities to act. "It [LSD] has got to go — it's a damnable thing. It's supposed to expand the mind but far as I am concerned it explodes it."[53]

As noted in Chapter 1, the LSD issue became the flashpoint for Vancouver's clash of cultures. One Kitsilano hippie flippantly mused about the possibility of putting LSD in the water supply, but what really sparked concern was LSD's perceived threat to the generation then in high school. Mayor Tom Campbell, never one to be indecisive, declared "War on Marijuana and LSD." To

Young Vancouverites enjoying an outdoor rock concert. Note the sign advertising speed in the middle of the photo. PHOTOGRAPHER UNKNOWN / GEORGIA STRAIGHT COLLECTION, UBC SPECIAL COLLECTIONS

this end, the mayor called for police action against drug dealing in Kitsilano and near the main public library downtown. Patrick McGeer, a local member of the BC Legislative Assembly, lobbied the provincial government to pass special legislation making possession illegal.[54] Not everybody was impressed with these actions. According to Alderman Harry Rankin, the public was being "whipped into a state of hysteria over LSD." He was particularly dismayed that on Fourth Avenue there were more "cops than hippies."[55]

In was in this context of growing cultural polarization that Vancouver's controversial underground newspaper, the *Georgia Straight*, was conceived in the spring of 1967. Dan McLeod and like-minded cultural progressives set up the paper, in part, because they believed the *Vancouver Sun* and *Province* were publishing misguided and ill-informed attacks on the drug culture.[56] *Straight* writers acknowledged that there were indeed some harmful impurities in LSD being sold, but they insisted that mainstream society had equally dangerous mass consumption habits, including watching television (the *Straight* headlined research, sponsored by the US Congress, which showed that "T.V. Rays Cause Brain Damage").[57] In the end, the *Straight* asserted that "materialist civilization" was "hypnotized, clobbered, stoned, and asphyxiated" far worse than the Fourth Avenue counterculture.[58]

The *Straight* also responded to what

The band Fireweed on the Malkin Bowl stage, 1973 Easter Be-In. SHARKIE PHOTO / GEORGIA STRAIGHT COLLECTION, UBC SPECIAL COLLECTIONS

it viewed as the exaggerated anti-drug "propaganda" campaigns in the local high schools. Cartoons parodied the "social ostracism" theme that had worked so well in the "halitosis scare" used to advertise mouthwash. The police and the "irresponsible" behaviour of Mayor Tom Campbell attracted the attention of *Straight* cartoonists on several occasions.

Initially the *Straight* mostly reprinted the work of American cartoonists, such as Ron Cobb, but two talented Canadians swiftly became local favourites. Rand Holmes produced the Harold Hedd series and was especially known for his depiction of the Vancouver police during the 1971 Gastown riot. Equally controversial, at least in the eyes of civic officials, were the Acidman cartoons of Peter "Zipp" Almasy, who later acknowledged that the creation of "Acid Man probably happened while I was drunk."[59] He recognized his limitations as a "good but imitative" artist who borrowed ideas and characters from Marvel comics, only "without that goddamn American censorship."[60] In his comic strips, Almasy did not promote love, peace, and goodwill for reaching an accommodation with culturally regressive civic officials. Instead he was inspired by the words of the American comic and social critic Lenny Bruce: "I spit in the face of authority."[61]

The Acid Rock Scene, 1966–69

Until the mid-1960s, Vancouver baby boomers enjoyed a pop music consensus that reflected the larger North American preference, spanning the range from 1950s Elvis Presley to the hipper early Beatles. The advent of acid rock, which hit Vancouver out of the blue, with Richter scale force, signalled the arrival of a counterculture movement that was deemed unacceptable by civic and parental authority. One devotee of the new sound recalled, "The music was great, the innovations were brilliant, the sentiments and ideals sometimes superb, the hedonism monumental."[62] In short, the San Francisco promise of a new cultural utopia proved to be irresistible.

After the first Trips Festival in San Francisco in January 1966, the popular Vancouver disc jockey Fred Latremouille noticed a dramatic increase in requests to play the popular bands of the San Francisco acid rock movement. He travelled to the Bay area to investigate this phenomenon himself,[63] and shortly thereafter local music impresarios organized Vancouver's own version of the Trips Festival, held in the summer of 1966 at the eastside Gardens Auditorium on the grounds of the Pacific National Exhibition. There were claims that Ken Kesey and the Merry Pranksters would appear, but most Vancouverites did not realize that many of them were hiding out in Mexico. What did arrive was a Pranksters-inspired multicoloured bus painted in a vivid sunburst of DayGlo (not the original "Furthur" model). The San Francisco representatives included Big Brother and the Holding Company with Janis Joplin, and the first acid rock ambassadors to Canada, the Grateful Dead.[64] The Dead, impressed with the heightened state of Vancouver's consciousness, stayed on for another week and played to a sold-out audience at the Pender Auditorium. Their free-spirited style also led to an impromptu concert at the bandstand on English Bay, causing a traffic jam and rapturous applause from bystanders.[65]

"Creative destruction" best describes the effect of imported acid rock.[66] Local R&B bands were just beginning to reach a critical mass in terms of their original lyrics and influence on the dance scene when the California musical earthquake hit. One observer noted that the Night Train Review, Kentish Steele and the Shantelles, and Soul Unlimited were, almost overnight, simply "floored by the psychedelic movement" and never really recovered their earlier momentum.[67] For the local musicians riding this new wave of musical adventure, the larger question became one of choice. Should they mimic the California scene or the emerging British interpretation, or should they develop their own local version of acid rock?

Aftershocks affected the local radio stations as well. The mainstream CBC, exhibiting the bureaucratic lethargy infusing its "high-brow" cultural mandate, simply ignored modern rock. But traditional rock

Bob Masse designed the poster for a series of shows the Grateful Dead did at the PNE Agrodome and Dante's Inferno. The popular local band The Collectors (later Chilliwack) opened for them. **BOB MASSE**

stations, still promoting the by-now-mainstream music of Elvis Presley and the Beatles, were directly exposed to the shock of psychedelia. Red Robinson, the music director of CFUN, ordered DJ John Tanner to remove Donovan's "Mellow Yellow" from the playlist on the assumption that it promoted "getting high." At the time, Robinson and others believed the song's refrain "electrical banana / is going to be the very next craze" was "a coded reference to getting a hallucinogenic high smoking dried banana peels."[68] Acid rock also shattered the traditional three-minute song length of mainstream radio, most notably with the Doors' classic "Light My Fire," which clocked in at just over seven minutes. This music simply did not fit the format for popular tunes played on AM radio, but it seemed tailor-made for the FM broadcast band. FM, with its ability to broadcast in stereo, was also technically more effective at capturing the nuances of the psychedelic beat.

After experiencing the Monterey Pop Festival during the 1967 Summer of Love, DJ Tim Burge improbably approached the "square" AM station CJOR and, to his surprise, landed a program. The station got more than it bargained for, as Burge featured such musicians as the Velvet

Tim Burge became the music director, and among the new staff were popular local DJs J.B. Shayne, Terry David Mulligan, and John Tanner.

Meanwhile, inspired by the success of underground media in the United States, unlicensed Radio Free Vancouver began broadcasting illegally at 650 on the AM dial in 1969. Not surprisingly, these "radio pirates" incurred the wrath of the Canadian Radio and Television Commission (as the CRTC was then known). In one irreverent outburst, the rogue station's announcers sent out a greeting: "We're just here to say hello and hope that everybody is together."[70] However, the fortunes of both Radio Free Vancouver and CKLG-FM soon began to wane. Even CFUN, the long-time "top 40" station which in 1967 had rebranded itself CKVN and featured "underground music", returned to its old singles format in 1970.

When the psychedelic sound hit Vancouver, there was considerable diversity on the local music scene, which encompassed soul music (as exemplified by the band Soul Unlimited) and blues (Hydroelectric Streetcar and the Black Snake Blues Band) as well as mainstream rock'n'roll. Other bands, including Spring, Mother Tucker's Yellow Duck, and the Collectors, developed their own unique compositions. What didn't appear was an identifiable psychedelic sound unique to Vancouver. Instead the Canadian west coast remained in the shadow of California's music, inspired especially by the folk, peace, love, and brother-

Underground, the Grateful Dead, and Jimi Hendrix. The station's owner, prominent church-going Vancouver businessman Jimmy Pattison, did not appreciate this venture into surrealist pop and hired Red Robinson as the new program director. Robinson quickly informed Burge his "hippie-dippy garbage" was unacceptable and told the DJ he should get a haircut.[69]

The success of the Beatles' *Sgt. Pepper's Lonely Hearts Club Band* and the continued appeal of the San Francisco sound eventually caught the attention of one of Vancouver's more progressive rock promoters, the radio station CKLG. In March 1968 the station established a new outlet featuring an underground rock format, which began broadcasting as CKLG-FM.

hood themes of the San Francisco bands. Particularly memorable concerts were the Grateful Dead's show at Pender Auditorium and an appearance by Jefferson Airplane at Brock Hall, the student centre on the UBC campus. The edgier and more nihilistic sound of the Doors from Los Angeles had some appeal as well.[71]

The United Empire Loyalists were an example of a British-influenced band, but they quickly made the transition to the new music coming out of California, and produced their own interpretation of the San Francisco sound. Coming from a blues/rock background, the United Empire Loyalists became well known locally for long instrumental jams, presumed to convey to the listener the experience of dropping acid. One exuberant reviewer described the band as "excellent food for the brains of space travellers."[72]

Papa Bear's Medicine Show, described as a merging of the Doors and Lovin' Spoonful, produced what was perhaps the most experimental sound in Vancouver. The group received critical acclaim for adding funk, zip, and an acid sound to the blues genre.[73]

The Pender Auditorium on the east side hosted the first wave of alternative acid rock bands from California. Closer to the hippie epicentre of Kitsilano, the Afterthought on Fourth Avenue briefly provided a stage for psychedelic bands, but declining revenues forced it to close in 1967. That same year the Grateful Dead played at Dante's Inferno, located in the downtown core on Davie near Burrard. Roger Schiffer, a local rock impresario, saw an opportunity to bring a version of San Francisco's Fillmore West to Van-

couver and reopened the club in the summer of 1967 as the Retinal Circus. It quickly established a reputation across Canada for featuring the latest sound coming out of Los Angles and San Francisco as well as Canada's leading psychedelic rock groups. City authorities were less impressed with this "centre of social destruction," and Mayor Campbell's office instructed the police to rigorously enforce the dance hall curfew that required eighteen-year-olds to leave the dance hall by ten o'clock.

That summer, thousands of young boomers could be found "hanging at the Circus" and listening to Country Joe and the Fish against a backdrop of swirling coloured water and oil images on the walls. One observer recalled that a state of otherworldly self-indulgence prevailed: "The audience would wander around, or sit and stare, or lie down, or do whatever felt right."[74] Although alcohol was restricted, the psychedelia-inspired boomers were probably already high. The Circus attracted attention in the local media as well as police surveillance and weekly raids. Bob Cummings of the *Georgia Straight* believed a clash of cultures was unfolding and the Circus "symbolized a new form of entertainment that is frightening to some deeply entrenched conservatives ... suppression by harassment is not tolerable in a free society."[75]

Psychedelic rock art appeared in storefront advertising along Fourth Avenue and in some of the hip outlets in Gastown, such as the Yellow Submarine record shop. The psychedelic theme was also popular in the posters promoting music venues and concerts. Bob Masse established a reputation as Vancouver's most talented psychedelic artist. While living in California, he came under the influence of the psychedelic poster artists of San Francisco, including Bill Griffin and Stanley Mouse, and began producing his distinctive, wildly colourful posters and handbills for shows at the Fillmore West and Avalon Ballrooms in San Francisco. He brought his SF style back home to Kitsilano, where he drew posters for the Afterthought and the Retinal Circus.

Perhaps the most improbable venue for acid rock in Vancouver was University Hill United Church, which offered a "trip without acid" service replete with electric guitars, strobe lights, and go-go girls. Church attendance was in decline, a consequence, according to liberal opinion of the 1960s, of "the excessive dogmatism and rigidity" of mainstream churches. One solution was to provide a more relevant and hip environment. Jim McKibbon, a guest "conductor" from the Anglican Church, was inspired

The local dominance of CFUN's Top 40 format had come to an end in 1967, when the station's new owners switched format and name, to CKVN. This bus advertisement promotes CKVN's March 1970 relaunch as a pop music station after having recruited the top DJs of the new music from rival CKLG-FM. KEN LESTER COLLECTION

to produce the imitation acid trip, "tracing birth through despair to re-birth," after "talking with people who have taken LSD and finding they fell back on conventional religious mystical terminology."[76] The service incorporated readings from beat poets Allen Ginsberg and Lawrence Ferlinghetti, accompanied by Bobby Taylor and the Vancouvers. "Take-off" was scheduled for 8 p.m. Sunday.

Moving On: 1970-1973

In late 1970, John Lennon pronounced, "The dream is over."[77] What really ended was the mythology about drugs moving society towards some kind of cosmic unity, breaking down moral boundaries, and heightening the collective social consciousness and political awareness. At the end of the 1960s there was declining interest in all aspects of psychedelia, even in San Francisco. Reflecting the usual cross-border delayed reaction, it was several months before the *Georgia Straight* confirmed Lennon's observations. The psychedelic scene in Vancouver was "moving on."[78]

But as the 1970s got underway, it became clear that hallucinogenic drugs were not going anywhere. In fact, the LSD experience was being tried by more and more teenagers who were not necessarily becoming part of the hippie counterculture. Despite the anti-drug efforts of civic officials, high-school students became the new cohort for experimentation. A 1971 Narcotic Addiction Foundation survey of 2,496 students

The ecstatic response to the Rolling Stones at their 1972 Vancouver concert suggested the wide appeal of classic rock throughout the psychedelic era. PHOTOGRAPHER UNKNOWN / GEORGIA STRAIGHT COLLECTION, UBC SPECIAL COLLECTIONS

showed that 40 percent had tried marijuana before the age of nineteen, while 22 percent had experimented with LSD at least once.[79] The *Ubyssey* suggested that for the 1970s generation of teenagers, "drugs as a form of social protest eventually became drugs as a form of social escape."[80] After the 1971 Gastown smoke-in, using drugs became less an act of defying authority than a means of attaining a personal high. What was particularly disturbing to those seeking collectivism through chemistry was the reported increase in cocaine use, as cocaine was seen as a drug that enhances the ego, in contrast to the ego-undermining effects of LSD.[81]

Some radical fringe groups questioned just how revolutionary getting high really was. For example, the proto-communist Diggers in San Francisco denounced Timothy Leary as a charlatan who "lured children into a ghastly trap from which there is no visible escape."[82] At UBC, the Campus Left Action Movement (CLAM), a Maoist organization, denounced the psychedelic revolution as nothing more than "bourgeois decadence."[83] Similarly, *Young Blood*, another radical media voice in Vancouver, condemned "death drugs" — supposedly LSD, speed, and cocaine — as "a weapon

in the man's bag of tricks. They are used to keep us apart and keep us from dealing with the real source of our oppression — the corrupt Canadian state and all its pig-forces."[84]

Acid rock remained popular for some time, although its eventual decline was inevitable. The Retinal Circus closed its doors in the fall of 1968, and the United Empire Loyalists and Papa Bear's Medicine Show dissolved, their members moving on to other bands. The last major California acid rock show featured the Doors and Jefferson Airplane in March 1969. When the CBC began broadcasting underground music that year, the standing joke was that "the trip was over."[85]

Vancouver's music scene became edgier, angrier, and more politicized in the early 1970s. Gone were the psychedelic illusions about society making a peaceful transition to tuning in, turning on, and dropping out. A much more hardened view of political reality emerged. Larger events — the Amchitka anti-nuclear demonstrations, the Gastown smoke-in, and the survival of the "People's Park" — occupied centre stage. Local musicians seeking a new image adopted a political activist identity.[86] The band Uncle Slug was held up as an example of progressive-minded musicians "who faithfully do benefits for the community" and worked towards "a liberated non-ripoff environment."[87] Although the aims of benefit concerts included consciousness-raising, some activists believed that not all causes were equal. Members of a high-minded group calling itself the Jesus People seized the public address system at one benefit

City of Love and Revolution

and began "haranguing the crowd." Alas, as one of the more upbeat benefit organizers sighed, "Everybody gets off on a microphone."[88]

Vancouver's rising feminist movement frequently made its voice heard as well. CKLG was singled out for the absence of women DJs and for ads catering to "the submissive stupid chick."[89] A local variation of the United States-based Women's International Conspiracy from Hell (WITCH) threatened to "trash" Uncle Slug for playing "Hooker," a musical number that presumably glorified the life of a prostitute. At a benefit for *Young Blood* in November 1971, more than 400 people in attendance were entertained by the spectacle of a dozen women attacking the Burner Boys onstage for their "cock rock" chauvinism. Bottles of milk were thrown at the public address system, and the benefit degenerated into pandemonium. Up to this point, the discourse about the meaning of rock had been conducted on what seemed to participants to be a higher philosophical plane. For example, Mike Flensburg, one of the local pop philosopher-kings, noted that "cock rock" was not a useful analytical tool insofar as the issue "goes beyond cocks. It goes generally into the areas of human emotions and directly into human sexuality."[90]

Charges of sexism and commercialism were ignored when major rock groups came to town, as the Rolling Stones did in the summer of 1972. Known for "Under My Thumb" and other celebrations of male chauvinism, the band did not incur the wrath of anti-sexist female activists but did attract the attention of small-time thugs. Representing the "lumpen elements" of

Led Zeppelin surrounded themselves with psychedelic paraphernalia but musically marked a shift to heavy metal. **PHOTOGRAPHER UNKNOWN / GEORGIA STRAIGHT COLLECTION, UBC SPECIAL COLLECTIONS**

Vancouver's eastside, a group dubbed the Clark Park Gang — after a park at 14th and Commercial Drive, where they were said to congregate — vowed to disrupt the show at the Pacific Coliseum. Inside the sold-out Coliseum a crowd of 17,000 fans were entertained by the revolutionary overtones of "Street Fighting Man" as 2,000 ticketless activists outside protested raucously because the concert was not free.[91] The demonstration became violent, and thirty-one police officers were injured after facing a barrage of rocks, bottles, smoke bombs, and even a Molotov cocktail. Although the event has been interpreted as rock-inspired class conflict, local unions and the B.C. Communist Party saw only hooligan-like behaviour.[92] As for the Rolling Stones, the band did not impress civic officials and did not return to Vancouver until 1989.

Shortly after the Stones' visit, Vancouver's rock enthusiasts turned their attention to the latest pop music fad, Led Zeppelin, an English group that took blues-based rock in the direction of heavy metal. In an interview after Led Zeppelin's first Vancouver concert in August 1971, the lead singer, Robert Plant, commented on the creative dynamic that was pushing rock music in new directions. Pop had moved away from the psychedelic, Plant said, because "you can't keep turning out the same thing," and that bands continuing with the same sound "haven't got anything going for them in the brains."[93]

Conclusion

In the early 1970s, psychedelic drugs and music went their separate ways. Pop music, driven by the relentless creativity of its composers and the profit calculus of the music companies to provide something new, jettisoned any pretence of creating a permanent drug-inspired counterculture.[94] In 1971, Bill Storey, a Vancouver rock commentator, concluded, "The dream, as the song goes, seems to be over. The counterculture lives on as the ideal of a few, but its existence is, at best, marginal. All that happened in the 1960s, as John Lennon pointed out, is that a lot of people grew their hair. Overall, the loquacious oracle of the Fab Four concluded that very little really changed. 'Music was always a business. Musicians were, and are, people who play for a living.'"[95]

Vancouver's local psychedelic bands displayed some merit, but they enjoyed limited commercial success. The United Empire Loyalists' only single, released in 1968, sold a few hundred copies and did not make it onto the charts. The band disappeared from memory until a compilation of local music from the period, *The History of Vancouver Rock and Roll, Volume 3*, featuring their single, was released in 1983. The psychedelic light shows put on by Addled Chromish and Electoplasmic Assault were innovative and lively but ephemeral. It is the psychedelic art of Bob Masse that has been most remembered. Featured in several international galleries, Masse's work has also been prominent at Hippie Daze, the annual celebration of the Sixties on Fourth Avenue in Kitsilano.

Given restrictive laws and LSD's limited profit margins, an indigenous drug industry comparable in size and influence to the music business did not emerge to push the psychedelic frontier. Moreover, Vancouver's drug scene did not make the transition to the mass religious movement envisioned by Timothy Leary. In 1980, Leary returned to UBC and was greeted with skepticism and mild contempt.[96] He told the students that getting high would remove the unnecessary pain and punishment inflicted by "the dead weight of [the] Judeo-Christian tradition of morality,"[97] but by the end of the lecture the heckling students had conspicuously dismissed him as a doddering fool.

As far back as 1968, at least one student dismissed as self-indulgent Leary's prescriptions and "the whole onanist-hedonist-pill-LSD society of American decadence," which had been uncritically absorbed by Vancouverites, particularly UBC students suffering from "a cowardness [sic] based on a degenerate absolute craving for pleasure and an absolute fear of pain."[98] In the end, Vancouver's psychedelic moment only confirmed the insight of the Buddhists, who saw the possibilities of the world as infinite but inherently unstable.

The 'Gastown riot' on the night of August 7, 1971, when Vancouver police ran amok using the pretext of an earlier, non-violent 'smoke-in' at Maple Tree Square, was the closest Vancouver came to the violent confrontations that marked the era in the United States. GLENN BAGLO PHOTO / VANCOUVER SUN

CHAPTER 5

Taking It to the Streets
Yippie Activism, 1970–71

The turmoil of 1960s America redefined the idea of revolution. Sixties radicals often repeated the traditional leftist mantra about liberation from economic oppression through the "destruction of property,"[1] but what distinguished less-mainstream cultural revolutionaries from those of earlier movements was their call for liberation from the moral constraints of "Uptight Pig Nation."[2] By freeing mind, body, and soul, baby boomers could indulge in what was really meaningful: the joys of drugs, sex, and rock'n'roll. Equally important was the idea that the process of revolution should be fun, irreverent, and colourful. Essentially it was to be the comedy of the absurd played out in the streets as "guerilla theatre." The kinkier the political drama, the greater the opportunity for coverage on the evening news. The audience was not the traditional constituency of the left, the industrial working class; instead a younger cohort made up of loose coalitions of blacks, students, and counterculture dropouts was to be the agent of change.

The most active wing of the cultural revolt was an "anti-party" phenomenon, known as the Youth International Party or "Yippies," which appeared on the scene in 1967. Philosophically, these activists attempted to bridge the gap between libertarianism and collectivism. At the more practical level of day-to-day politics they sought to accelerate the politicization of longhair dropouts, at the same time introducing New Left students to the counterculture lifestyle.[3]

Although the designation Youth International Party suggested Yippies had a larger global agenda, Vancouver was the only non-US city to entertain a "revolution for the hell of it." Between April 1970 and the August 1971 Gastown riot, there were twenty-five recorded incidents of youth protests in the Vancouver/Victoria area, and Yippies were either the instigators or at the centre of these events.[4] Although there were other fringe activist groups, including Diggers, the Vancouver Liberation Front, and the Partisan Party, the Yippies had the greatest public exposure.[5] Vancouver's Yippies are of some note because they highlight the cross-border transfer of American popular culture. They also point to the influence Americans in Canada had on the propagation of anti-Americanism.

Vancouver came rather late to the Yippie party. The issue of the Vietnam War was not as pressing north of the border, and the Kitsilano counterculture, enjoying the blissful otherworldliness of the West Coast, was content to remain politically indifferent, basking in the mellow vibes associated with Stanley Park Be-Ins, street theatre, and psychedelic dance venues. No one on the local scene was comparable to such dynamic characters as Abbie Hoffman and Jerry Rubin. Until the spring of 1970, Yippie action remained south of the border.

American Yippie, 1967–70

Until the massive nationwide anti-war demonstrations in the spring of 1967, the counterculture and peace activists moved in separate circles.[6] Throughout the formative years of the drugs, sex, and rock'n'roll rebellion, hippie dropouts remained unin-

The Easter Be-Ins continued to draw large, peaceful crowds — here, thousands enjoy the vibe at the 1973 Be-In at Lumberman's Arch in Stanley Park. But for more and more hippies, 'being' was no longer enough. SHARKIE PHOTO / GEORGIA STRAIGHT COLLECTION, UBC SPECIAL COLLECTIONS

volved with the issues of the day. Sober and idealistic political activists, on the other hand, were not content to "turn on, tune in, and drop out." They were committed to ending the Vietnam War, organizing public rallies and teach-ins, and working within the reform wing of the Democratic Party to achieve this end.[7] Spontaneity, unpredictability, and the use of street theatre were not part of their tactics.

Abbie Hoffman, who had earlier taken part in the drive to register black voters in Mississippi, was a self-described "action freak" in search of a movement.[8] After a brief and stormy relationship with the black-dominated Student Non-violent Coordinating Committee (SNCC), he turned his attention to the flourishing underground scene on the Lower East Side of New York. Hoffman was particularly impressed with the outrageous street-theatre antics of a San Francisco group commonly known as the Diggers. He realized that New York's apolitical hippie culture could relate to street theatre that made a statement against oppression, and an opportunity to try out this new tactic presented itself in spring 1967. A demonstration sponsored by the patriotic group "Support Our Boys in Vietnam" has been identified as

Taking It To the Streets

the moment when the counterculture spilled over into the anti-war movement.[9]

Hoffman "spontaneously" organized a group of activist-minded hippies, sporting capes and flags, who joined the march and offered flowers to supporters of the war. Interviewed after the event, Hoffman memorably observed, "The cry of 'flower power' echoes through the land. We shall not wilt."[10] He recognized that the flowers "playfully" offended the marchers. More importantly, he understood that "colorful tension" appealed to the evening news shows on television, driven as they were by Neilsen ratings. He made sure the media was informed in advance of a potentially "violent confrontation," and the networks seized the opportunity to boost their evening news market share.

Hoffman later explained that the seemingly absurd way of protesting was informed by the avant-garde ideas of playwrights Samuel Beckett and Peter Weiss, whose *Marat–Sade* was exciting controversy on both sides of the Atlantic. The new style, described as *surrealpolitik* or theatrical politics, was ideal for the telegenic age of action and images. As for the spoken word, Hoffman avoided the long-winded New Left exposés regarding the excesses of American materialism and imperialism. Instead he "trained for the one-liner, the retort jab, and sudden knockout put-ons."[11]

The immediate purpose of *surrealpolitik* was to end the Vietnam War. There was also an expectation that future wars could be prevented by creating an egalitarian utopia in which aggressive impulses were curtailed by drugs, sex, and rock'n'roll. Woodstock, the ultimate rock event of 1969, was cited as an example of what the future would look like.[12] The anarchist-inspired hip utopia governed by the "pleasure principle" would be a celebration of personal freedom, spontaneous acts of generosity, volunteerism, and a non-hierarchical division of labour.

Throughout 1967, New York was entertained by several examples of *surrealpolitik*. Soot bombs went off in the foyer of the building that housed Consolidated Edison, a huge New York utility which symbolized polluting, coal-burning capitalism; "See Canada Now" posters were plastered all over the army recruiting centre at Times Square; and marijuana joints were mailed out to thousands of New Yorkers randomly selected from the phone directory. Probably the most publicized prank took place at the New York Stock Exchange, where Hoffman and others threw dollar bills from the balcony and then burned the money in front of the hastily assembled TV news cameras.

In October 1967, Hoffman brought the street theatre of the absurd to a huge demonstration at the Pentagon near Washington, DC, where he first joined forces with Jerry Rubin, the California guru of political theatre. Both rejected the "pompous and pretentious" posturing of the New Left,[13]

believing an eye-catching prank — a mass public exorcism of the Pentagon's evil spirits by levitating the concrete behemoth 300 feet in the air — would be more effective in getting media attention. Instead of promoting a physical confrontation, Hoffman and his pranksters placed flowers in the barrels of the soldiers' guns, and flirtatious hippie girls teased the soldiers with chants about making love not war. Hoffman and his supporters were a small minority among the 50,000 protesters, but they garnered more media attention than any other group at the Pentagon demonstration.[14]

At a New Year's party to mark the beginning of 1968, Hoffman, Rubin, and assorted friends came up with the idea of the Youth

Abbie Hoffman's book Woodstock Nation was a foundational text for the Yippie movement founded by Hoffman and Jerry Rubin.

International Party. This unusual political phenomenon would have no formal organization. Instead, its creators expected that Yippie behaviour in New York, Chicago, and San Francisco would in and of itself inspire "14-year old freaks in Kansas" and across the nation.[15] Through the pursuit of the "pleasure principle" and an appeal to the younger generation's preference for action and imagery, a revolution would be born.

It was perhaps the must undemanding revolution in recorded history, requiring little more of its supporters than to drop acid, groove to rock music, and grow their hair long. No self-discipline or personal sacrifice was required. Hoffman explained, "I don't like the concept of a movement built on sacrifice, dedication, responsibility, anger, frustration and guilt ... You want to have more fun, you want to get laid more, you want to turn on with your friends, you want an outlet for your creativity."[16]

Such impulsive behaviour did not lend itself to coordinating activity with other leftist groups. This became clear when groups from the entire left-wing spectrum converged on the Democratic National Convention, held in Chicago in late August 1968. The convention was the last chance for the Democrats to address the war by nominating a peace candidate, which was why it was important for left liberals to be there. But Yippies, members of the black power movement, and other radicals saw the convention as a chance to embarrass America on the world stage. These groups believed the real danger was posed not by the Republican Party but by left liberals who thought they could reform capitalism. Although Hoffman and Rubin attended pre-convention meetings of the National Mobilization Committee (MOBE), an anti-Vietnam War group, in the end the Yippies "did their own thing."[17] In particular, they ignored pleas for non-violence from David Dellinger, a prominent pacifist in the anti-war movement. Hoffman later conceded that he was more interested in provoking a major police overreaction to be recorded "for all the world to see" on network television. This would discredit the Democratic Party and remind young people across "Amerika" of the violent nature of the behemoth. To raise the pre-convention tension, Yippies circulated rumours that Chicago reservoirs would be contaminated with LSD, and Yippie girls disguised as hookers would spike delegates' drinks with hallucinogens. Thousands of "freaks" from across America would come to the city, be exposed to the inherent violence of the "American beast," and return home intensely politicized.[18]

The organizers' expectations were dampened as events unfolded. In spite of a national call for counterculture solidarity, only a few thousand Yippies appeared in Chicago's Grant Park for a demonstration, where they were soundly beaten by the police. Yippie leaders were then disappointed that mainstream America either supported the police or were indifferent to the plight of the longhairs.[19] As for the younger boomers, most remained intent on reforming the Democratic Party and eventually emerged as the George McGovern wing, which won the presidential nomination in 1972 but ultimately lost the election to Richard Nixon.

Hoffman, Rubin, and six other activists — the Chicago Seven — were charged with conspiracy to cross state lines to incite a riot. In 1970, after a notorious trial, they were found not guilty of conspiracy, but Hoffman, Rubin, and three others were convicted of crossing state lines to foment violence. The trial and the ensuing lengthy appeal process distracted them from political activity.

After Chicago, the Yippies continued their theatrical protests, but with less dramatic flare and enthusiasm. In contrast to other movements, they maintained a minimal degree of structure and authority, which over time inevitably led to chaos and lack of direction. The absence of structure, procedure, and party discipline also allowed egotistical posturing to run rampant. Women especially bore the brunt of the chauvinist impulses of male Yippie leadership, and prominent female activists like Robin Morgan preferred "to go it alone," independently organizing their own Yippie-style protests against the sexist stereotyping of the Miss America pageants.[20] Others within the movement were suspicious of the Hoffman/Rubin circus of excessive self-promotion and their pursuit of media star status.[21]

In August 1970, three hundred Yippies stormed Disneyland but misjudged the shock value of raising the flag of the Vietnamese National Liberation Front over Tom Sawyer's Island.[22] When people stopped taking offense at Yippie pranks, and when those pranks became predictable and un-newsworthy, the group's *raison d'être* came into question and it simply faded away.

Yippie comes to Vancouver, 1968–69

At first, Vancouver's hippie community was unaffected by the Yippie political theatre unfolding south of the border. In response to Mayor Tom Campbell's politicization of the hippie issue (as mentioned in Chapter 1, he described hippies as a "cancerous growth that is invading society"), there was a growing sense that longhairs should "fight politics with politics," and in March 1968 about four hundred people crowded into the Retinal Circus for the first meeting of a group calling itself the Alternative City Government. Organizers wanted to set up "free" coffee houses, establish a committee to monitor the police, and gain permission to hold an Easter Be-in in Stanley Park — not exactly the stuff of Yippie pranks.[23] Nothing of lasting importance came of these early efforts, but the issue of police harassment came up again the next year.

After the events of the Democratic Con-

October 24, 1968: The UBC Faculty Club is occupied by about 1,200 students, egged on by visiting Yippie co-founder Jerry Rubin. ARNIE BANHAM PHOTO / UBC REPORTS

vention in Chicago were televised, Yippie leaders earned remunerative book contracts and were in demand as speakers on university campuses. In the fall of 1968, the UBC student society's special events committee invited Jerry Rubin to visit the Vancouver campus. He readily accepted the invitation. Rubin recognized the cultural revolution in his own country was running into the wall of the Nixon/Republican reaction, but he saw some potential in the younger generation on Canada's West Coast.

Rubin's short visit was expected to be an entertaining but frivolous event on a rather staid middle-class campus. At the end of an impromptu lunch hour "be-in," the wild-haired, cape-clad Yippie leader disingenuously asked, "Is there any place on campus you are not allowed to go?" A small handful of eager undergraduates shouted, "The Faculty Club."[24] Rubin later admitted the occupation was not entirely a spontaneous act of Yippie theatre, as he had planned the event with a group of student radicals the previous evening.[25]

What did surprise the California longhair was the estimated 1,200 students who gathered on the steps of the Faculty Club, effectively disrupting the quiet lunch of the tea-sipping faculty. One liberal-minded professor welcomed the students "as long as you don't break things,"[26] but the expectation of civilized behaviour quickly proved to be naïve. The students, impressed with Rubin's uninhibited "toking up," proceeded to launch a pot party of their own in the for-

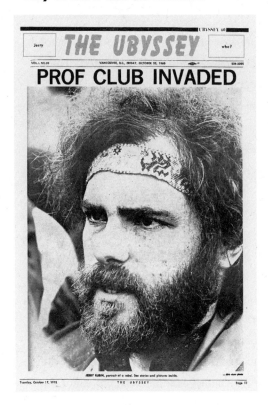

Rubin's visit and the Faculty Club occupation dominated the front page of The Ubyssey, *the campus newspaper.*
THE UBYSSEY, ALMA MATER SOCIETY ARCHIVES

mal dining room. In the course of the occupation, some $5,000 in liquor and other club belongings were "liberated and some minor damage was done to the furniture."[27]

Not all of the professors shared the open-minded tolerance of their liberal colleagues. Classics professor Malcolm McGregor was particularly upset that a single American "troublemaker" could so disrupt the peaceable kingdom. "I'm disgusted. The guttersnipe comes up from the United States and organizes this thing and all the students follow along like sheep."[28] Students, on the other hand, recalled the spontaneity and carnival atmosphere that lasted until the early hours of the next day.

Over the course of the next year the theatrical posturing of American Yippies was covered in the university's student paper and the local underground press. Joachim Foikis, the self-described "Town Fool," introduced Vancouver to the idea of street theatre with decided Yippie overtones. In April 1969 the Fool attracted some media attention by distributing kazoos and tambourines to down-and-outers on Skid Row. Later that summer, unemployed students offered a program of plays, puppet shows, comedy routines, and political theatre, aimed mostly at a younger audience, in the city's squares and parks.[29]

Vancouver Yippie is born

In 1969, as Yippie public events south of the border were becoming less well received, Jerry Rubin announced, perhaps prematurely, the "Death of Yippie." He pessimistically observed that "the war roars on, the San Francisco scene is gone, pot and acid are being challenged by speed and smack, Nixon has replaced Johnson, and white racism is stronger than ever . . . America proved to be deaf, and our dreams proved to be innocent."[30]

The Yippie spirit continued to flicker on Canada's West Coast, however, perhaps in part because cultural oppression was less pervasive there than it was south of the border. Canada was generally a less violent country, with fewer people in jail, and authorities were willing to support social welfare initiatives like Cool-Aid house, which provided short-term accommodation for people who would otherwise be on the street. The New Democratic Party brought a strong element of social justice to the political and social arena, and Canada tended to accept other cultures rather than requiring them to conform to the white, Anglo-Saxon mainstream.

British Columbia was by no means a utopia. Mayor Tom Campbell, not content to be part of the "silent majority," continued venting his anti-hippie rhetoric, and throughout the year there was an increase in the number of street people being charged for vagrancy and marijuana possession. At the end of August 1969, the social democrats of the New Democratic Party, who were at times sympathetic to youth issues, lost the provincial election. Clearly, higher authority could not speak to the concerns of the youthful rebels, and that fall the *Georgia Straight* ran a cover story suggesting the counterculture would have to be more militant in defence of its culture.[31] But despite mounting cultural tensions, Vancouver's activists had not reached Rubin's point of despair.

In January 1970, radical students at Simon Fraser University, including a handful of American draft dodgers, worked with the *Georgia Straight* to organize a "high energy" fundraising concert on behalf of American White Panther John Sinclair, who had been imprisoned for the insubstantial misdemeanour of marijuana possession. The fundraiser was unusually successful by the standards of such events.[32] It was also the first time a broad diversity of groups came together for one purpose, and it signalled the possibility of a new kind of revolutionary activity demarcated along generational lines.

The SFU students, recognizing an affinity with the more activist-minded hippies from the Kitsilano and Commercial Drive neighbourhoods, met with politicized hippies and

Joachim 'Kim' Foikis brought street theatre to Vancouver in the late 1960s, proclaiming himself the 'Town Fool'. The Canada Council made it semi-official in 1968, awarding Foikis a grant to pursue his vocation. VANCOUVER SUN

members of the Committee to Aid American War Objectors in April 1970 to form the nucleus of a new revolutionary movement. Thus, Americans having their own particular interests played a role in fomenting Canadian anti-Americanism.[33] The new group distinguished itself from the mainstream American movement by identifying itself as the "Northern Lunatic Fringe" of the Youth International Party.[34] Vancouver's Yippies were well aware of ominous developments south of the border, including the US invasion of Cambodia, and were initially preoccupied with American concerns, but they soon began to organize on issues specifically affecting the city and remained optimistic that they could advance the revolution here. Like their American cousins, they kept their distance from the traditional left, notably the Young Communist League and the eager reformers in the youth wing of the New Democratic Party.[35]

The Vancouver Yippies took a page out of the Abbie Hoffman playbook as they devised their basic strategy. First of all, it was important they manufacture a public image for the cultural revolt taking place in the city. Ideally, they would be portrayed as a part of the cultural vanguard that was on the verge of replacing mainstream culture. To achieve critical mass, the Yippies sought to "turn straights into hippies; turn hippies into revolutionaries."[36] They established an underground paper, the *Yellow Journal*, published out of an office in Gastown, which contained stories publicizing the themes of

American imperialism abroad and cultural oppression at home.[37]

Yippies harboured a keenly developed sense of their cultural oppression by the mainstream. They saw the occasional act of measured discrimination against longhairs as comparable to the treatment of blacks in the segregated south. After a few minor incidents involving security guards in the Hudson's Bay department store cafeteria, the Yippies concluded they had become

A toy pig was attached to a police cruiser clearing the way for a Yippie-organized anti-war demonstration in downtown Vancouver in the fall of 1971. It highlighted the playful nature of the Yippies, generally more noticeable in Canada than in the United States. PHOTOGRAPHER UNKNOWN / GEORGIA STRAIGHT COLLECTION, UBC SPECIAL COLLECTIONS

Vancouver Yippies were well aware of the excesses American 'pig nation' and warned of similar developments in Canada. **KEN LESTER COLLECTION**

the "white niggers" of Vancouver,[38] and the image of blacks sitting at a segregated Woolworth's counter prompted a Vancouver version referred to as the "Bay Sip-In." Following the guidelines proposed by Abbie Hoffman in his movement-founding book *Revolution for the Hell of It*, the media was alerted in advance to the introduction of Yippie theatre to Vancouver on 8 May 1970.[39]

After a few hours of leisurely sipping coffee, the Yippies were satisfied that they had unnerved the Bay's anti-longhair management.[40] They had not completely exorcised their pent-up grievances, however. Incensed by the American invasion of Cambodia and by the Ohio National Guard's shooting of four students at Kent State University during an anti-war demonstration on 4 May, the protesters headed for the United States consulate that evening. There, they burned the American flag and removed the Great Seal of the United States from the building's façade.[41] Several arrests were made, and one demonstrator later received a two-and-a-half-year sentence for freeing a prisoner and assaulting a police officer.

What really put Vancouver Yippies on the media radar screen was the so-called Blaine invasion on 9 May. Working in collaboration with the Vancouver Liberation Front, the Yippies led an estimated four to five hundred protesters in an illegal border crossing at the Peace Arch, followed by the symbolic occupation of the border town

City of Love and Revolution

of Blaine. Described as the first Canadian invasion of the United States since the War of 1812, the incident was widely covered in the newspapers and on TV stations in the Pacific Northwest.[42] What particularly caught the attention of media was the destruction of commemorative plaques and the shocking anti-imperialist slogans spray-painted on the Peace Arch. The invaders also "attacked" the border town of Blaine, singling out the Bank of America for a spree of window-breaking. Later, a passing freight train was pelted with rocks, which caused some $50,000 in damages to the new automobiles, destined for Vancouver dealers, on an open autorack. In response to the Canadian sacking of their community, the local population physically assaulted some of the Yippie invaders, prompting their retreat back across the border.[43]

Although the border incident met the basic objective of getting free publicity, these overt displays of anti-Americanism failed to generate much enduring support on the home front. Nor did the physical assaults by Americans produce any sympathy for the hapless Canadian activists in the mainstream Vancouver newspapers. Even the presumably sympathetic NDP, labour unions, and university students remained relatively quiet. George Muir, a Conservative Member of Parliament, was more vocal, calling the Canadian radicals a bunch of "hoodlums, queers, and just plain fools."[44]

A new direction for Yippies: 'All politics are local'

After the well-publicized direct attacks on the U.S. consulate and the border town of Blaine, Yippies turned to more pressing local issues. In 1970 the "prison industrial complex" became a major issue for American radicals outraged by overcrowding in prisons and the number of inmates convicted without due process. Growing prison unrest across the United States culminated in violence at the Attica Correctional Facility in New York, where prisoners rioted for better living conditions in 1971.[45]

Local Yippies took note of these events, if only because some of them were facing

Damage to United States consulate on Georgia Street. Yippie-inspired property damage was less common in Vancouver than south of the border. VLAD PHOTO / GEORGIA STRAIGHT COLLECTION, UBC SPECIAL COLLECTIONS

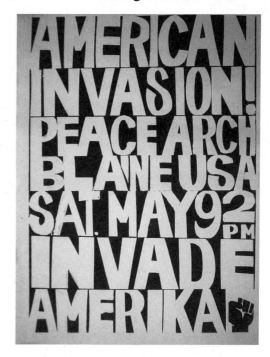

Trying to reverse the course of American imperialism, Canadians advertise their intention to invade the border town of Blaine, 30 kilometres south of Vancouver. KEN LESTER COLLECTION

judicial prosecutions and the prospect of receiving long-term sentences. Moreover, radicals saw the fear of imprisonment as a major factor deterring more people from becoming revolutionaries. So in July 1970, Vancouver Yippies informed the local media that their next public event would be a Sunday demonstration outside Oakalla prison in the nearby municipality of Burnaby.[46]

The Yippie-sponsored weekend "Be-out" did not disappoint the media. Participants donned colourful costumes and war paint, and sang popular American protest songs. Particularly amusing were the "Find a Narc in the Crowd" contest and a joint-rolling competition. The more activist-minded, intent on making a statement, tore down part of the prison's outer fence but did not venture past the phalanx of RCMP and prison guards.[47] By evening the Yippies had retreated from the park without further confrontation.

To keep activists out of prison, the *Georgia Straight* created a People's Defense Fund to pay for legal assistance for the growing number of longhairs being arrested. The paper also published a widely distributed manual that outlined a person's basic legal rights at the point of being arrested. Yippie public events — including dances and concerts — brought in revenue for these endeavours. To reach a wider audience, they sought the support of popular local bands including Uncle Slug and the Burner Boys.[48]

In addition to helping with the legal defence fund, Yippies made a major effort to help the local counterculture gain "free" access to basic necessities, opening a Free Store on West 7th Avenue, where customers were told to "give freely and take freely." The local Salvation Army and St. Vincent de Paul thrift stores were recommended as more traditional but cooperating outlets. Shoplifting was discussed, but readers were cautioned that stealing goods worth more than $50 was considered a serious offence.[49] The local YMCA, churches, and Cool-Aid were known to provide low-cost accommodation, and sleeping on the beach or in

City of Love and Revolution

Stanley Park was an option in the summer. As for food, several bakeries were willing to give away day-old bread, and scavenging at food outlets like Safeway, while not always a reliable source, was encouraged. The Yippies also continued the tradition established by the San Francisco Diggers and organized "feed-ins" at Jericho Beach and English Bay during the summer months.[50]

The search for free goods and services was a trademark characteristic of the Yippies, one not particularly well received by the general public. When Rubin addressed UBC students in 1968, he emphasized a point that had great appeal to the younger boomers unwilling to defer their basic gratifications: "Everything is free and we deserve everything. We want it now."[51] When the definitive counterculture movie *Woodstock* appeared at a local theatre, Yippies caused a minor street incident by demanding free entry. The theatre manager, concerned about rental costs and other overhead expenses, was less than charitable about the new lifestyle. "Why should they get in free? Everyone else pays. It's a good movie. The price is not exorbitant."[52]

The Gastown Riot

In the confrontation between the counterculture and the mainstream, the issue of drug use was more likely to lead to violent

The new counter-cultural imperialism: Happy warriors from Canada breach the 49th parallel and march into Blaine, May 1970. PHOTOGRAPHER UNKNOWN / GEORGIA STRAIGHT COLLECTION, UBC SPECIAL COLLECTIONS

outbursts than sex and music. Downtown Yippies, otherwise known as the "Gastown Dopes," actively challenged the "fascist" marijuana laws and occasionally promoted small gatherings or "smoke-ins." They were, in effect, recasting the law to agree with their own lifestyle and habits, but there was a larger political objective in play as well, inspired by Abbie Hoffman's idea that the marijuana issue was an opportunity to mobilize a base of support among the growing number of users — millworkers from New Westminster, renegade biker gangs, and middle-class university students.[53]

Mayor Tom Campbell, who held more conventional views about the legitimacy of the Narcotics Control Act and what constituted proper behaviour in public, was not happy that Gastown was "becoming the drug capital of Canada."[54] Much to the dismay of Campbell and other Vancouver civic authorities, the rule of law was further called into question when a federal Royal Commission raised questions about the enforcement of the drug laws. In April 1971, the Le Dain Commission, established by the Pearson government and charged with surveying Canadian habits and attitudes towards recreational drug use, released an interim report on the non-medical use of drugs. This report recommended that police officers use less draconian measures in the control of the use of soft drugs. There was also an implication that the laws themselves were outdated.[55] Vancouver's counterculture immediately recognized the report's significance. It opened a legal black hole that set the stage for violent confrontations in the summer of 1971.

Mayor Campbell largely ignored the Le Dain Commission's interim report and remained committed to strict enforcement of existing laws, giving Vancouver police a mandate to confront the perceived problem of growing drug use, especially in the Downtown Eastside. In July 1971 the mayor outlined a new strategy, for dealing with what was seen as a deteriorating situation. He urged Gastown operators of beer parlours, rooming houses, and restaurants to police their own premises and drive drug users into the streets. Undercover police would patrol bars to facilitate their ejection.[56] Once on the street, the users were subjected to an intimidating police control measure known as "saturation patrolling." Police would cordon off a specified area, block escape routes through alleys, and then detain and search everyone within the area. This measure was known as "Operation Dustpan" because its objective was to once and for all sweep the streets clean of the "filthy" drug culture. Gastown, according to some local accounts, was becoming a police state, and Yippies, the most active members of the neighbourhood's counterculture, were singled out in the police crackdown.[57]

These new measures re-enforced the Yippies' contemptuous stereotyping of the police, which dated back to a street theatre levitation of the police department in April 1970.[58] Borrowing from the imagery of the Chicago Democratic Convention, the Vancouver Yippies publicized the idea of police officer as "Pig," with a distinctly Vancouver irreverence. This insulting caricature appeared in newsletters and *Georgia Straight* cartoons, and in conversations overheard by police on the beat. In response, police displayed their hostility by targeting youths with particular haircuts, clothes, and street behaviours.[59]

To counter the growing police surveillance and harassment, local Yippies Ken Lester and Eric Sommer distributed posters and placed an advertisement in the *Georgia Straight* calling for a "Grasstown Smoke-In" on Saturday, 7 August 1971. Realizing the possibility for violence, they emphasized the event was "to be a peaceful sharing" celebrated with "a joyous high energy."[60]

It was a warm summer evening as a few hundred people gathered in Maple Tree Square at the centre of Gastown to dance to bongo drums and recorded music of the Grateful Dead. A half dozen Yippies appeared carrying an "eight-foot-long simulated marijuana cigarette." Ken Lester commanded attention by reading a petition calling for the legalization of marijuana. He then proceeded to burn a copy of the Narcotics Control Act. With Yippie flags flying, the assembled multitude chanted, "Legalize dope" and "We hate the pigs."[61] They were, however, far outnumbered by weekend fellow-travellers, curious onlookers, and some "suspicious characters."[62]

These latter might have included undercover police officers, who monitored the situation and reported that the gathering was being manipulated by radical elements who wanted to cause a confrontation with the police. The police later reported to an inquiry into the riot that one of the most provocative instigators was a known American draft dodger, who shouted, "Power to the people ... F...k the pigs, f...k the mayor."[63] As darkness fell, the officer in charge, Inspector Abercrombie, on the pretext that he had received reports of windows being smashed — which turned out to be false — ordered the crowd to disperse. Four mounted patrolmen immediately appeared, wielding riding crops, to break up the "smoke-in."[64]

Shortly thereafter, an estimated eighty helmeted policemen armed with nightsticks began moving towards the Maple Tree Square area. Although there were provocations from both sides, the police held the balance of power and meted out the most violence. Several longhairs and uninvolved

The attack on a shipment of new cars shows the harder edge of the Yippie-led Blaine invasion. The Straight's photo retoucher helpfully points out a rock leaving a protester's hand. PHOTOGRAPHER UNKNOWN / GEORGIA STRAIGHT COLLECTION, UBC SPECIAL COLLECTIONS

bystanders were clubbed by nightstick-wielding police officers, and blood spilled onto the street. The event was covered by CBC reporters and the local newspapers, which confirmed the excessive police violence.[65] Reports the next day indicated that twelve people had been taken to hospital, seventy-nine were in custody, and thirty-eight were charged with various offences.

This was Vancouver's first taste of mass violence since the unrest of the 1930s and the Grey Cup riots of the mid-1960s, but the city was spared the scale of bloodletting that had occurred in Chicago three years earlier.[66] Reaction on radio talk shows and in the newspapers was strongly divided. Art Phillips, a young city councillor, urged that immediate steps be taken to investigate the incident, and the provincial Ministry of the Attorney-General quickly set up a commission, headed by Justice Thomas Dohm, to interview eyewitnesses and make recommendations. Although the Dohm Commission raised questions about the Yippies' intention to deliberately provoke violence,[67] it singled out the "excessive" behaviour of the police and condemned them for overreacting, a conclusion supported by the BC Civil Liberties Union.[68] The City of Vancouver prosecutor's office recommended that five officers be charged, but prosecution did not materialize because of resistance from Mayor Campbell and the police union.[69]

City officials and Gastown merchants also moved quickly to create a more civilized and tolerant climate. The following weekend a street party was held in the neighbourhood. Local bands played for free, and thousands danced in the streets, which were closed to traffic. Merchants provided free watermel-

ons, hot dogs, and popcorn. An estimated 15,000 were in attendance, and the twenty or so police officers on the scene ignored the public displays of drinking and marijuana smoking.[70]

The counterculture returned to the scene as well. There were longhaired, braless teenage girls and shirtless males with headbands, all mingling without any particular street agenda. Yippie spokesmen promised that they would work towards "keeping the event peaceful."[71] Reminiscent of the first act of flower power in New York in 1967, a local longhair offered a police officer a flower, possibly as an act of reconciliation.

In the end, the police assault on the youthful drug users did not expand the base for the cultural revolution. What the Yippie leaders failed to understand was that soft drug usage was now common among the middle class, and these "straights" could enjoy the delights of getting high without signing on to the Yippie cause. The counterculture activists also did not see that the people inclined to support them during the riot were essentially "undesirables" — street toughs from the eastside, biker-gang miscreants looking for action, and rebels without a cause from downtown pool halls. They were generally younger males looking for trouble, with no long-term ambitions to transform or improve society.[72]

Berkeley déjà vu: The People's Park comes to Vancouver

The course of Vancouver Yippie activism was determined by immediate lifestyle issues, a calculation of what would catch the attention of a broad cross-section of middle-class youth and generate interest among the media, and an understanding of events in the United States. These considerations were reflected in the decision to occupy a parcel of undeveloped land near the Georgia Street entrance to Stanley Park in the late spring of 1971.

Two years after acquiring fourteen acres of prime land between the Bayshore Inn and Stanley Park, the Four Seasons hotel chain began drawing up development plans in the fall of 1969. The next step was to acquire all the remaining waterfront property bordering Coal Habour, which was owned by the federal government. The development proposal called for three thirty-three-storey apartment buildings, three lower-rise eight-storey buildings, and a fourteen-storey hotel. Public reaction to the proposal, expressed in letters to the editor, court cases, and discussions at city council, was overwhelmingly negative.[73] By the end of 1970, the project was in limbo, with neither side gaining ground.

Vancouver Yippies recognized that a continuation of the impasse would eventually play into the hands of the developers. Now was the time to act if they were going to stop

Taking It To the Streets

Sometimes the police appeared to be less menacing than Yippie rhetoric suggested. PHOTOGRAPHER UNKNOWN / GEORGIA STRAIGHT COLLECTION, UBC SPECIAL COLLECTIONS

the Four Seasons chain from turning the site into "a religious Mecca for the worship of plastic."[74] Money was raised to buy saplings and flowers, and peat moss, shrubs, and a variety of garden tools were donated. The media was alerted, and the *Georgia Straight* invited the community to come down to witness the creation of a new park.[75]

Parks had a special attraction as enclaves of public space where members of the Rousseau-inspired counterculture could return to a state of nature. They believed that, ideally, parks should remain non-industrial and non-commercialized for all time, and every effort should be made to expand their area and restrict the further encroachment of urbanization. In a perfect world, parks would also accommodate the lifestyle of the counterculture, which was facing resistance from mainstream society. There was nowhere longhairs could go to sleep and "do their own thing" on the downtown streets. They were constantly being hassled for gathering in groups — which they preferred to describe as "tribes" (a term borrowed from U.S. west coast counterculture). Vancouver's Stanley Park was faulted for not being open to the new music, organic concessions stands, or counterculture educational classes.

Vancouver Yippies were particularly impressed by the short-lived "people's park" that had so inspired counterculture activists in Berkeley, California.[76] In that case, Americans had acted decisively to protect public space, seizing an empty lot owned by the University of California at Berkeley that was slated to be the site of

dormitories and other university buildings. Berkeley's students and street people had an alternative vision, occupied the land in April 1969, and renamed it the "people's park." The occupation immediately led to a confrontation with the university and sparked a *cause célèbre* among liberal-minded people throughout the Bay area.[77] The counterculture underground in Vancouver had followed the developments in Berkeley closely, and they vowed that the Four Seasons land would be "a place to come to, be at, and go from" — in short, a successful version of the Berkeley experiment, which ended after a month when the National Guard was sent in by Ronald Reagan, governor of California at the time.

The liberation of the Four Seasons land began on a Saturday morning at the end of May 1971. A few dozen longhairs approached the fenced-off area adjacent to Coal Harbour, cut a hole in the fence, and proceeded to "liberate" the site. Although they "officially" named it "All Seasons Park," some, in recognition of the Berkeley antecedent, called it "People's Park." Caught up in the spirit of the moment, some described the event as "a symbolic attempt to inspire people and give them confidence to take back the earth."[78]

The occupiers proceeded to give their liberated territory some revolutionary legitimacy. The media and city officials duly noted the presence of North Vietnamese and National Liberation Front flags. Curiously, a Canadian flag was also prominently displayed.[79] In an effort to make the liberated park a self-sustaining and viable long-term community, gardens were planted, and makeshift dwellings erected. Next came a children's playground and a baseball diamond, and pieces of sculpture soon dotted the landscape. In the words of its urban cultural pioneers, it was to be a "people's park" founded on "a hope."[80]

The idea was not welcomed by civic authorities. Nine people were arrested for tearing down the fence, although those who managed to set up makeshift lodgings on the land were not forced to leave. Mayor Campbell was appalled by the spectacle. "The young people showed a complete disregard for authority," he noted. "This is a breakdown of society."[81] Yet the mayor was not prepared to use force and said it was a problem for the Four Seasons hotel chain and the federal government to deal with. Campbell recognized that public opinion was split over the proposed development for the site. Moreover, the local NDP took up the cause, as did Harry Rankin, a prominent figure on city council. This gave the Yippie effort some significant political traction.

Throughout the summer, Four Seasons and the federal government remained inde-

The Yippies were behind the 1971 occupation of All Seasons Park at the entrance to Stanley Park and were effective in their use of mainstream news media in the occupation's early days. PHOTOGRAPHER UNKNOWN / GEORGIA STRAIGHT COLLECTION, UBC SPECIAL COLLECTIONS

cisive about the course of development. In June, a city plebiscite was held in which 51 percent of Vancouver residents voted to buy the land — but this number fell short of the necessary 60 percent for approval. Meanwhile, the site's population continued to grow; by midsummer there were an estimated three to four hundred inhabitants. The social highpoint was an "informal" wedding between "Crazy Horse" and his bride, Arlene. In the course of the ceremony, rice was thrown and a nude couple approached to offer their best wishes.[82]

Inevitably tension developed, but it was not between the longhairs and conservative, intolerant, church-going Vancouverites. Rather, it was the employed service sector workers living in high-rise apartments on the other side of Georgia Street — store clerks, bartenders, and bank tellers — who were pitted against the lifestyle excesses of the underclass dropouts. At night, amplified music rocked the neighbouring renters, who had to go to work the next day. They asked Police Chief John Fisk to enforce the anti-noise bylaws, but he responded by noting that the squatters were on land over which the city had no jurisdiction.[83]

Mayor Campbell visited the site on two occasions and explained to his critics that the occupation was not an issue for city hall to resolve. Others in the city government were reluctant to press the issue. City police monitored the situation but made no further arrests. Health authorities, when asked to comment on the sanitation conditions in

Yippies exhibited a 'joyous high energy' during the All Seasons Park occupation. PHOTOGRAPHER UNKNOWN / GEORGIA STRAIGHT COLLECTION, UBC SPECIAL COLLECTIONS

the park, which had become an unappealing, smelly eyesore strewn with garbage, remained quiet. One official, not willing to be identified by name, commented, "It is just too hot a potato politically."[84] After being on the political firing line for his handling of the Gastown riot, Campbell was now taken to task for tolerating the "squatters in the park." Later in August he explained that his policy was actually a clever ploy to isolate the "young vagabonds" in a specific area, thereby deflecting them from "camping all over like in Stanley Park and Kitsilano."[85]

By the end of the summer, the Yippies and other activists, having established the park, were long gone, leaving behind a ramshackle community of transients from across Canada. There was little sense that they were cultural pioneers building a society of the future. Instead, the park people spent their days panhandling and their nights drinking cheap wine and smoking marijuana while singing refrains from the latest Rolling Stones album. The co-operative spirit of the heady days of June was replaced with bickering and infighting. As food resources became scarce in September, the occupants began stealing from each other. One newspaper reporter sent to the park observed that it looked more like a chaotic "Bedouin camp" than "a launch pad

for a revolution."[86]

Over the winter the transient population declined to less than a dozen; no Yippies were to be found among them. As the weather warmed the following spring, Alderman Art Phillips expressed concern that the park would again become a teeming shantytown. The National Harbours Board, which still controlled the centre of the Four Seasons Park site, was particularly anxious that the issue be resolved. Bill Rathie, chairman of the Vancouver port authority, contacted the mayor's office to request that measures be taken to remove the remaining "squatters" on federal government land, but the mayor was not available. His secretary explained he was at the dentist having an impacted molar attended to.[87]

Rathie quickly grew impatient with the civic authorities' unwillingness to act and ordered the National Harbours Board police to tear down the shacks and remove the occupants. They razed four lean-tos, and out straggled the survivors of the revolutionary occupation, including four mangy dogs and a dozen half-starved young teenagers. One of them, a sickly girl in need of medical attention, was taken to hospital. The rest were driven to the Cool-Aid house in Kitsilano.[88] Only makeshift toilet facilities and what appeared to be a primitive rainwater supply system remained. Garbage was strewn everywhere, and rats were spotted scouring the wreckage.[89] The next day some activists attempted to build a lean-to on nearby land, but the harbour police evicted them as well.[90]

After a year and a half of drama in the park, the Four Seasons development did not materialize. In August 1972, Four Seasons officials officially announced the company would not proceed with plans for the multi-tower complex. They blamed the waffling National Harbours Board, which had reneged on earlier promises regarding the acquisition of waterfront property, as well as the growing criticism from activists on city council, most notably Harry Rankin.[91] A particular thorn in their side was legal challenges by Leslie Phillips, a long-time city resident and retireee, who wanted to save the park entrance for future generations.[92]

Interestingly, Four Seasons officials had tolerated the occupation of the site, and did not mention the Yippie action as a factor in stopping the development. Nonetheless, Yippies have taken some credit for the demise of the project in their official history.[93] In 1977, the Four Seasons site was officially annexed to Stanley Park, thus freeing more public space from the surrounding concrete jungle and fulfilling the Yippie vision for the land.

Conclusion

In spite of the apparent success of the park occupation, there were continuing problems with the Vancouver Yippies' organization and finances. In the fall of 1970, the *Yellow Journal* offices had been broken into, and the paper's remaining cash reserve — fifty dollars — was stolen.[94] The paper published

its last issue in late 1970. With the demise of the Four Seasons park in the spring of 1972, there was a sense that the scene was moving on.[95]

In hindsight, it's clear that Vancouver reacted with a great deal of restraint when confronted with the spectacle of a Yippie cultural revolution, in contrast to what happened south of the border. Although there was street violence during the Gastown riot, it is significant that both sides attempted a reconciliation the following weekend. Lester, Sommer, and other Yippies were not prosecuted for conspiracy, as the Chicago Seven were. Similarly, the Four Seasons Park ended with a whimper, and there was no violent confrontation during the course of the occupation. In the case of Berkeley's People's Park, University of California authorities asked for a police intervention, and in a fit of overreaction the National Guard was called in. One student was killed and several dozen protesters were wounded after the police opened up with shotgun volleys.[96]

Although Canadian Yippies were inspired by Berkeley's People's Park and by other events in the United States, there is no evidence of an international Yippie conspiracy in Canada.[97] Nor was the RCMP able to document any connections to foreign Communist regimes, whose bureaucratic administrations were, in any case, detested by Yippies. Canadian Yippies were indigenous, spontaneous, and not terribly original. Most importantly, they were much less confrontational than their American counterparts. Whatever American influences drove them initially were soon replaced by local preoccupations. External pressures, such as police surveillance and harassment, may actually have unified Yippies. As for internal problems related to the movement itself, there were accusations of sexism and publicity-seeking, as there was in the United States, but these, as well as criticism of Ken Lester's leadership, such as it was, were muted. (Lester, one of the organizers of a movement noted for its lack of organization, worked on the *Yellow Journal* and helped come up with the idea for the Grasstown Smoke-In, but his greatest contribution is as an observer of events and a collector of ephemera from the movement and the era, making him an invaluable resource for historians.)

In the end, Yippies withdrew from the scene without much attention from either the police or the media. Many of them, upon entering their thirties, simply began working at regular jobs and supporting their families. Others ended up in the anarchist movement (Groucho Marxist). Lester eventually moved on to the music scene, getting involved with the punk rock group DOA in the late 1970s, before relocating to Whistler to build his

Winter 1972: Police dismantle the rough-and-ready structure that served as the People's Park presence for Greeanpeace. The nascent environmental movement had been formed the previous summer. VANCOUVER SUN

dream mountain chalet and retreat.[98]

While hippies are pleasantly remembered during the annual Fourth Avenue Hippie Daze, Yippie-inspired events are not accorded quite the same attention. In 2008, the company redeveloping the old Woodward's building in Vancouver's Downtown Eastside commissioned artist Stan Douglas to create a mural of the Gastown Riot of August 1971. The Vancouver police chief, Jim Chu, expressed dismay at Douglas's piece and contacted the artist to ask him to reconsider the project. Police spokesman Tim Fanning, conscious of the past controversy, explained, "Who wants to have a piece of history that isn't something that they are proud to put up."[99] Gregory Henriquez, the Woodward's project's chief architect, concluded, "Luckily, we don't live in a society where the police chief has any say over public art."[100] It was a denouement that few in 1971 would have foreseen.

CHAPTER 6

'Peaceniks' and Protest

Vancouver's Disarmament and Anti-War Movement, 1961–72

The noisy but orderly October 1971 protest against nuclear testing on Amchitka Island was Vancouver's largest peace demonstration to that date. An estimated nine to ten thousand protesters, mostly students from local high schools, shouted anti-nuclear slogans as they passed the American consulate on Burrard Street. Newspapers in Paris, London, New York, and Seattle covered the event.

Vancouver peace marchers welcomed their new status on the international protest stage with enthusiasm. Closer to home,

Rand Holmes's caricature of US president Richard Nixon, which appeared in a December 1971 issue of the Georgia Straight, *proposed a Reichian explanation for militarism and the arms buildup.* RAND HOLMES / GEORGIA STRAIGHT COLLECTION, UBC SPECIAL COLLECTIONS

their hopes were also raised. Student leader Robert Stowe predicted that Prime Minister Pierre Trudeau would respond to public sentiment and withdraw Canada's military from NORAD (North American Air Defence Command, the joint US-Canadian military organization responsible for air and sea defence), stop shipments of nickel for American armaments production, and call for an emergency meeting of the United Nations Security Council to stop nuclear testing.[1] Such was the heady mindset of the rising generation of Vancouver baby boomers.

The anti-Amchitka protest distinguished Vancouver's anti-war movement from others in Canada by linking nuclear weapons testing to the emerging environmental movement.[2] This event also marked the beginning of an indigenous peace/environmental movement completely independent of foreign influences. Up to that time, many Vancouver peace initiatives had been driven by the local Communist party, reflecting the Soviet Union's position regarding American nuclear superiority, or by American "peaceniks," who sought to coordinate Vancouver's anti-Vietnam war initiatives, which called for an end to Ottawa's collaboration in the war, with their own larger objective of getting the United States out of Vietnam.[3]

The American peace movement, 1961–72

Throughout the twentieth century, the limits to the American liberal tradition of public protest were most clearly defined in the context of challenges to national security policy. During the early Cold War years, the US peace movement was monitored by the FBI, which effectively infiltrated Communist front organizations. Later, the cause of anti-Vietnam war protesters was undermined by CIA and Army G-2 Counterintelligence Corps operations. Among the general public, the American Legion and other patriotic organizations strongly expressed their antipathy to "peaceniks and communist sympathizers." However, it was internal fissions, not the inhospitable external climate, that irreparably harmed the effectiveness of the protest movement by the late 1960s.[4]

In the early 1960s, peace organizations were divided between moderate mainstream groups and those dominated by the Communist Party of the United States (CPUSA) and its various front associations. It was easy for the FBI to monitor, and the media to criticize, this separate "un-American" movement. At the time, CPUSA groups vigorously denied having any foreign connections, but recent scholarship has documented operational ties to the Soviet Union.[5]

A Communist Party anti-nuclear demonstration at Victory Square in downtown Vancouver, early 1960s. VANCOUVER SUN

The mainstream of the Cold War peace movement was represented by the Committee for Sane Nuclear Policy (SANE). Created in 1957, SANE included prominent artists, actors, and public intellectuals. Organizers made a considerable effort to screen its membership so no radicals, especially those with ties to the Soviet Union, were allowed to join. This kept SANE independent of foreign influences and meant it was able to maintain some credibility even at the height of the Cold War.[6]

The first major issue for the peace movement was the massive strategic arms buildup of the Kennedy administration. John F. Kennedy campaigned for the presidency on the issue of a "missile gap," and within a year of his taking office in 1961, the United States had a strike force of 1,700 intercontinental bombers, several dozen intercontinental ballistic missiles (ICBMs), and 80 Polaris missiles.[7] The CPUSA, acting on instructions from Moscow, spearheaded a unilateral nuclear arms reduction movement

'Peaceniks' and Protest

designed to turn public opinion against the government's policy of maintaining strategic superiority. The protests were vocal, but given the legacy of McCarthyism, which stoked US fears of communist subversion, their effect on national public opinion was inconsequential. SANE, on the other hand, organized a march to the United Nations Plaza in New York, highlighting the "overkill" capability of the American arsenal. The 1961 event drew an estimated 25,000 supporters. SANE also focused on political lobbying, supporting candidates who worked for an end to the arms race and, as the Vietnam War began to escalate, an end to the war.

American universities became the centres of protest for members of the baby boom generation speaking out against the war. The political middle ground shifted to the left, and SANE came to be viewed as far too

The Bay-area campus of Berkeley was a hotbed of anti-war activism, and events there were closely followed by Vancouver peace activists. BERKELEY POSTER COLLECTION, UBC SPECIAL COLLECTIONS

moderate. As for the peace initiatives of the CPUSA, the Communist Party was almost completely ignored and contemptuously dismissed by the campus peace movement.[8] New organizations appeared, notably Students for a Democratic Society (SDS) and the Student Nonviolent Coordinating Committee (SNCC). Almost from the beginning, campus protests were more confrontational and less respectful of state authority than the demonstrations in major urban areas. Berkeley, home of the Free Speech Movement and the Vietnam Day Committee, was initially one of the most active campuses. The Vietnam policies of the Johnson administration were vehemently challenged during teach-ins, and on one occasion a figure of President Lyndon Johnson was burned in effigy.[9]

The expansion of the draft pool fuelled the racial and generational conflicts. Ever since 1918 the US Selective Service System had drafted men to fill the armed forces' needs to staff bases in the United States and overseas. As more soldiers were needed to fight in Vietnam, the number of young men drafted doubled to 35,000 per month in 1965 and then to 40,000 per month in 1967. However, those enrolled in university or special training programs were exempt, which meant the number of young black men drafted was disproportionately high — a fact highlighted by the actions of the black civil rights movement and student anti-draft protests on university campuses.

The protests had a negligible effect on public support for the war. This was due less to the public's perception that anti-war protesters were driven by communism or had any connections to a foreign power, however, than to the public's disgust at the protesters' overtly anti-American behaviour. One observer has suggested that it was this aspect of the movement that most alienated mainstream opinion.[10] A patriotic sensibility prevailed even among the twenty-one to twenty-nine age group, reflected in the fact that as late as March 1966, 71 percent of Americans in that age group believed the US intervention in Vietnam was not a mistake.[11]

In 1967, the number of troops deployed to Southeast Asia reached 485,000, and new recruits were desperately needed so more could be sent. As a result, the student deferment was removed in stages — undergrads would be called up first, then graduate students, then married students — from the list of items that could shield a person from the draft. In response, protests reached a fevered state on campuses, and the anti-war movement in the larger northern cities from San Francisco to New York grew exponentially. The general strategy was to influence the media, public opinion, and Congress in support of a US withdrawal — the protesters were not supporting the Vietnamese communists but simply said the United States should not be involved. In short, the movement remained essentially in the mainstream of consensus politics.

The turning point for American public perception of the war came in 1968. The change can partly be attributed to the effective use of popular culture to spread the anti-war message, although the public was less impressed by the use of "vulgar" street theatre antics. More importantly, the spring 1968 Tet offensive by the National Liberation Front (NLF) insurgency in Vietnam appeared to contradict the US government's claim that it was winning the war and that the NLF was incapable of such an offensive.[12] Anti-war demonstrations gained momentum, peaking with gatherings of over 500,000 protestors in New York and Washington.

Just as the anti-war movement reached its zenith, fissures began to appear. At the Democratic Convention in Chicago in summer 1968, the Yippies refused to cooperate with the National Mobilization Committee (MOBE), and members of the black civil rights movement also made it clear they had their own agenda. Within SDS, the "crazies" were beginning to appear, activists who turned to violence and bizarre ways of protesting the war and who openly welcomed a communist victory. One SDS-affiliated group, the anarchist Up against the Wall Motherfuckers based in New York, caused

The city's university campuses served as another vector for the Berkeley/San Francisco influence, frequently hiring Berkeley alumni (who were sometimes draft dodgers) to teach. **COURTESY STEPHEN DUGUID**

particular havoc. Progressive Labor, a stridently Maoist sect that had broken away from the CPUSA, added its own uncompromising political agenda to the movement.[13]

At the level of national politics, the Democratic Party spawned a more moderate anti-war movement around the unassuming Minnesota senator Eugene McCarthy, and Senator Robert Kennedy added his support to those critical of "Johnson's War." This wing of the Democratic Party offered a national base of support and consequently attracted some activists from SDS and even more radical groups.[14] The election of President Nixon with the support of "the silent majority" signalled the emergence of a powerful challenge to the message of the peace activists. At the same time, "Vietnamization" of the war saw a withdrawal of American troops as South Vietnamese soldiers were trained and equipped to carry on the war. In May 1970 there was a flare-up of protest over the US invasion of Cambodia, and four students were shot to death by National

The Communist Party of Canada organized this anti-nuclear arms demonstration in downtown Vancouver in the mid-1960s. The CP emphasized the impact of Cold War politics on women and children. PHOTOGRAPHER UNKNOWN / THE FISHERMAN COLLECTION, UBC SPECIAL COLLECTIONS

Guard troops at a Kent State University anti-war demonstration. Nonetheless, anti-war sentiment continued to grow among Americans, and the Nixon administration pursued peace negotiations with North Vietnam. By the time the Treaty of Paris was signed in December 1972, ending the Vietnam conflict, the nationwide anti-war movement had collapsed.

The peace movement in Vancouver, 1961–65

Throughout the early 1960s the Vancouver peace movement was divided between a moderate wing and a more vocal and activist group of Communist supporters. What these groups had in common was a concern about the arms race and the growing prospects of nuclear war. Until the mid-1960s, the mainstream anti-nuclear weapons activists in Vancouver, while well informed about the Aldermaston marches (which protested the Atomic Weapons Research Establishment near the village of Aldermaston in England) and the activities of SANE across the border, did not have any lasting direct ties to their like-minded comrades in the United States or Great Britain.

Local Communist activists and their associated peace organizations, on the other hand, were largely devoted to advancing the Soviet Union's strategic interest. To this end, the Communist Party of British Columbia (CPBC) organized demonstrations and used its weekly newspaper (the *Pacific Tribune*), the BC Peace Council, and "a very attractive float" in the PNE parade as means to propagate unilateral disarmament and stop the deployment of nuclear weapons in Canada.[15] Communists calculatedly used innocent untutored children as a particularly effective way of getting their point across. The Communist organizations ostensibly shared the larger concerns of the mainstream peace movement, but their actions were not always convincing.[16] It was no coincidence that issues affecting the Soviet Union had a direct impact on the timing of CPBC protests. For example, the 1961 Berlin crisis, when East Germany closed the border between East and West Germany and began building the Berlin Wall, sparked a burst of demonstrations and letter-writing campaigns calling for Canada to support disarmament and the signing of a German peace treaty. CPBC actions showed a certain bias, as they consistently presented the Soviet Union as the sole power promoting disarmament and the United States as the "imperialist aggressor."[17] Communist supporters also conveniently overlooked the series of dangerously polluting atmospheric nuclear tests conducted by the Soviet Union between 1961 and 1964.

Among the moderate peace-movement

groups, the University of British Columbia Nuclear Disarmament Club (UBCNDC) maintained its credibility by disassociating itself from any particular foreign power. There were reportedly some Communists in the organization, but efforts were made to isolate or expel them, and Directing Secretary Dorothy Thompson made it clear on several occasions that the group had no ties to any religious, political, or ethnic organizations and was only concerned with "human survival."[18] Despite this, the RCMP occasionally conducted surveillance on the assumption that UBCNDC was compromised by the influence of either Trotskyists or Soviet sympathizers.[19] The UBC group was informally tied to the Combined Universities Campaign for Nuclear Disarmament (CUCND), a large, national, "ban the bomb" movement.

Off campus, the Vancouver chapter of the BC Committee on Radiation Hazards also promoted nuclear disarmament. Its members, including scientists, educators, and some local journalists, were moderate peace activists who, having no larger political agenda, focused on the dangers of nuclear war and sought to broaden their base by working with labour unions and school boards. To reach a wider audience, they sponsored anti-nuclear parades, petitions, screenings of documentary films about the effects of the bombing of Hiroshima and Nagasaki, and booths at the Pacific National Exhibition.[20]

In November 1961, UBCNDC worked

The Peace Arch crossing at Blaine was a popular venue for demonstrations with an anti-American theme. This 1970 demonstration focussed on Richard Nixon and the role of the US in Vietnam. JACK PHILLIPS PHOTO / PACIFIC TRIBUNE

with the Committee on Radiation Hazards during "Disarmament Week" to highlight such issues as US production of nuclear weapons (many people believed the US had pulled so far ahead in the arms race that it should scale back its arsenal), their possible deployment on Canadian soil, and the danger of atmospheric — as opposed to underground — nuclear tests. The groups used visually arresting actions, such as burning a ten-foot BOMARC missile in the UBC main mall, in an effort to capture media attention, but the protests remained civil and, on occasion, entertaining. The non-communist peace activists did not display any particular animus towards the United States, drawing equal attention to the Soviet Union's atmospheric testing and reckless rhetoric, which did not inspire confidence in Soviet intentions.[21] Despite these efforts to maintain a semblance of neutrality, campus hawks occasionally expressed their indignation at the campus anti-nuclear movement.[22] There were, however, no reported incidents of violence or uncivil behaviour.

The Kennedy administration's strategic arms buildup did not attract widespread attention in Vancouver, but the October 1962 Cuban Missile Crisis triggered alarm across the city.[23] The rising anxiety was

reflected in the debate over the deployment of nuclear weapons in Canada in the form of the nuclear warhead on the medium-range BOMARC missiles. The BC Peace Council, essentially a front organization for the CPBC, recognized this as an opportunity to gain political support and shift the nuclear balance of power in favour of the Soviet Union.[24] However, the council's demonstrations were conspicuous for their lack of boomer-aged students as the Peace Council attracted an older crowd in an attempt to cultivate a certain middle-class respectability and credibility.

On campus, the UBCNDC response to the missile crisis focused on two issues: the deployment of nuclear-tipped BOMARC missiles on Canadian soil and atmospheric weapons testing. Like the nation in general, Vancouver was split on the BOMARC issue. In a campus referendum at UBC, 47 percent of students voted against accepting nuclear arms under any conditions.[25] The effort to end atmospheric testing resonated with the public, though it was of no consequence for the negotiation of the 1963 Partial Test Ban Treaty between the United States and the Soviet Union, which prohibited nuclear weapons testing in the atmosphere, under water, or above ground.

In early 1965, CUCND evolved into the Student Union for Peace Action (SUPA),[26] an organization usually associated with the birth of Canada's New Left movement (which in many ways parallelled its American counterpart).[27] There is no evidence that the RCMP deliberately undermined SUPA, but there were reports of stepped-up police surveillance on university campuses, including UBC.[28] With the onset of the Vietnam War, SUPA's focus shifted from anti-nuclear activities and peace to aiding American draft dodgers in Canada and organizing demonstrations against American military action abroad. After a brief and noisy interlude, the organization was "co-opted" in the summer of 1967 when the federal Liberal government lured away a number of actively engaged SUPA leaders to staff the more politically acceptable Company of Young Canadians.[29]

The Vietnam war protest comes to Vancouver, 1965–67

The first stirring of Canadian academic discontent over the war in Vietnam occurred at UBC, a campus uniquely affected by the anti-communist excesses south of the border. In the 1950s, during the McCarthy era, the New York-based Institute of Pacific Relations faced criticism for its views of communism and Communist China, and the institute's director, William Holland, eventually accepted a position in the Asian Studies program at UBC. Other prominent Asian scholars, including William Willmott, soon followed, and they quickly created one of North America's leading centres for studying Far Eastern politics and society. In spring 1965, after the Johnson administration escalated US involvement in Vietnam, Willmott circulated a letter, signed by prominent local authorities, urging Ottawa to demand a ceasefire and the eventual withdrawal of American troops from Vietnam.[30] The Vancouver media paid little attention, but the petition was headlined in the Communist newspaper, the *Pacific Tribune*.[31]

The Vietnam War marked the beginning of a countercultural instance of a Canadian–American "special relationship" — the continentalization of dissent. From the beginning, UBC's anti-war activists had close ties with the Berkeley anti-war movement. When the Vietnam Day Committee at Berkeley called

This photo of a burning papièr-maché *Bomarc missile appeared in the November 10, 1961 issue of* The Ubyssey. *University campuses were a focal point of early anti-war and anti-nuclear activities.* THE UBYSSEY, ALMA MATER SOCIETY ARCHIVES.

FIRST SUCCESSFUL firing of Bomarc missile was recorded by Nuclear Disarmament club Thursday in Buchanan quadrangle as part of "disarmament week."

for international support in October 1965, UBC activists staged a campus teach-in.[32] The content of the event reflected American concerns about the role of the military-industrial complex and its recruiting efforts on campuses. Although this was not a major concern in Canada, UBC professor Norman Epstein did caution students against accepting positions "that would help to keep the war going."[33] Much to the dismay of Professor Willmott, the moderate non-communist speakers addressing the teach-in were heckled and ridiculed by a small number of radical students. He was concerned that the movement would be delegitimized if it were seen to represent the interests of the Soviet Union or any other foreign power.[34]

After the United States began massive bombing north of Vietnam's seventeenth parallel in the spring of 1966, UBC students established their own Vietnam Action Committee, which was the centre of anti-war activity throughout 1966. It worked with the Vancouver Vietnam Day Committee (VVDC),[35] an off-campus group, to organize a demonstration in downtown Vancouver on 28 March 1966. The VVDC coordinated the city's various protest groups and had strong support from labour unions, local churches, and the provincial New Democratic Party (NDP). In short, almost from the beginning the VVDC was influenced by a politically moderate base.[36]

This was in contrast to the first off-campus event, a poorly attended anti-Vietnam war demonstration in March 1965 organized by the Communist Party's BC Peace Council. By that fall, however, the CPBC recognized that it was not drawing large enough crowds and decided to work with other groups, such as churches, unions, and the NDP. This "United Front" strategy produced better results in October 1965, when an estimated five hundred Vancouverites turned out to protest.[37] The CPBC presented the war as a clash between the working class and the imperialist values of the capitalist ruling class. In addition to mobilizing workers against capital, it promoted solidarity with Third World communist movements and opposed the American commitment to contain communist expansion in the developing world,[38] but the group's voice became lost in the larger chorus of anti-war sentiment, especially after it refused to criticize the Soviet invasion of Czechoslovakia in 1968.

The NDP was careful not to associate itself with the CPBC. Nor was the party particularly anti-American, given that its union base, dominated by the International Woodworkers of America (IWA), was closely tied to the American trade union movement.[39] The NDP provided some modest financial support to the VVDC, shared its mailing lists with anti-war organizers, and encouraged local constituencies to publicize demonstrations.[40]

Similarly, the United Church qualified its criticism of the American intervention in Vietnam. Historically, prominent religious institutions had not taken up foreign policy issues, and the United Church, at times referred to as the religious arm of the NDP, was the first church to address the Vietnam war. Church authorities admitted the issue was a "complicated one."[41] They were not against American efforts to contain communism per se, but criticized the American reliance on military force as the primary policy instrument. United Church officials noted that the church had been active in Vietnam for more than twenty years and had more than 150 missionaries working there. They wanted "to use the millions squandered by the USA" for reconstruction, and argued for Christian missionaries to "have control" of that money to build schools, hospitals, and irrigation projects, thus winning the hearts and minds of the people.[42]

The non-communist groups from the political mainstream quickly came to dominate the anti-war movement, and they established a pattern that was followed in the years ahead, holding the largest demonstrations in the early spring and the fall. The March 1966 event started at City Hall and ended in a rally at the downtown courthouse on West Georgia Street (now the Vancouver Art Gallery). On the steps of the courthouse, Professor Willmott reminded the demonstrators, "We are not anti-American, . . . [but] join with the best Americans in urging their government to disengage the West from an impossible war."[43] A decidedly moderate tone prevailed. The marches were generally orderly and non-violent, but police were

An anti-Vietnam war demonstration in Stanley Park organized by the Vietnam Action Committee. Their anti-war activities tended to attract an older, middle-class base. PHOTOGRAPHER UNKNOWN / GEORGIA STRAIGHT COLLECTION, UBC SPECIAL COLLECTIONS

on hand, and Vancouver organizers relied heavily on properly trained parade marshals to get the demonstration from its assembly point to the final rally. To this end, they encouraged marchers to be "highly spirited" but peaceful. If trouble broke out, the marshals were trained to isolate people trying to disrupt the demonstration.[44] Over the course of the various rallies, divergent views were expressed and usually tolerated. For example, two UBC forestry students, who stated that they did not necessarily want the United States to stay in Vietnam, raised the question of "the Viet Cong getting out" as well.[45] However, the general view was that "ideological differences" would be "pushed aside as the need for a Canadian anti-war movement becomes more evident."[46]

In November 1966 a second UBC teach-in drew a modest turn-out of only fifty people, but the dialogue was spirited and occasionally spiced with comic relief. About twenty pro-war science and engineering students attended what *The Ubyssey*, the UBC student newspaper, described as a "bitch-in," waving posters bearing slogans like "Bomb the Cong," "The Dove of Peace is a Commie Chicken," and "Napalm Burns Good like an Incendiary Bomb should."[47]

Peace activists at off-campus demonstrations occasionally had to endure taunting and public criticism as well, which contributed to their sense of solidarity. One participant, Daphne Morrison, observed that after singing a few bars of "We Shall Overcome," one felt "right at home."[48] Demonstrations developed a sense of community, and a comfortable ritual quickly emerged, which involved singing classics of the American civil-rights movement and, curiously enough, "O Canada." Protesters could easily identify each other by their sartorial preference for wearing the "same old gaudy and strictly uniform dress." After noisily marching through downtown, they gathered in front of the courthouse for informative speeches that "hardly anybody listened to." Instead, they entertained themselves, "generous with the joints." Not much was learned about the war, but "the guitars sound good up front," and after the festivities were over, people drifted off, "feeling that [they had] spent the afternoon in one of the best possible ways."[49]

In general, anti-Vietnam War activists were earnest, sincere, and serious, especially motivated to garner public attention and media coverage and, ultimately, to change government policy. There was also a baby boom identity factor.[50] Daphne Morrison described everyone "thinking and acting" the same way, and frequently indulging in a sense of moral superiority. "All together now: we're right, we're young, and we're beautiful. And we're free," she wrote.[51] There was also a social component, manifested in a feeling of comradeship, and one

City of Love and Revolution

The Yippies organized this anti-war demonstration on the steps of the provincial courthouse — now the Vancouver Art Gallery — on April 18, 1970. A more strident and anti-American tone is evident. **VLADIMIR KEREMIDSCHIEFF PHOTO**

participant even recalled marching as a progressive opportunity for finding a date.[52]

Canadians quickly realized that the best critics of the war were the Americans themselves, and American expertise was seen as an effective way to influence Canadian public opinion. Robert Scheer, a member of the Berkeley Free Speech movement, advised Vancouver activists and was occasionally invited to be a speaker.[53] In 1966, Yale academic Staughton Lynd was asked to recount his controversial visit to North Vietnam, and in 1967 the prominent American pacifist David Dellinger came to Vancouver with his message advocating non-violent protest within acceptable legal boundaries.[54] Dellinger noted the presence of a large American expatriate community in the city, including a core of activist academics teaching at the universities and a contingent of over a thousand Americans in the draft dodger community, who would be motivated to protest the war.[55]

As for style, the Canadians tapped into the popular "we shall overcome" rhetoric of the Civil Rights Movement.[56] Demonstrations were generally timed to highlight what was happening south of the border.[57] The only thing not imported was the confrontational style and sense of moral outrage. By the fall of 1966, the Vietnam Action Committee at UBC had emerged as an effective voice of moderate anti-war criticism, as was the VVDC, which was made up of non-affiliated Vancouver residents with no particular larger political agenda. At a VVDC meeting held in July 1966, anti-war activists concluded that, in order to be effective, "We have to remain a single issue committee."[58] Even their anti-Americanism was muted. One early memo issued a guideline for public behaviour: "Our official policy is that we are opposed to flag burnings."[59]

The publicity surrounding the growing voice of protest by moderate organizations helped attract over 2,500 anti-war demonstrators to the VVDC's protest rally in the spring of 1967. Similar demonstrations occurred simultaneously in other cities across Canada, though these were much smaller. In Edmonton, an estimated two hundred demonstrators marched down Jasper Avenue; a Halifax event attracted about a hundred marchers; and only a few hundred were present in Toronto. Vancouver was becoming the leading anti-war centre in Canada.[60]

In 1967 the VVDC also provided assistance to over a hundred draft dodgers who crossed the border at Blaine, Washington, hoping to resettle in Canada. This action raised questions about what the organization's priorities should be. If the draft-dodger issue received the most attention and energy, would that compromise the initial objective of ending the war as quickly as possible? Also unresolved was the issue of whether the movement should call for peace negotiations, which legitimized the American position, or for immediate and unconditional withdrawal of US troops.[61] Vancouver organizers did however consistently agree on the importance of learning from the American experience and, most of all, of maintaining moderation in time of protest.

The Berkeley connection continued into 1967, when the VVDC was renamed the Spring Mobilization Committee. The committee noted that it was "in constant touch with the west coast anti-war organizations in the San Francisco area," notably *Ramparts* magazine and the Berkeley anti-war movement. The groups worked together to coordinate visiting speakers, train parade marshals, and implement strategies to inform (and use) the media. Initially, Vancouver organizers received some modest financial assistance from the Seattle Day Committee.[62] Their American sponsors asked only that they coordinate scheduled protests with demonstrations in the United States.[63] The VVDC even consulted the Berkeley activists on modest organizational changes, such as renaming the Spring Mobilization Committee the Coordinating Committee, which in turn became the central body for future anti-war protests.

What was different about Vancouver's demonstrations as 1967 unfolded was the absence of tension and confrontation. The CPBC and other radical movements were not invited to speak and remained barely visible. Instead, the NDP remained the most prominent political party on the peace front. Its popular national leader, Tommy Douglas, was often a featured speaker. He offered restrained criticism of the United States, saving his best line for Ottawa. "There are many hawks and doves in Washington," he famously observed, "but there are only parrots in Ottawa."[64]

Like the CPBC, the provincial NDP saw certain political advantages in its anti-war stance. Aside from the psychological benefits of cultivating the "moral high ground," the party saw the war as an opportunity to distance itself from the BC Liberal Party, its main rival in opposition to the ruling Social Credit Party. British Columbia's NDP was the most consistently critical anti-war provincial party in Canada. The war issue was frequently raised in the BC legislature, and the party enjoyed widespread support from labour unions, teachers, and the growing number of politically active draft dodgers in Vancouver.[65] The one potential disadvantage of opposing the war was the possibility of being labelled pro-Soviet communist sympathizers, but the BC NDP insisted that it was primarily anti-war and not anti-American.[66]

The Guernica theme — innocent peasants vs. weapons of mass destruction, this time in an Asian setting — is echoed in this drawing, which appeared in the Georgia Straight. ARTIST UNKNOWN / GEORGIA STRAIGHT COLLECTION, UBC SPECIAL COLLECTIONS

'Peaceniks' and Protest

The anti-war movement also gained a base of support in the counterculture media, most notably the *Georgia Straight*. After the first issue of the *Straight* was published in the spring of 1967, articles criticizing American military operations and the complicit role of Canada's government and the arms industry appeared every week. The paper provided a voice for American draft dodgers and occasionally echoed the sentiment of the growing draft resistance community by calling for those facing the draft to "Desert Now."[67] The American connection was strengthened by the Underground Press Syndicate, which was essentially the media pipeline for the American New Left. The critical American voice was presented in articles by the most prominent war resistors: Abbie Hoffman, Tom Hayden, and Eldridge Cleaver.[68]

The fragmentation of protest, 1968–70

The coordination of Vancouver demonstrations with the American protest schedule continued into 1968. However, that year a distinct Canadian focus began to develop; organizers were less concerned about spe-

cific American issues and less reliant on speakers from Berkeley. Their priority now was to link the war with community issues. Canadian complicity was highlighted by singling out defence contracts to Lenkurt Electric, a Lower Mainland company; Armed Forces recruiting sites; and federal Liberal Party headquarters in British Columbia.

The Coordinating Committee appeared to be on a secure organizational footing. It rented offices on West Pender Street and hired a full-time staff member. Opposition to the Vietnam War was reaching its peak, and the *Sun* and *Province* were paying more, and more respectful, attention to the local resistance. There was some evidence that younger high-school students were getting involved and that the protest movement was even spreading to the suburbs.[69] The long-term prospects for anti-war activism had never looked better.

However ideological fissures, the bane

Young NDP activists sought to cultivate a distinct identity to distinguish themselves from other political formations on the left, including both the Communist Party and the Yippies. PHOTOGRAPHER UNKNOWN / GEORGIA STRAIGHT COLLECTION, UBC SPECIAL COLLECTIONS

of progressive movements generally, were starting to appear within the peace movement in Vancouver. Most of the mainstream communists were staid and unobtrusive, but other leftist groups, including the Young Socialists (Trotskyists) and the Young NDP, proved more energetic and excitable. The most ideologically driven were New Left groups from the UBC and SFU campuses, and high-minded but politically non-aligned faculty. The Coordinating Committee tolerated their intellectual pretensions but expressed some dismay at the stinginess of SFU faculty, who contributed the modest sum of ten dollars from a fundraising drive.[70] More supportive were counterculture elements, especially the *Georgia Straight*, which stepped up its anti-war efforts by sponsoring fundraising events and providing ample publicity for anti-war groups.

On the other side of the protest fence, there was some resistance to the anti-war demonstrations, but even the anti-communist voices on city council were balanced by progressive critics such as Harry Rankin. Mayor Tom Campbell did not consider himself an anti-war activist, but he did support the right to public dissent. In April 1968 he even proposed that Vancouver be selected as the site for a peace conference. Canada was an "ideal country" to host the talks, he said, because "it had not taken any real stand ... and we had sold grain to the Chinese."[71] Most of the criticism levelled at the anti-war movement came from the NDP. In 1965, party member William Deverell had scolded the VVDC for not working hard enough to gain new supporters for the NDP: "You are simply blowing off steam by marching once or twice a year. It's a release for frustration,"[72] suggesting it would be better for activists to join the party and ensure it became the government in the next election.

In the wake of the summer of violence in the United States in 1968, local police became more alert to any such tendencies in Vancouver. They responded quickly to a series of bomb threats on the assumption that the threatening letters were produced by a "peacenik-type writer."[73] No charges were laid, however, and the streets of Vancouver flowed with peace and love rather than anti-war rage. The Coordinating Committee judged that it was plateauing in 1968 and made an effort that fall to expand and "get the support of as many organizations as possible."[74] Draft dodgers, who had been involved with the movement from the beginning, were becoming more vocal that year, and students from UBC and SFU joined in ever greater numbers.[75] A reported thirty groups took part in an anti-war demonstration on 26 October. However, the Coordinating Committee was not particularly effective at screening new participants, which meant that radical groups, including the Young Socialists and the Maoist Communist Party of Canada (Marxist-Leninist) (CPC–ML), were infiltrating the mainstream movement.

This growing radicalization unfolded in Canada much the same way it did in the United States. In February 1969 the American anti-war movement issued a call for demonstrations around the world. The Vancouver Coordinating Committee responded by convening a special meeting to organize a demonstration that April. Over a hundred activists attended the planning meeting, including "a suspicious number of young people." A debate quickly developed between the moderates and the radical groups, which included the CPC–ML, New Left student radicals, and some SFU faculty members. The main point of contention was the purpose of the upcoming demonstration. Should it be limited to a call for American withdrawal from the war, or should the local anti-war movement support a more radical view, one which encouraged the victory of the Vietnamese National Liberation Front?[76]

The contending sides in the debate agreed to disagree and held their demonstrations on two separate days in April. The younger radicals, sporting coolie hats and red armbands, waved North Vietnamese flags at their protest on Saturday. The next day, Coordinating Committee chairperson Hilda Thomas and the moderate wing called for American withdrawal from the war and an end to Canadian complicity.[77] What surprised everybody was the turnout of about a thousand counter-demonstrators, who held their own event in support of "Fair Play for the USA" at the Queen Elizabeth Theatre. Among other demands, this group of contrarians called for the "communist aggressors" to withdraw their troops from Vietnam and issued a warning to the NDP about its naïvety regarding communist agitators in its ranks.[78]

The *Georgia Straight* downplayed the significance of the split between radicals and moderates as a minor dispute over "logistics and themes."[79] Nonetheless, a weakened central organization and little overall discipline meant there was a greater chance of mayhem breaking out, and in August 1969, despite the efforts of the moderates to maintain a semblance of civility, events spiralled out of control. Prime Minister Pierre Trudeau was scheduled to speak at the Vancouver Armoury, and protestors gathered to disrupt the event. One woman, in addition to making clear her contempt for Canadian complicity in Vietnam, voiced her outrage at patriarchy. Her message was clearly expressed in a brightly painted sign aimed at the "playboy" prime minister: "Hustle wheat not women." Trudeau, perhaps indiscreetly, issued a sharply worded retort for which he was pelted on the side of his head with a rotten banana.[80] Such was the nature of Canadian confrontation and conflict.

As the more radical anti-war activists abandoned the Coordinating Committee, the moderate wing of the peace move-

'Peaceniks' and Protest

Despite the fact that the 1960s was a decade of militant labour activism, and the trade union movement was prominent in the anti-war movement, the redneck, anti-hippie worker was a common media trope. Here, anti-Communist counter-demonstrators at a February 1970 protest. Hank Vogel is the man in the middle of the photo. VLADIMIR KEREMIDSCHIEFF PHOTO

City of Love and Revolution

'Trudeaumania' was a distinctly Canadian manifestation of the Age of Aquarius, as the rakish politician captured the Canadian imagination as youthful justice minister and subsequently, prime minister. PHOTOGRAPHER UNKNOWN / GEORGIA STRAIGHT COLLECTION, UBC SPECIAL COLLECTIONS

ment regrouped and began to work more closely with the NDP and the labour movement. Inflation was sweeping Canada, and the BC Federation of Labour was quick to emphasize that the "fantastic sums being spent on armaments, the Vietnam War and other commitments" were to blame, not the wage demands of organized labour.[81] The NDP also recognized that the war was a convenient issue to use to differentiate itself from the federal Liberal Party, which under Trudeau had steadily encroached on the NDP's traditional territory on the left.[82] Environmental issues were also being tied to the Vietnam War. Activists claimed that American chemical and biological warfare was undermining "the ecological balance of the entire earth." Coordinating Committee chair Hilda Thomas even vowed to introduce the war issue into the civic elections,[83] though this had minimal effect on the outcome.

In October 1969, several hundred people gathered peacefully at the UBC Student Union Building to listen to rock bands and anti-war lectures, and to participate in student discussion forums.[84] (Interestingly, almost the same number of students turned out the same day to join in campus fraternities' Bids War, a drive to recruit students for what the frats claimed was the "real social life."[85]) The following month, Dr. Benjamin Spock, the American authority on child rearing, entertained an overflow crowd at the Queen Elizabeth Theatre and called for Canadians to step up their protests.

An anti-war demonstration held at the downtown courthouse on 15 November 1969 was, in the estimation of William

Despite Trudeau's stance of independence from Washington, he never distanced himself from the illegal bombing campaign in Cambodia and Laos — to the displeasure of the anti-war movement. The sign is a reference to the prime minister's famous taunt of some Québecois workers who had lost their jobs. PHOTOGRAPHER UNKNOWN / GEORGIA STRAIGHT COLLECTION, UBC SPECIAL COLLECTIONS

Willmott, the largest to date.[86] Speakers from the NDP and labour movement were featured, and radical groups were noticeably underrepresented. The event remained orderly and non–confrontational, and no policemen were visible. Police Inspector Bud Errington later commented that the rally and marches "were a tribute to the city and its citizens," and that "it's always a pleasure to hear about peaceful protest rallies."[87] Even Mayor Campbell refrained from issuing any disparaging remarks. Overall, dissent within the rule of law was a respected Canadian tradition and only a few political "hotheads" offered an occasional outburst of indignation.[88]

1970 as turning point

Throughout 1970, President Richard Nixon's policy of "Vietnamization" accelerated the rate of American troop withdrawals beyond initial expectations. However, Nixon's decision to invade Cambodia in an effort to disrupt Viet Cong supply routes reignited protests across American campuses. The one at Kent State University in Ohio proved to be the most tragic. In spite of these events, Vancouver's anti-war movement remained relatively quiet throughout the summer and fall of 1970. The estimated four hundred protesters who turned out for a 30 May demonstration were substantially fewer than participated in the demonstra-

tion the previous fall. For the first time, organizers met some resistance from city authorities over the use of Victory Square, the traditional site for annual Remembrance Day ceremonies. Alderman Halford Wilson called protesters "gutless pussy cats . . . helping the Commies." Others on council responded that Wilson's rhetoric was overheated and uncalled-for. The demonstration was eventually held at City Hall itself and gained the support of Alderman Art Phillips, a rising political star and future mayor.[89]

Outside council chambers, opposition to anti-war demonstrations was tainted with working-class hostility. In May, for example, demonstrators were confronted by a counter-demonstration with a dozen or so pickets supporting US policy in Vietnam.[90] One of the pro-US demonstrators, Hank Vogel, a Teamsters member, enthusiastically waved a placard declaring himself a "working man" and "an Imperialist Pig. I support US action in Vietnam."[91] A scuffle involving some enraged "peaceniks" ensued, and Vancouver police eventually intervened and, without making any arrests, encouraged cooler heads to prevail. This was an example of the city's unique protest character, in which the police acted less as adversaries to the movement and more as arbitrators intervening between different points of view to maintain civil order.

In the early fall of 1970, Vancouver's city council was divided on whether to allow a demonstration scheduled for October to go ahead. Curiously, the issue was resolved

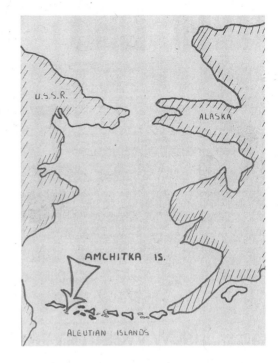

when the chief of police, John Fisk, gave his approval for the event.[92] But the political climate was not conducive to protest. Early in October the Front de libération du Québec, a radical nationalist group, kidnapped James Cross, the British trade commissioner, and murdered Pierre Laporte, the Quebec labour minister, and the federal government invoked the War Measures Act, suspending civil liberties across the country. In this atmosphere of heightened state security, there was a disappointing turnout for the late October demonstration in Vancouver, and only a few hundred stayed for

The fishing vessel Phyllis Cormack, *which would be rechristened* Greenpeace, *the flagship of the environmentalist fleet.* PHOTOGRAPHER UNKNOWN / GEORGIA STRAIGHT COLLECTION, UBC SPECIAL COLLECTIONS

'Peaceniks' and Protest

Distorted Amchitka map overstates island's proximity to Asia and the Soviet Union, thereby suggesting that other countries besides Canada were threatened by the tests. ARTIST UNKNOWN / GEORGIA STRAIGHT COLLECTION, UBC SPECIAL COLLECTIONS

the speeches at the courthouse.[93] At the same time the Coordinating Committee was facing severe financial problems that forced its move to free accommodation at the Vancouver Free University in the Commercial Drive neighbourhood. At the end of the year, the committee changed its name again to the Vancouver Vietnam Action Committee (VVAC).

The withdrawal of troops, imposition of the War Measures Act, and dissension in the anti-war movement all served to dampen support, but another factor accounting for the waning numbers was heightened concern about nuclear weapons testing. In

August 1970, several hundred demonstrators participated in a series of Hiroshima memorials to underline the possibility of the Vietnam War escalating into a nuclear war, and weapons testing in Alaska changed the direction of Vancouver protests.

'Don't Make a Wave': The Amchitka nuclear test

In 1964, US president Lyndon Johnson had announced a new defence initiative, the development of the Spartan anti-ballistic missile defence system designed to protect North American cities. For the Spartan to be effective, the United States needed to test a new generation of nuclear warheads. These weapons were normally detonated underground in the Nevada desert, but the Atomic Energy Commission (AEC) decided that the projected multi-megaton explosions posed a threat to the structural integrity of buildings in nearby Las Vegas.[94] The AEC suggested sparsely populated rural Alaska as an alternative, and pinpointed Amchitka Island in the fog-shrouded Aleutian chain, about 1,400 miles west of Anchorage, as the most suitable site. In addition to being extremely remote, Amchitka, which was only forty-two miles long and two to four miles wide, was uninhabited and therefore considered by the AEC to be an ideal site for a small-scale nuclear explosion. The first test, in 1965, received virtually no coverage in the Vancouver media and only passing reference in *The Ubyssey*.

A second, larger (about one megaton)

test occurred on 2 October 1969. This time the detonation was preceded by extensive coverage in the Canadian media. What surprised many was the spontaneous and unprecedented one-day protest by various groups from Greater Vancouver at the Peace Arch border crossing. The most visible activists were environmentally concerned students and faculty from UBC, who organized transportation to the event.[95]

While activists in Portland and Seattle expressed some apprehension, and American environmentalists in the Sierra Club identified nuclear testing as a concern, there was no substantial response from American activists and little criticism in Anchorage of nuclear testing.[96] As a result, the BC chapter of the Sierra Club formed an independent Canadian-based group, the Don't Make a Wave Committee (DMWC), to protest future testing in the Aleutians.[97] The continentalization of the peace movement did not extend to the budding environmental movement, and it was in this area that Vancouver developed a unique protest identity. With its counterculture, progressive unions, and social democratic traditions, the city provided a much more viable base for a sustained criticism of "war craziness and environmental degradation."[98]

Meanwhile, the AEC announced a third test in the Aleutians, codenamed Cannikin, which was scheduled for October 1971 and estimated to be on the order of five megatons. The pressing issue for the DMWC was how to publicize the issue and raise public

Vancouver high schools closed for the day as thousands of students attended the October 6, 1971 demonstration against the Amchitka tests. The huge crowd filled Alberni Street, behind the US Consulate on Georgia Street. GEORGE LEGEBOKOFF PHOTO / PACIFIC TRIBUNE

awareness. Two of the key organizers, Jim Bohlen and Irving Stowe, decided to play on latent anti-American sentiment among Canadians and on their Cold War fears of a nuclear apocalypse.[99] The specific strategy was to connect the Amchitka test to the acceleration of the arms race and the potential damage from tidal waves, earthquakes, and radiation leakage. Potential damage to animals and marine life was a special concern of the environmentalists.

DMWC member Bill Darnell, who saw the importance of product branding as a means of capturing public attention, came up with an appropriately catchy moniker for the nascent organization: Greenpeace.[100] Shortly thereafter, the now ubiquitous and instantly recognizable logo made its appearance. The media quickly warmed to early DMWC initiatives as it launched an ecological campaign to inform the public of the dangers of nuclear testing and weapons. With the next test looming, the group bought a converted fishing trawler, the *Phyllis Cormack*, renamed it *Greenpeace*, and prepared to sail into Alaskan waters to protest at the test site.

The AEC delayed the test until early November, and bad weather forced the

Greenpeace to return to Vancouver. Nonetheless, through these bold actions the environmental movement established a strong base of support among students at UBC and SFU. Non-student groups also provided aid and encouragement, including the BC Federation of Labour and, somewhat surprisingly, the Greater Vancouver Real Estate Board.[101]

Shortly before the original date for the Canniken blast, support for the anti-nuclear movement quickly spread through local high schools as younger students, wishing to establish their own distinct boomer identity in the midst of the counterculture revolution, realized that taking an anti-nuke stance was an easy way to seize the moral high ground.[102] This youthful enthusiasm spilled over into the streets in early October 1971, when school officials unofficially gave them the day off in order to attend a protest. The *Province* reported that some students saw it as an opportunity to skip class, but most were at least minimally informed about the issue.[103] An estimated 10,000 "rebels with a cause" marched outside the American consulate, at the same time enjoying their unauthorized but tolerated midweek break. Student leaders presented a letter calling on the United States "to take the lead in the ending of nuclear testing through restraint, example, and negotiation."[104] Sergeant Gordon Dalton of the Vancouver Police was pleased with their overall "peaceful and orderly" conduct. The only reported incident involved an adventurous student who fell

off the roof of the Tilden rent-a-car garage across from the demonstration site and crashed through the roof of a shed.[105]

Despite Greenpeace's last-minute effort to sail the *Greenpeace* north for a second time in early November, the AEC test went ahead as scheduled. On 7 November, UBC's geophysics department recorded a tremor measuring 7.0 on the Richter scale and three mild shockwaves in the Greater Vancouver region.[106]

After the massive anti-Amchitka turn-out in October 1971, a November anti-war demonstration organized by the Vancouver Vietnam Action Committee went relatively unnoticed by the media and the general public. At the time, organizers believed the anti-Amchitka enthusiasm would translate into greater support for the anti-war movement, but some activists acknowledged that the Amchitka protest could turn out to be competition for the VVAC.[107] The VVAC continued to criticize the war and also tried to downplay the importance of a victory by the Viet Cong. At the same time it dealt with internal disruptions "by some freaks called Yippies." On the first of a series of "peace days" during the first week of November 1971, Yippie activists shouted the new slogan "Get off your ass and stop the blast." These antics did not resonate with the general public, nor did they change the AEC's plan to proceed with the Canniken test blast the next day.[108] On the last of the peace days, only a few hundred marched, signalling the imminent demise of the anti-war movement.[109]

A pessimistic mood prevailed at an

The protest against nuclear tests at Amchitka grew out of a much broader view of environmental issues, and within a few years Greenpeace was taking on the whaling industry. In this famous image, Greenpeace activists in rubber Zodiacs prepare to confront a Soviet factory ship, the Vostok, *in 1975.* REX WEYLER PHOTO

"anti-war action conference" held early the next year in Vancouver. The main question on the minds of those in attendance was "After Amchitka, what?" There was a brief interlude of optimism when one union representative suggested that discussing the immorality of the war — which he described as "ecocide in Indochina" — was not enough. It was also politically useful to explain, as the BC Federation of Labour had tried to do earlier, that the war, and not union wage demands, was the main reason for inflation and the wage-and-price controls that the Trudeau government had imposed in an attempt to control inflation.[110] Public opinion, however, remained unchanged.

Also of consequence for the anti-war movement was the serious decline in contributions from long-time supporters. The NDP continued to criticize American actions in Vietnam, but in 1972 the party contributed only a modest fifty dollars to the peace campaign coffers. Financial support from the unions also waned, and the CPBC-dominated United Fishermen and Allied Workers' Union refused a request to use its hall in east Vancouver for fundraising activities. Even the election of an NDP government in the August 1972 provincial election did not help. After making some brief critical comments about the intensified American bombing campaign in December, the party turned its attention to social reform at the provincial level. Foreign policy issues quickly faded from its agenda.

The VVAC's final demonstration, in the fall of 1972, was sparsely attended, and early the next year the group disbanded.[111] Remnants of the organization ended up in the Canadian Peace Congress, while many of the younger members gravitated to Greenpeace and the environmental consciousness it promoted.[112] The enthusiasm of the younger boomers was now focused on the issue of pollution and the dangers posed by US oil tankers carrying Alaska crude close to the coast of British Columbia.

Conclusion

Like their anti-war comrades south of the border, the activists leading Vancouver's anti-nuclear weapons groups and the VVAC were dedicated, well-organized, hard-working, and exceptionally diligent in keeping the peace issue before the media. What was most remarkable was their self-reliance and their endless hours of unpaid labour, often unrecognized by the numerous weekend demonstrators.

The movement maintained a degree of cohesiveness and internal discipline and did not come to be dominated by radical political movements with their own agendas. In particular, activists promoting the policies of foreign Communist powers, notably the Soviet Union, were effectively isolated.[113] Except in the case of the CPBC, with its Soviet ties, the historical record generally confirms a single-minded determination to maintain credibility by remaining independent. The long shadow of the American anti-war movement extended into Vancouver, but this did not impede the movement, at least in the early stages.

The history of the peace movement shows that Vancouver, in contrast to many American cities, did not descend into the abyss of violent confrontation. To be sure, the issues that fuelled American protest — race, student radicalism, and the draft — were not part of the Vancouver scene. Also absent was the repression faced by their US counterparts: the surveillance, infiltration, and provocation by the FBI, police, and broad-based patriotic organizations. The political balance on Vancouver's city council and the fairness of local civic authorities moderated the confrontation as well. Also, it should be emphasized, movement organizers consistently insisted on peaceful tactics, and protesters consistently followed their lead.[114]

In the end, events beyond the control of the Vancouver anti-war movement precipitated its demise. After the turmoil of the US invasion of Cambodia and the Nixon administration's policy of de-escalation, the local media ceased covering Vietnam as a pressing issue from 1971 onward. Complicating this lack of interest, the Amchitka nuclear weapons test overshadowed the war.

In retrospect it is not clear what the peace movement accomplished. The general public in Vancouver remained either unconcerned or skeptical of the American intervention in Vietnam. While the United Church opposed the war, Anglicans were ambivalent, and other churches were non-committal; Roman Catholics and the more fundamentalist Christian denominations based in the Fraser Valley supported America's anti-communist crusade.[115] As for the effect on government, Vancouver activists' demonstrations in front of the US consulate had no effect on Washington's weapons testing policy or the strategy of Vietnamization: consular reports to the US State Department expressed no concerns. The impact on Ottawa was also inconsequential. Vancouver demonstrators did not realize at the time just how much the Trudeau government opposed both the war and nuclear weapons, for reasons not directly related to those of the peace movement.[116]

The Vancouver peace movement was less ideologically driven than its Toronto counterpart. Toronto peaceniks were sometimes so anti-American that they called for the expulsion of US draft dodgers. Vancouver's progressive community, in contrast, welcomed war resisters.[117] Many American exiles in Vancouver were amazed at their warm reception. People were sometimes politely indifferent, but more often they were overtly sympathetic; there was "little criticism and even some congratulations."[118]

Finally, examination of Vancouver's peace movement sheds some light on the relationship famously described by Prime Minister Trudeau as similar to that between an elephant and a mouse. Vancouver activists were consistently informed by and supportive of American peace initiatives. When an indigenous movement emerged in Vancouver, Americans showed complete indifference.

In a 1971 interview, Greenpeace activist Bob Hunter bemoaned the absence of US support for his organization's initiatives. For their part, Hunter and his environmental comrades had responded to American developments in the peace and environmental movements almost daily.[119] But when it came to the *Greenpeace* voyage, no print or electronic media in any American city took notice. Even in Alaska, site of the Amchitka tests, most US activists had never heard of the *Greenpeace*. Isolated from the American progressive community, Vancouver charted the future of the environmental protest alone, for now.

The 1970s saw a migration of Vancouver's counterculture to its own version of the suburbs: the Gulf Islands, the upper Fraser Valley, or — as here — the North Vancouver foreshore. SHARKIE PHOTO / GEORGIA STRAIGHT COLLECTION, UBC SPECIAL COLLECTIONS

CONCLUSION

Who Owns Sixties Vancouver?

In 1973 the United States withdrew from Vietnam, the world entered a severe oil crisis, and Canada descended into an economic recession. Fewer hippies were seen in the Kitsilano neighbourhood, Yippies no longer actively engaged in street theatre, and the Vancouver Free University had closed its doors.

Change was in the air. Mayor Tom Campbell decided not to run in the 1972 civic election and retreated from the public spotlight. There were signs that his cultural *bête noire*, the hippies, were also retreating — to the North Shore, the Gulf Islands, and the upper Fraser Valley.[1] Their acid rock music had evolved, and for the seventies generation heavy metal and, later in the new decade, punk rock dominated the scene. Vancouver was moving on from the sixties.

The legacy of that era is still a contested subject, both for those who lived through it and for the historians currently writing about it.[2] There is virtually no remaining tension in Vancouver about the Vietnam War, nor any residue of antagonism over black–white race relations. Differences of opinion still exist, however, about the effects of drugs, the sexual revolution, and the assault on traditional values. A basic synthesis has yet to appear, so a state of interpretive malaise prevails; only when the boomer generation completely passes on will some kind of consensus emerge.

Local critics such as David Morton point to the effect drugs and the sexual revolution had on the family.[3] When using drugs became a recreational pursuit rather than a marker of cultural revolt, it had little consequence for middle-class families, who had the financial resources and support network

City of Love and Revolution

to quit. However, the sixties legitimized the use of illegal drugs, many of which are worse now than the ones prevalent in the 1960s, and their growing use among the city's poorer citizens, especially those living on and around East Hastings Street, has produced horrendous consequences, especially as it's much more difficult for them to escape their addictions.[4] They may successfully complete a detox program, but when they return to their usual milieu, with drugs accessible and no other options, they are much more likely to fall into addiction again.

As for "love is all you need," the incidence of sexually transmitted diseases rose steadily throughout the sixties and seventies, and the media-induced commodification of sex undermined the mystical allure of romantic love, replacing it with the physical allure of multiple partners. However freedom to choose often became condemned to choose, and what became familiar in Vancouver's social landscape, as elsewhere around the country and indeed Western society, was a rising divorce rate and increasing acceptance of the single-parent family.

Another questionable outcome of the boomer-dominated decade was the emergence of a cult of youth, the "forever young" syndrome.[5] "Young" and "old" were no longer valid distinctions — after the sixties, all ages shared an adolescent fascination with the same dress, speech codes, music, film, and consumer preferences. This inevitably led to juvenile revolt, a decline in parental authority, and loss of respect for the wisdom of elders. A corollary to this was the fact that many denizens of sixties Vancouver

Rock radio DJ John Tanner and musician Craig McCaw atop the Vancouver Planetarium, where McCaw was putting on psychedelic light shows using the planetarium's equipment, circa 1974. COURTESY JOHN TANNER

turned their backs on traditional religious authority, descending into an abyss of self-absorption and spiritual self-help in order to transcend technological society and attain a state of cosmic consciousness and inner tranquility. Some of the paths to this cosmic state included transcendental meditation (TM), Hare Krishna, and Zen Buddhism. The Buddhism-inspired yoga movement presented itself as a cure-all for a range of ills, both individual and social, and has even been proposed for treating heroin addiction. Other individuals focused on the use of herbs, zone therapy, and special exercises as an alternative to drugs. After a period of incubation in southern California, new-age therapeutic approaches such as primal scream therapy and (which stands for Erhard Seminars Training, after Werner Erhardt, the psychotherapist credited with developing the method) also arrived in Vancouver.[6]

Dominique Clement, an authority on the human rights movement, celebrates some aspects of 1960s Vancouver.[7] He notes that several pieces of human rights legislation enacted during the Trudeau era (1968–84) can be traced to the activism of the sixties. There is also evidence that the Canadian state became less inclined to control citizens' behaviour. Although a variety of new drugs — STP, MDA, and crack cocaine — appeared on the scene, most of the hippie middle class didn't go beyond marijuana, magic mushrooms, and LSD. Laws related to these drugs were less rigorously enforced, and the public sale of marijuana on Hastings Street today far surpasses anything witnessed during the smoke-ins of the riotous summer of 1971.

If sex was reduced to a commodity in the marketplace, sex education in the school system did give kids an informed view of the risks involved and introduced the possibility that they could make rational choices. The existence of Vancouver's large and self-confident gay community was accepted in the 1970s, if not yet celebrated as part of mainstream culture. Like the drug laws, the laws governing the erotic behaviour of "consenting adults" were less rigorously enforced, and massage parlours and other establishments catering to the city's libidinal needs proliferated. Sex was now free from inhibition, commitment, and government oppression. A recent study indicates that sex-related businesses offering pornography, erotic toys, commercial striptease, and sexual tourism contribute significantly to the Vancouver economy.[8]

Student life changed too, as high schools relaxed dress codes and rules relating to attendance and other behaviour. Out at UBC, reforms included creation of a "relevant" Arts One program, student participation on hiring committees, and construction of a new Student Union Building.[9] UBC students established a legitimate protest identity of their own, organizing the first large-scale neighbourhood recycling program in hopes of converting people to "spaceship earth thinking."[10] Recycling containers and programs have since become a ubiquitous feature of modern life.

Although some were disappointed that sixties activism did not lead to the replacement of capitalism by some form of socialism, businesses did change in positive and substantial ways. After hippies targeted the "straight" vibe at the Bay and Eaton's, management began to allow staff to sport longer hair, wider belts, and flared pants. The stodgy *Vancouver Sun*, recognizing a new readership market, hired Bob Hunter away from the *Georgia Straight* to write on gestalt therapy, peyote ceremonies, edgy psychologists like R.D. Laing, and environmental issues. "Hip" consumerism was embraced throughout the city. Even in the downtown core, far away from the action on Fourth Avenue, the commercialization of avant-garde culture flourished. New businesses, inherently risky operations, popped up to sell organically grown foods, records featuring the new music, new-age books, Indian cotton clothing, and a yoga-based lifestyle.

Viewed in the context of North America, sixties Vancouver is a test case of a relatively new international phenomenon: the transfer of mass culture across political borders. The city provides insight into how mass culture is transmitted through music, television, and travel. Canadians, historically skeptical of all things American — especially trade, investment, and political pressure — became more open to all three, and for a brief period Vancouver demonstrated how a universal "sense of a new age dawning" trumped a nationalist consciousness confined by borders.

As the counterculture waned and the anti-war movement collapsed, another wave of change appeared on the historical stage. Interestingly, the social and cultural movements of the seventies were in part a reaction to the sixties' incomplete commitment to reform. The rise of the feminist and native rights movements was unrelated to the broader cultural issues of the sixties and marked the beginning of narrowly focused identity politics in Vancouver. Ultimately, the longevity and enduring historical impact of these two movements surpassed the counterculture enthusiasms of the sixties.

By the early 1970s, Vancouver women, disillusioned by the chauvinism of the long-haired progressive male, but impressed by the effectiveness of Yippie-style street theatre, began developing their own initiatives to "combat the patriarchy." In May 1971, five local members of the US-based Women's

As the Be-Ins faded into memory, Hare Krishna accolytes began to appear in Stanley Park. SHARKIE PHOTO / GEORGIA STRAIGHT COLLECTION, UBC SPECIAL COLLECTIONS

International Conspiracy from Hell (WITCH) were arrested for painting "This degrades and exploits women" on a storefront window displaying a bikini-clad cyclist.[11] More practically, the Free University and the Vancouver Women's Caucus (VWC) offered self-defense courses for hitchhikers and encouraged women drivers to pick up women thumbing rides. Less flamboyant but more pragmatic political organizations appeared. The VWC was created by local activists and academics in 1968 and soon focused its attention on the abortion issue. In May 1970 the VWC attracted widespread media attention for sponsoring the "Abortion Caravan" to Ottawa,[12] an initiative that is generally given substantial credit for the subsequent liberalization of Canada's laws dealing with abortion and reproductive rights. Other issues that received attention included access to childcare, discrimination against women in the professions, "pink collar" unionization, and sexual harassment in the workplace. At UBC, seventy scholars and younger activists produced a report on the status of women at the university to document inequities in hiring and salaries on campus.[13]

Stirrings of Native discontent in the early 1970s also led to a local movement of historical significance. Vancouver's Natives, impressed by the activism of the American Indian Movement (AIM), especially AIM's 1970 occupation of Alcatraz Island in San Francisco Bay, decided to speak out against police harassment. Even more than the Yippies of Gastown, First Nations people bore the brunt of police excesses in Vancouver's

Downtown Eastside. Native activists sought the help of local Yippies and like-minded activists to address the harassment issue. Instead, some of the longhairs frivolously turned the protest flyers into paper airplanes, and "none of the freaks" turned out to rally against police mistreatment of Natives.[14] The message to the First Nations was clear: they would have to work to right historical injustices on their own, without the help of the hippies.

Similarly, the nascent environmental movement was a reaction to the limitations of sixties activism, specifically the US-based Sierra Club's neglect of the antinuclear testing campaigns of its Vancouver branch. In turn, Canadian environmentalists became less preoccupied with American issues and focused on French testing in the South Pacific. Greenpeace was at the forefront of this new environmental movement and soon captured the attention of the local and international media.

The Greenpeace Foundation, established in 1972 by a group of environmentalists led by the journalist Ben Metcalfe, gave Vancouver its most enduring legacy of the sixties. Using Vancouver as its base, Greenpeace planned an even more audacious exploit than the journey to Amchitka: an assault on Mururoa, the atoll that was the French testing site in the South Pacific.[15] The French proved to be much more hostile adversaries than the Americans, ramming *Greenpeace III* and later attacking Canadian protesters in international waters.[16] The protests garnered sensational worldwide media attention and made Greenpeace one of the world's most recognizable brands.

The *Terminal City Express*, a short-lived underground alternative to the increasingly mainstream *Georgia Straight*, noted that all the news through the winter of 1973 seemed to be American — dollar devaluations, repatriated POWs, and Alaskan oil pipeline suits. However, breaking through the American news hegemony was the Greenpeace story, the one most likely to be remembered

Another outcome of the sixties — and in part at least a reaction to the ethos of gratification of (male) urges — was 'second wave' feminism, which encouraged young women to form expectations different from those of their mothers. **PHOTOGRAPHER UNKNOWN / GEORGIA STRAIGHT COLLECTION, UBC SPECIAL COLLECTIONS**

that year.[17] Forty years later, Greenpeace is still celebrated in Vancouver, lending its name to the city's public service award and gaining regular attention in the media. The organization embodies a deeply rooted psychological impulse that transcends the sixties. As Bob Hunter observed before his death in 2005, Greenpeace tapped into our "instinctive fears of extinction and hopes for survival."[18] Perhaps the preoccupation with hope, instinct, and survival is the best way to remember sixties Vancouver.

NOTES

Introduction: Images of a Hipper Era

1. "The City 1966-1975," *Vancouver Sun*, 3 December 1975, C9.
2. John Mackie, "Peace, Love, and Happiness," *Vancouver Sun*, 18 April 2009, D1. John Tanner, standing six foot six, was affectionately known as "Long John."
3. Dennis Cocke was elected New Westminster's Member of the Legislative Assembly in the 1972 election that put an end to two decades of rule by the Social Credit Party under W.A.C. Bennett. Cocke became a cabinet minister in Premier Dave Barrett's government, in office from 1972 to 1975.
4. Abbie Hoffman, *Revolution for the Hell of It* (New York: Dial Press, 1969).
5. Captain John Deighton, affectionately known as "Gassy Jack," was the first settler on the site of what was to be Vancouver.
6. James Law, "Happy Hippie Daze," *Kitsilano Views*, 16 August 2006, 1–2.
7. "Great Bus Stop Bust," *Georgia Straight*, 5 May 1967, 1.
8. Ibid.

Chapter 1: Hippies and Their Discontents

1. "Dropouts with a Mission," *Newsweek*, 6 February 1967, 92–95.
2. "1,000 Hippies Turn-on in Park," *Vancouver Sun*, 27 March 1967, 1.
3. James J. Farrell, *The Spirit of the Sixties: The Making of Postwar Radicalism* (New York: Routledge, 1997), 204.
4. "Diggers," in *The ABC-CLIO Companion to the 1960s Counterculture in America*, ed. Neil A. Hamilton (Santa Barbara, CA: ABC-CLIO Press, 1997), 80.
5. William L. O'Neill, *The New Left: A History* (Wheeling, IL: Harlan Davidson, 2001), x.
6. La Monica Everett-Haynes, "A Different Type of Hippie Hype," *UA News*, 19 March 2008, http://uanews.org/node/18838.
7. "Summer of Love," in *The Columbia Guide to America in the 1960s*, ed. David Farber and Beth Bailey (New York: Columbia University Press, 2001), 249.
8. Ibid.
9. David Laskin, "Storybook Vancouver: Pervasive Brooding in a Beautiful Setting," *New York Times*, 13 June 2006, 4.
10. Industrial Development Commission of Greater Vancouver, *Annual Report*, nos. 10 to 16, 1961 to 1967.
11. Allen Ginsberg, *Howl and Other Poems* (San Francisco: City Lights Books, 1996).
12. Ray Murphy, "Big Problems Face Our Youth," *Pacific Tribune*, 24 May 1963, 7.
13. Memo, Vancouver City Clerk to Bryn Lloyd, 31 May 1968, 79B5-12, Vancouver Archives. This memo was a summary analysis by the city clerk's office of Vancouver's changing cultural scene from 1965 to 1968.
14. Local papers, for instance, noted that many

dropouts from Vancouver high schools were in the Kitsilano district. See Bob Wilson, "Hippie Drop-Outs Return," *Vancouver Sun*, 17 October 1967, 15.

15. See Maureen Kirkbride, "Home was Hippie Hollow," *The Ubyssey*, 16 September 1977, 4; Verne McDonald, "Psychedelia Fades Away," *The Ubyssey*, 16 September 1977, 11; and Chris Emmott, "Hippies Hop to Acid Shop," *The Ubyssey*, 17 March 1967, 7.

16. See Emmott, "Hippies Hop"; and Lois Atkinson, "Fourth Avenue," *Vancouver's Leisure Magazine*, March 1974, 14–15.

17. Ruth M. Jones, "Here's the 'Scene' in Hippie Heaven," *Vancouver Sun*, 28 July 1967, 4A.

18. See Jim Robinson, "The Unhappiest Hippies," *Vancouver Life Magazine*, 13 January 1968, 2–4; and "Hippie Request for Concert Finds Park Board Not Deaf," *Vancouver Sun*, 4 August 1967, 3.

19. Stephen Brown, "'Be-in' Snarls Park Traffic," *Vancouver Province*, 15 April 1968, 1.

20. Harry Rankin, Special Committee on Hippies, 15 July 1968, 79B5-13 Vancouver Archives.

21. Daniel Bell, *The Cultural Contradictions of Capitalism* (New York: Basic Books, 1976), 3–32.

22. Bob Masse, interview by Lawrence Aronsen, 26 August 2006.

23. A sizable number of hippies travelled to Vancouver from San Francisco when it became clear that Haight-Ashbury was not developing into a utopian hippie enclave. See Edward Thorpe, "The Hippie Is Dead ... Long Live the Yippie," *Vancouver Sun*, 30 October 1968, 5; and Bob Quintrell (host), "Festivals and Happenings: Vancouver's Human Be-in," 7 O'Clock Show, CBC, aired 30 May 1967 (the actual event was held on 26 March 1967), available on the CBC Digital Archives Website, http://archives.cbc.ca/society/youth/clips/3160/.

24. "1,000 Hippies Turn-on in Park," *Vancouver Sun*.

25. "The Hippies: The Philosophy of a Subculture," *Time*, 7 July 1967, 18–23.

26. Kirkbride, "Home was Hippie Hollow."

27. H. Michael Williams, "How to Keep in the Pink," *The Ubyssey*, 21 January 1966, 9.

28. Ibid.

29. In the fall of 1966 the largest drug bust to date in the city showed that the problem had indeed spread to Vancouver's west side. Vancouverites were surprised to read that young people were increasingly engaged in the use of a new generation of hallucinogenic drugs, such as LSD, and marijuana. See "Police Make Record Number of Drug Arrests This Month," *Vancouver Sun*, 23 November 1966, 3; and "Marijuana Seized, Police Tell Court," *Vancouver Sun*, 23 November 1966, 12.

30. See Tom Wayman, "LSD: Gate Opener to Heaven or to Hell," *Vancouver Life Magazine*, September 1966, 36–41; "The Scourge of Drugs upon the Land," *Vancouver Province*, 11 October 1969, 5; and Nicholas Steed and Eileen Johnson, "Marijuana and the Middle Class," *Vancouver Life Magazine*, 11 January 1968, 15–17. At the same time, marijuana was increasingly featured on the Canadian flag and elsewhere in an attempt to marry the drug culture with Canadian culture. See "Oh, Cannabis, Glorious and Free," *Georgia Straight*, 15 December 1967, 16.

31. The Keir quotation is from an unidentified, undated clipping in the Ken Lester Collection, Vancouver, BC. The term "hippie" was not used in internal civic documents until early 1967; the term was surely borrowed from a San Francisco reporter, who first used it in a 1965 newspaper column.

32. There were reports of young male university students cruising Fourth Avenue and harassing hippie girls in pursuit of sexual favours. See "The Hate-4th Scene," *Georgia Straight*, 28 June 1967, 3.

33. Paul Manning, "Love, Drugs, and a Kind of Living: What's It All About ... This Hippie Thing?" *Vancouver Province*, 8 November 1969, 5.

34. Photographs from various communal events featured in the *Georgia Straight* clearly show hippies' unique dress and hairstyles. See Joe Ellis, "We Have Gathered Together in a Grassy Meadow," *Georgia Straight*, 8 September 1967, 3; and Don Slade, "Super Human Be-In," *Georgia Straight*, 11 August 1967, 1.

35. Lone Star College, Kingwood, "1960–1969," in *American Cultural History: The Twentieth Century*, http://kclibrary.lonestar.edu/decade60.html (accessed 1 October 2006).

36. The Golden Lotus (1967) and The Naam (1968) remain the most prominent pioneering hippie eateries of their era. "Golden Lotus," *Georgia Straight*, 26 July 1967, 17. The Naam is still in operation today.

37. Donna Mason, "If It's Happening ... It's on Fourth Ave," *Vancouver Province*, 8 April 1967, 5.

38. Red Robinson, Rockbound: *Rock'n'roll Encounters* (Surrey, BC: Hancock House: 1983).

39. Valerie Hennell, "The Love Generation," *Vancouver Life Magazine*, September 1967, 23.

40. "Activist artist," *Georgia Straight*, 22 September 1967, 11.

41. Photographs, sketches, and cartoons of nude women were a staple of the *Georgia Straight* in its early years (1967 to 1970).

42. "1,000 Hippies Turn-On in Park," *Vancouver Sun*.

43. Quintrell (host), "Festivals and Happenings: Vancouver's Human Be-in."

44. See "Invitation Super Human Be-In," *Georgia Straight*, 8 March 1968, 1; and "Super Human Be-In," *Georgia Straight*, 22 March 1968, 1.

45. Brown, "'Be-in' Snarls Park Traffic."

46. Ibid.

47. See James Reid, "It's in the Pot," *The Ubys-*

sey, 10 March 1967, 6; "The Only Bad Thing About Pot Is the Rap," *Georgia Straight*, 19 May 1967, 10. The group's message was widely popularized in the local media. Reid's letter was also sent to the mayor directly. Letter, James Reid to Mayor Campbell, 17 November 1966, 45C2-39, Vancouver Archives.

48. See Allan Fotheringham, "The Beginnings of Tom Campbell," *Globe and Mail*, 21 September 1972, 1; and "Campbell won't seek fourth term as mayor of Vancouver," Globe and Mail, 21 September 1972.

49. See "Mayor Tom Campbell," *Vancouver Sun*, 21 January 1967; and Sandra Thomas, "Museum looking for hippie memorabilia," *Vancouver Courier*, 21 December 2003, 2.

50. Tom Campbell, telephone interview by Lawrence Aronsen, 10 October 2006.

51. Alf Strand, "Police Drug War Backed by Mayor," *Vancouver Sun*, 8 March 1967, 1.

52. See "City Opens War on Marijuana, LSD," *Vancouver Sun*, 28 February 1967, 1; and Strand, "Police Drug War Backed by Mayor."

53. Dr. J.L. Gayton, "An Open Letter to All Young People and Parents: DANGERS OF LSD (Lysergic Acid Diethylamide)" [dated 10 March 1967], *Georgia Straight*, 13 March 1967, 15.

54. "Hippie Society Slammed for Runaways' Problem," *Vancouver Sun*, 2 November 1967, 49.

55. Ibid. See also "City Opens War on Marijuana, LSD," *Vancouver Sun*, 28 February 1967, 1; and Strand, "Police Drug War Backed by Mayor."

56. Stan Shillington, "Dope Roundup of 84 Launched," *Vancouver Sun*, 12 June 1969, 1.

57. Paul Smyth (former RCMP constable), interview by Lawrence Aronsen, 30 September 2006.

58. "Hippies: Good or Bad," *Vancouver Province*, 5 June 1967, 5.

59. See "Two Charged after Sit-in at Café," *Vancouver Sun*, 12 June 1967, 27; and "Hippies Harass Hamburger Haven, *Vancouver Sun*, 13 June 1967, 45.

60. Letter, Dorothy I. and Thomas A. Cacchioni to Mayor Campbell, 22 February 1967, 79B5-11, Vancouver Archives.

61. Mason, "If It's Happening ... It's on Fourth Ave."

62. Letter, G.H. Baylow to Mayor Campbell and council, 10 May 1967, 546B1-9, Vancouver Archives.

63. "Violence / Love Street," *Georgia Straight*, 28 June 1967, 4.

64. Report, Patrol Superintendent T. Dixon to Mayor Campbell, 29 August 1967, 79B5-13, Vancouver Archives.

65. Report, Chief Constable R.M. Booth to Mayor Campbell, 28 March 1967, 106D5-2, Vancouver Archives.

66. Report, Dixon to Campbell.

67. Alf Strand, "Will Wield Big Stick Tom Vows," *Vancouver Sun*, 12 December 1968, 43.

68. See Report from the Special Committee of Council re: Hippie Situation, 10 October 1967, 79B5-12, Vancouver Archives.

69. Reports from the Special Committee of Council re: Hippie Situation, 11 July 1968 106D5-2; and 15 July 1968, 79B5-13, Vancouver Archives.

70. Letter, Ken Armstrong to Mayor Campbell and aldermen, 17 February 1968, 79B5-15, Vancouver Archives. Armstrong emphasized, for example, that "several hundred teen age girls, many from Kitsilano are reported to have become pregnant."

71. Letter, Harold Kidd, Kitsilano Ratepayers' Association, to Ronald Basford, 20 March 1968, Vancouver Archives.

72. See reports from the Sub-Committee of the Special Committee of Council re: Hippie Situation, 8 July 1968, 79B5-2; 11 July 1968, 79B5-2; and 24 July 1968, 79B5-14, Vancouver Archives. See also report from the Special Committee of Council re: Hippie Situation, 15 July 1968, 79B5-13, Vancouver Archives. In addition to housing and food assistance, the committees recommended an open dialogue between hippies and members of city council.

73. See George Peloquin, "City Council To Continue Involvement in Cool-Aid," *Vancouver Sun*, 21 August 1968, 18; and "Council Cool-Aid Voted for Hippies," *Vancouver Province*, 17 July 1968, 23.

74. "Hippie House Row Reaches New Heights," *Vancouver Province*, 7 August 1968, 23.

75. Campbell's views concerning hippies were well known in Vancouver. As a result, the mayor's political opponents used his extreme anti-hippie rhetoric for their own political advantage. For example, in a pre-election interview Art Phillips commented, "I am not a reactionary. Personally, I think that hippies are important as an extreme reaction and reflection of the problems of our society." See George Peloquin, "Can TEAM COPE with the NPA?" *Vancouver Sun*, 26 November 1968, 6.

76. See "Hippies Hold Be-in Sunday at City Hall," *Vancouver Sun*, 6 May 1968, 1; Lorraine Shore, "Hippies 'Capture' City Hall," *Vancouver Sun*, 16 May 1968, 1; and "Suspend *Georgia Straight*?" *Vancouver Province*, 21 September 1968, 27.

77. These subjects took on greater prominence in alternative periodicals in 1970. See, for example, Irving Stowe, "Greenpeace Is Beautiful," *Georgia Straight*, 4 November 1970, 19; J. Arthur, "Ecology Happening," *Georgia Straight*, 28 January 1970, 17; Rick Doucet, "Out of the Closets and into the Streets," *Georgia Straight*, 31 August 1970, 9; "International Women's Day," *Georgia Straight*, 4 March 1970, 17; "Peace and Vibes," *Georgia Straight*, 15 July 1970, 5; and "Oakalla Shaken," *Georgia Straight*, 15 July 1970, 3.

78. "Bad Trips To Increase, Says Narcotics Expert," *Vancouver Province*, 8 November 1969, 19.

79. "The Peace Sleep," *Georgia Straight*, 31

December 1969, 5.

80. Muz Murray, "Street Communication Turn Over a New Leaf," *Georgia Straight*, 10 September 1969, 4.

81. "Fourth Avenue Images," *Georgia Straight*, 22 October 1969, 4. Author Ron Verzuh also identifies 1970 as the turning point in the decline of Vancouver's hippie movement.

82. Harry Rankin, "What Makes a Hippy?" *Pacific Tribune*, 8 September 1967, 4.

83. Hippie Daze (now called Summer of Love) has been held annually by the Kitsilano business community since 2005 to "celebrate" the counterculture. While historical pictures and various events at the festival suggest a heartfelt reflection of the past, they obscure the reality that many Kitsilano merchants did all they could to remove hippies from the area during the late 1960s. See Kitsilano 4th Avenue Business Association, "Hippie Daze Photos," http://www.kitsilano4thavenue.com/qs/page/2541/150/-1.

84. John Luce, "Haight–Ashbury Today: A Case of Terminal Euphoria," *Esquire* 72 (July 1969): 68, quoted in Allen J. Matusow, *The Unraveling of America: A History of Liberalism in the 1960s* (New York: Harper and Row, 1984), 302.

85. One Digger wrote about the increasing problem of violence and its connection to drugs in the neighbourhood saying, "Pretty little 16-year old middle-class chick comes to the Haight to see what it's all about and gets picked up by a 17-year-old street dealer who spends all day shooting her full of speed again and again." See Underground Press Syndicate, "Diggers Put Down Haight," *Georgia Straight*, 5 March 1967, 3.

86. William L. O'Neill, (New York: *New York Times* Books, 1971), 253–54.

87. See also local typologies of hippies that divided them into good and bad: for example, Max Wyman, "Hippies Could Rule World, Nurture Them, Says Prof," *Vancouver Sun*, 28 July 1967, 12.

88. "The Problem," *Georgia Straight*, 9 July 1969, 11.

89. "Cool-Aid Gets Help from UBC," *Vancouver Province*, 20 November 1970, 14.

Chapter 2: Liberating Higher Education

1. Bruce Serafin, "Cultural Workers and Muslim Hats," in *Vancouver: Representing the Postmodern City*, ed. Paul Delany (Vancouver: Arsenal Pulp Press, 1994), p. 88.

2. Ibid.

3. Todd Gitlin, *The Sixties: Years of Hope, Days of Rage* (New York: Bantam Books, 1987), 353.

4. This phrase was popularized by the founders of the VFU in its first year of operations.

5. See Jane Lichtman, *Bring Your Own Bag: A Report on the Free Universities* (Washington, DC: American Association for Higher Education, 1973), 9–10; and "Free University," in *The ABC-CLIO Companion to the 1960s Counterculture in America*, ed. Neil A. Hamilton (Santa Barbara, CA: ABC-CLIO Press, 1997), 109.

6. See Kirkpatrick Sale, *SDS* (New York: Random House, 1973); and James Miller, *Democracy Is in the Streets: From Port Huron to the siege of Chicago* (Cambridge: Harvard University Press, 1994).

7. See Tom Hayden, *The Port Huron Statement: An Agenda for a Generation*, June 1962 (available online at The Sixties Project website, http://www2.iath.virginia.edu/sixties/HTML_docs/Resources/Primary/Manifestos/SDS_Port_Huron.html); Tom Hayden and Dick Flacks, "The Port Huron Statement at 40," *The Nation*, 5 August 2002, 18–22; and Maurice Isserman, *If I Had a Hammer: The Death of the Old Left and the Birth of the New Left* (New York: Basic Books, 1987), 209–14.

8. Alexander Bloom and Wini Breines, eds., *Takin' It to the Streets: A Sixties Reader* (New York: Oxford University Press, 1995), 74.

9. Hayden and Flacks, "The Port Huron Statement at 40."

10. Bloom and Breines, *Takin' It to the Streets*, 74.

11. Miller, *Democracy Is in the Streets*, 179.

12. Gitlin, *The Sixties*, 151.

13. See Harvard Sitkoff, *The Struggle for Black Equality, 1954-1980* (New York: Hill and Wang, 1981); and Kathy Emery, Sylvia Braselmann, and Linda Reid Gold, "Introduction: Freedom Summer and the Freedom Schools," Mississippi Freedom School Curriculum website, http://www.educationanddemocracy.org/FSCfiles/A_02_Introduction.htm.

14. See Waldo Martin, "Holding One Another: Mario Savio and the Freedom Struggle in Mississippi and Berkeley," in *The Free Speech Movement: Reflections on Berkeley in the 1960s*, ed. Robert Cohen and Reginald E. Zelnik (Berkeley: University of California Press, 2002), 83–102; and Ruth Rosen, "A Passion for Justice: A Gentle Warrior's Fight for Free Speech," *Chronicle of Higher Education*, 10 (January 1977): B7.

15. Paul Lauter and Florence Howe, "What Happened to the 'Free University'?" *Saturday Review*, 20 June 1970, 80–96. There is some dispute about where exactly the first free university was established; however, much of the evidence suggests the first school was either Berkeley Free University or Free University of New York.

16. Bill Draves, *The Free University: A Model for Lifelong Learning* (Chicago: Follett, 1980), 23–36.

17. See H. Junker, "Free University: Academy for Mavericks," *The Nation*, 16 August 1965, 78–80; Johnathan Eisen and David Steinberg, "The Student Revolt against Liberalism," *Annals of the American Academy of Political and Social Science* 382 (March

1969): 83; and Peter Bart, "Students of Left Set Up Colleges," *New York Times*, 12 December 1965, 1.

18. The *Berkeley Barb*, a local underground newspaper, printed course information for interested students (obtained through a special order from the New York Public Library).

19. Jeff Lustig, "Free U of Berkeley: Developing the Left," *Free Student* (May/June 1966): 7.

20. Nora Sayre, "Free University," *New Statesman*, 1 April 1966, 463.

21. "Universities, Free Style," *Newsweek*, 10 January 1966, 59–60.

22. See *Free University of New York Fall Catalog, 1965*, and *Free University of New York Winter Catalog, 1966*, Nora Sayre Papers, Manuscripts and Archives Division, New York Public Library.

23. Sayre, "Free University," 463.

24. Ibid. The quotation about "a commie-tool" was credited to a 1966 piece in the *New York Journal-American*.

25. Murray N. Rothbard, "Egalitarianism and the Elites," *The Review of Austrian Economics* 8 (1995): 48.

26. See Fred M. Hechinger, "Free Universities: No Grades, No Exams — And Now, No Schools," *New York Times*, 22 August 1971, E9; and Lewis S. Feuer, "Berkeley and Beyond," *Change in Higher Education* 1, 1 (January/February 1969): 47–49.

27. The evolution of Rochdale College is documented in several issues of *This Magazine Is About Schools*.

28. John Baillie, interview by Julian Benedict, 1 December 2006; see also "College Drop-Outs Plan to Organize a Free University in Vancouver," *The Ubyssey*, 10 October 1969, 22.

29. See the *Constitution and Bylaws* of the Vancouver Inner City Service Project Society 1969, 600-D-54 Vancouver City Archives; Vancouver Inner City Service Project Society, "You and the Inner-City," 27551, University of British Columbia Rare Books and Special Collections—Pamphlets Collection; Max Beck, email interview by Julian Benedict, 8 August 2006. Beck was instrumental in getting many of Vancouver's social service organizations, like VISP, off the ground.

30. According to former VFU coordinator Jerry Barudin, he received a salary of roughly $150 per month, which was paid almost exclusively out of student registration fees. Jerry Barudin, interview by Julian Benedict, 30 July 2006.

31. Official course calendar, Vancouver Free University, 1969, Ken Lester Collection, Vancouver, BC (hereafter KLC). Ken Lester was a prominent counterculture activist in Vancouver who also edited and wrote for several underground newspapers in the city. He is best known for coordinating the so-called Grasstown Smoke-In.

32. See "Free University Proves Big Draw," *Vancouver Sun*, 22 August 1970, 9; Leslie Plommer, "Teachers, Students Want To Learn: Free U Does Just That," *Vancouver Sun*, 4 September 1970, 13; Wilf Bennett, "University Runs on Shoestring," *Vancouver Province*, 24 September 1970, 15; "New Courses at the Free University—879-7856," *Georgia Straight*, 7 October 1970, 22; "Free U Examines Media," *The Ubyssey*, 9 October 1970, 2; "Winter Term: 100 Enroll at Free U," *Vancouver Sun*, 28 December 1970, 8; "Vancouver Free University," *Georgia Straight*, 14 September 1972, 8–9; Teya Ryan, "Back to Learning through Free U," *Vancouver Sun*, 1 December 1972, 26; Phil Hanson, "Free U Entrenched as Key Part of Hip Establishment," *Vancouver Sun*, 11 September 1973, 38; and Charles Wolverton, "Free University Holds Its Classes in Homes," *Vancouver Province*, 6 July 1973, 42.

33. Plommer, "Teachers, Students Want to Learn."

34. Roger Mattiussi, interview by Julian Benedict and Lawrence Aronsen, 11 November 2006. Mattiussi took over as a VFU coordinator when Jerry Barudin accepted a salaried position elsewhere.

35. In October 1969, eight faculty members of the PSA Department were suspended after they went on strike to obtain greater autonomy for hiring new faculty and granting tenure to professors already in the department.

36. Don Currie, "Need Sober Analysis of Student Movement," *Pacific Tribune*, 17 January 1969, 5.

37. Mattiussi, interview by Benedict and Aronsen.

38. Jacques Khouri, "Creative Motorcycle Course: Try 100 m.p.h. on Your Violin," *Vancouver Sun*, 15 May 1971, 13.

39. Mark Marcinkiewicz, email interview by Julian Benedict, 13 July 2006.

40. The popularity of sustainable lifestyles incorporating beekeeping is discussed in Richard W. Langer, *Grow It! The Beginners Complete in-Harmony-with-Nature Small Farm Guide* (New York: Avon Books, 1972), 276–303.

41. For an overview of the counterculture's views on religion and capitalism, see Douglas T. Miller, *On Our Own: Americans in the Sixties* (Lexington, MA: D.C. Heath, 1996), 199–210.

42. "Free U: Closing, Opening," *Georgia Straight*, 20 January 1971, 7; and KLC.

43. Adding sex education courses to the existing curriculum in British Columbia had been the subject of increasingly intense discussion since the early sixties; however, substantive changes were not introduced until the late 1960s in the Vancouver area. See "Sex Education Launched in Schools," *Victoria Colonist*, 10 February 1968, 14; and "Sex Course Ready in Fall," *Vancouver Sun*, 13 March 1968, 15.

44. "Learning How To Love," *Vancouver Province*, 7

January 1971, 23.

45. This information was part of a one-paragraph course description offered by Clive and Lynn Stenning, the married couple who originally instructed the course.

46. "Ask the Teacher," *Vancouver Sun*, 9 January 1971, 4.

47. "Learning How to Love," *Vancouver Province*.

48. Official course calendar, Vancouver Free University, KLC.

49. Numerous books discuss Reich's theories on this issue. See Myron R. Sharaf, *Fury on Earth: A Biography of Wilhelm Reich* (New York: St. Martin's Press, 1983); and Wilhelm Reich, *Children of the Future: On the Prevention of Sexual Pathology*, trans. Mary Higgins and Chester M. Raphael (New York: Farrar, Straus and Giroux, 1983).

50. Official course calendar, Vancouver Free University, fall 1970, KLC.

51. Ibid., spring 1971, KLC.

52. See back issues of the lesbian-feminist magazine *The Pedestal* (1970–73), Simon Fraser University Archives.

53. Official course calendar, Vancouver Free University, supplement, 1974, KLC.

54. One calendar from 1972 explained that the course was restricted to women "because it is impossible to teach anything of even a marginally technological nature to mixed male/female classes for the simple reason that men quite erroneously assume a natural superiority in these matters and tend to dominate all proceedings to no good purpose whatsoever."

55. See "Minister Names Head," *Vancouver Sun*, 26 February 1973, 13; "John Bremer: 'Interaction Counts, Not Revolution,'" *The Peak*, 25 July 1973, 4–6; and Dan Mullen, "The Educator Who Says Nothing Is Impossible," *Vancouver Province*, 21 July 1973, 5.

56. See Norbert Rogan, "Free U 'Cosmic Party,'" 7 July 1973, np, KLC; and "Free U for Kids," *Vancouver Sun*, 5 January 1974, 49.

57. Interview by Julian Benedict with a former director of the Britannia Community Centre, 12 November 2006.

58. Daniel Wood, interview by Julian Benedict, 12 November 2006. This interview clarified the links between the emerging NDP educational ethos and the changing nature of the VFU.

59. Greg Quill, "Rochdale: Sex, Drugs and Tax Breaks," *Toronto Star*, 1 March 2006, F1.

Chapter 3: 'The Sodom Of the North'

1. "RCMP Raiders Hunting French Sex Novel Here," *Vancouver Sun*, 14 October 1961, 1,2. See also Peter Birdsall and Delores Broten, *Mind War: Book Censorship in English Canada* (Victoria: Canlit, 1978), 20.

2. Alex MacGillivray, Editorial, *Vancouver Sun*, 1 December 1971, E 2.

3. See, for example, W.E. Mann, "Canadian Trends in Premarital Behaviour: Some Preliminary Studies of Youth in High School and University," *Bulletin: The Council for Social Service* (December 1967): 1–63; Christabelle Sethna, "The University of Toronto Health Service, Oral Contraception, and Student Demand for Birth Control, 1960–1970," *Historical Studies in Education* 17, 2 (2005): 265–92.

4. These questions were raised in Michel Foucault, *The History of Sexuality: An Introduction*, vol. 1 (New York: Random House, 1978); Alice Echols, *Daring to be Bad: Radical Feminism in America, 1967–1975* (Minneapolis: University of Minnesota Press, 1989); and Theodore Roszak, *The Making of a Counter Culture: Reflections on the Technocratic Society and Its Youthful Opposition* (Berkeley: University of California Press, 1995).

5. As Edward Shorter points out in *Written in the Flesh: A History of Sexual Desire* (Toronto: University of Toronto Press, 2005), 169, it was difficult to make consistently accurate observations on sexual behavior prior to the 1970s, because data from the international polls conducted by the Durex condom company was not yet available.

6. Doug Owram, *Born at the Right Time: A History of the Baby Boom Generation* (Toronto: University of Toronto Press, 1996), 269–70.

7. Shorter, *Written in the Flesh*, 23–24.

8. Allan Petigny, "Illegitimacy, Postwar Psychology, and the Re-Periodization of the Sexual Revolution," *Journal of Social History* 38, 1 (Fall 2004): 63–79. See also Ira L. Reiss, *The Social Context of Premarital Sexual Permissiveness* (New York: Holt, Rinehart and Winston, 1967).

9. For a discussion of the term "cold war Puritanism" see Anne M. Boylan, "Containment on the Home Front: American Families During the Cold War," *Reviews in American History* 17, 2 (June 1989): 301–5; Elaine Tyler May, *Homeward Bound: American Families in the Cold War* (New York: Basic Books, 1988).

10. This scene was frequently presented in the popular 1950s family sitcom *I Love Lucy*.

11. May, *Homeward Bound*.

12. Sharon Jayson, "Most Americans have had premarital sex, study finds," *USA Today*, 19 December 2006, http://www.usatoday.com/news/health/2006-12-19-premarital-sex_x.htm.

13. A bestseller on American campuses was Steven Marcus, *The Other Victorians: A Study of Sexuality and Pornography in Mid-Nineteenth-Century England* (New York: Basic Books, 1966), which was considered to be the definitive critique of the "pretentious" morality of the nineteenth century.

14. Beth Bailey, "Sexual Revolutions," in *The Sixties: From Memory to History*, ed. David Farber (Chapel Hill: University of North Carolina Press, 1994), 245–46.

15. Patricia Cohen, "New Slant on the 60's: The Past Made New. Experts Are Reassessing a Tumultuous Decade," *New York Times*, 13 June 1998.

16. This suggestive phrase is taken from Christopher Lasch, *The Culture of Narcissism: American Life in an Age of Diminishing Expectations* (New York: Norton, 1979).

17. Barbara Ehrenreich, *The Hearts of Men: American Dreams and the Flight from Commitment* (New York: Doubleday, 1983); Walter M. Gerson and Sander H. Lund, "*Playboy* Magazine: Sophisticated Smut or Social Revolution," *Journal of Popular Culture* 1, 3 (Winter 1967): 218–27.

18. Helen Gurley Brown, *Sex and the Single Girl* (New York: Random House, 1962).

19. See Helena de Bertodano, "Sex and the Octogenarian," *London Telegraph*, 26 June 2003, http://www.telegraph.co.uk/culture/books/3597396/Sex-and-the-Octogenarian.html.

20. Ibid.

21. David Allyn, *Make Love, Not War: The Sexual Revolution; An Unfettered History* (New York: Routledge, 2001), 101.

22. Timothy Miller, "The Sixties-Era Communes," in *Imagine Nation: The American Counterculture of the 1960s and 70s*, ed. Peter Braunstein and Michael William Doyle (New York: Routledge, 2002), 327–51; *Polyfidelity: Sex in the Kerista Commune and Other Related Theories on How to Solve the World's Problems* (San Francisco: Performing Arts Social Society, 1984).

23. Alan J. Matusow, *The Unraveling of America: A History of Liberalism in the 1960s* (New York: Harper and Row,1984), 279.

24. See Herbert Marcuse, *One Dimensional Man: Studies in the Ideology of Advanced Industrial Society* (Boston: Beacon Press, 1964).

25. See Sandra Thomas, "Those Were the Gays," *Vancouver Courier*, 28 July 2006, 1.

26. This is the author's recollection of buying such products in East Vancouver in the early 1960s.

27. "Red Light District Preferable to Call Girl Racket," *Vancouver Sun*, 21 February 1959, 1; "City Call Girl Centre Highly Organized," *Province*, 14 April 1960, 8.

28. "Camp Followers Top VD Problem," *Vancouver Sun*, 24 September 1965, 2.

29. Doug Collins, "Morality Crusade Launched by Rising Disease Rate," 15 August 1964, *Globe and Mail*, 8.

30. "Camp Followers Top VD Problem."

31. Bruce Ryder, "Undercover Censorship: Exploring the History of Regulations of Publications in Canada," in *Interpreting Censorship in Canada*, ed. Klaus Peterson and Allan Hutchinson (Toronto: University of Toronto Press, 1999), 147.

32. "Suggestive Poses Pull Playboy off Streets," *Province*, 31 October 1967.

33. Jack Moore, "Censored: Now a New Philosophy," *Vancouver Sun*, 16 January 1965, 3.

34. John Huitson, former BC film censor, interview by Lawrence Aronsen, 7 April 2008. See also Malcolm Dean, *Censored! Only in Canada: The History of Film Censorship—The Scandal off the Screen* (Toronto: Virgo Press, 1981).

35. "Film Censorship in B.C. 'Most Lenient,'" *The Province*, 14 September 1967, 39.

36. Historians have generally overlooked the culturally progressive appeal of the NDP in the turning-point election of 1972. See, for example, Patricia Roy and John Herd Thompson, *British Columbia: Land of Promise* (Toronto: Oxford University Press, 2005), 163–67. The author recalls the "hipness" of Dennis Cocke, a cabinet minister in the first NDP government. The combination of three lovely daughters and unrestricted petting parties in his family rumpus room produced a cultural revolution of sorts.

37. "Movie Censorship Attacked by MLA," *Vancouver Sun*, 3 March 1964, 1. The NDP's recommendations were quickly adopted. See "Film Censorship in B.C. 'Most Lenient,'" *The Province*.

38. "The Second Sexual Revolution," *Time*, 24 January 1964, 7–12.

39. Ken Lamb, "Everywhere That's Merry," *The Ubyssey*, 22 March 1955, 2.

40. This was the observation of one student activist writing from the perspective of middle age. See Stan Persky, "Sex History: From Making Babies to Making Whoopie," *Vancouver Sun*, 16 September 2000, A23.

41. "Frosh Ripe for Picking On," *The Ubyssey* 11 September 1962, 4.

42. "A Squinty Look at the Library," *The Ubyssey*, 21 September 1965, 1.

43. "Clubs Day's a Bash for Unwary Frosh," *The Ubyssey*, 10 September 1963, 9.

44. See "Dorm Jail Ludicrous to South," *The Ubyssey*, 9 March 1965, 1.

45. Ian Cameron, "New Group Bucks Birth Control Ban," *The Ubyssey*, 8 January 1965, 1; Tony Bond, "Birth Control Laws Are Laughable," *The Ubyssey*, 2 November 1965, 7.

46. Owram, *Born at the Right Time*, 268.

47. "25-cent Safes for SUB Cans," *The Ubyssey*, 30 September 1969, 9; see also "Sub Washrooms Modernized: Prophylactic Popularity Rises," *The Ubyssey*, 7 October 1969.

48. "Sex Course Comes to UBC," *The Ubyssey*, 21 November 1969, 19.

49. "Birth-Control Information Ok for City High

Schools," *Vancouver Sun*, 23 February 1971, 7.

50. "Where Love Is," *The Ubyssey*, 5 February 1971, 4.

51. Protests against the "Break the Dull Steak Habit" first occurred at the 1968 Miss America Pageant and spread across the United States in 1969.

52. "Where Love Is."

53. "Playboy Typifies Perversion," *The Ubyssey*, 21 November 1967, 9.

54. Leah Fritz, "A Woman's View," *The Ubyssey*, 16 February 1971, 6.

55. "Godiva," *The Ubyssey*, 6 February 1973, 4.

56. "Relationships and Sex Going Strong at UBC," *The Ubyssey*, 6 February 1987, 7.

57. Ibid.

58. In 1967, approximately 56 percent of Vancouver's population was under twenty-six years of age. Cited by Danny Baceda in an interview with *Vancouver Sun*, 29 October 1967, 29.

59. Danny Baceda quoted in Bonita Lee, "Virgin Hunting in the Concrete Jungle," *The Ubyssey*, 18 October 1968, *Page Friday* 13.

60. This sweeping, albeit impressionistic, generalization is based on interviews the author conducted in February 2008 with Warren Coughlin, Bernie Douglas, and Paul Boyle, formerly devout Catholics who came of age in the late 1960s.

61. Joan McTavish, a former downtown go-go dancer, interview by Lawrence Aronsen, 4 February 2008.

62. Lee, "Virgin Hunting in the Concrete Jungle," *Page Friday* 7.

63. Ibid., *Page Friday* 13.

64. Helen Gurley Brown's *Sex and the Single Girl* was a bestseller in Vancouver, and copies were widely circulated from the public library. *Cosmopolitan* was on sale in news outlets, bookstores, and a variety of chain grocery stores.

65. Lee, "Virgin Hunting in the Concrete Jungle," *Page Friday* 9.

66. "Should We Give the Pill to Teen-age Patients?" *Vancouver Sun*, 5 May 1968, 3.

67. Lee, "Virgin Hunting in the Concrete Jungle," *Page Friday* 8.

68. Ibid., *Page Friday* 13.

69. Daniel Francis, *Red Light Neon: A History of Vancouver's Sex Trade* (Vancouver: Subway Books, 2007).

70. John Mackie, "Surviving on the Strip: Penthouse Reaches 60," *Vancouver Sun*, 29 September 2007.

71. "Philliponi Pledges Call-Girl Probe," *Vancouver Sun*, 14 January 1959, 12.

72. Francis, *Red Light Neon*, 87–92.

73. Becki Ross and Kim Greenwell, "Spectacular Striptease: Performing the Sexual and Racial Other in Vancouver, B.C., 1945–1975," *Journal of Women's History* 17, 1 (2005): 144.

74. Ibid., 158.

75. "Nudes Turn Prudes for A-G," *Province*, 31 December 1971, 11.

76. "Clubs Want Complete Bottomless Ban," *Vancouver Sun*, 24 March 1972, 38.

77. Bob Cummings, "Total Sexuality," *Georgia Straight*, 31 May 1969, 8. See also Peter Toole, "My Days with Playboy; The Ideal Lover," *Georgia Straight*, 11 May 1971, 12–13.

78. Rebecca Klatch, "The Formation of Feminist Consciousness among Left and Right-wing Activists of the 1960s," *Gender and Society* 15 (December 2001): 791–815; Sara Evans, *Personal Politics: The Roots of Woman's Liberation in the Civil Rights Movement and the New Left* (New York: Vintage, 1979).

79. Letter to the editor, *Georgia Straight*, 15 July 1970, 5.

80. Norman O. Brown, *Life Against Death: The Psychoanalytical Meaning of History* (Middleton, CT: Wesleyan University Press, 1959).

81. "3000 Cast Their Eyes on Nude-in," *Vancouver Sun*, 24 August 1970, 2. See also Carellin Brooks, *Wreck Beach* (Vancouver: New Star Books, 2007).

82. "3000 Cast Their Eyes on Nude-in," *Vancouver Sun*.

83. Lorne and Betsey, "Groping Through Group Marriage," *Georgia Straight*, 11 November 1971, 4.

84. Personals ads, *Georgia Straight*, 19 May 1967, 11.

85. Lani Almas, "Sex Ads Found Wanting," *Georgia Straight*, 15 July 1970, 18.

86. "Straight Responds to Women's Demands," *Georgia Straight*, 16 April 1971, 3.

87. See, for example, "Female Sexuality and the Liberated Orgasm," *Georgia Straight*, 2 December 1969, 12–13; and "Women's Liberated," *Georgia Straight*, 8 April 1971, 1.

88. "Cynthia Plaster-Caster," *Georgia Straight*, 25 April 1969, 15.

89. Ron Verzuh, *Underground Times: Canada's Flower-Child Revolutionaries* (Toronto: Deneau,1989), 67.

90. Shorter, *Written in the Flesh*, 167–73.

91. Neil Watson, interview by Lawrence Aronsen, 14 May 2008.

92. Kevin Griffin, "The Pioneers in Vancouver's Queer History," *Vancouver Sun*, 16 August 2007, D.19.

93. Ibid.

94. Watson, interview, 14 May 2008.

95. Ibid.

96. Quoted in Jeanette A. Auger, "A Modest Proposal," *Georgia Straight*, 31 May 1972, 23.

97. Watson, interview.

98. Norton, "Sexual Revolutions."

99. Ira E. Robinson and Davor Jelicka, "Change in

Sexual Attitudes and Behavior of College Students from 1965 to 1980: A Research Note," *Journal of Marriage and the Family* 44 (1982): 237–40; Robert R. Bell and Kathleen Coughey, "Premarital Sexual Experience Among College Females, 1958, 1968, and 1978," *Family Relations* 29 (1980): 353–57.

100. Jack Wasserman, "Saloon Crawler's Notebook," *Vancouver Sun*, 19 October 1971, 15.

101. Paul Raugust, "Vancouver Goes Boom in the Night," *Province*, 13 March 1974, 13.

102. "Playboy 'Sex' Good Clean fun," *Vancouver Sun*, 2 June 1972, 9.

103. Janet, "Rape: The Ultimate Come-on," *Women Can*, 5 July 1974, 8.

104. Douglas T. Miller, *On Our Own: Americans in the Sixties* (Lexington, MA: D.C. Heath, 1996), 296–97

105. Young Boys 'Cost $10' in Baths," *Vancouver Sun*, 26 September 1975, 8.

106. "Sex Rules Vital," *Province*, 20 February 1967, 23.

107. Patricia Anderson, *Passion Lost: Public Sex and Private Desire in the Twentieth Century* (Toronto: Thomas Allen, 2001).

Chapter 4: Getting Higher

1. The "acid rock" experience has been vividly described in Tom Wolfe's *The Electric Kool-Aid Acid Test* (New York: Picador, 2008).

2. "Trips Festival," in *The ABC-CLIO Companion to the 1960s Counterculture in America*, ed. Neil A. Hamilton (Santa Barbara CA: ABC-CLIO Press, 1997), 308–9.

3. Wolfe, *Electric Kool-Aid Acid Test*, 236.

4. Neil Douglas, local rock band guitarist, interview by Lawrence Aronsen, 12 August 2008.

5. Tom Campbell, interview by Lawrence Aronsen, 12 November 2006; see also "Campbell Memorable Mouth," *The Ubyssey*, 16 September 1977, *Page Friday* 6.

6. Tom Campbell, interview. See also "Rid City of LSD—Mayor," *Vancouver Sun*, 8 March 1967, 1.

7. Paul Rutherford, "Made in America: The Problem of Mass Culture in Canada," in *The Beaver Bites Back*, ed. David Flaherty and Frank Manning (Montreal: McGill-Queen's University Press, 1993), 260–80.

8. For an overview of drug control legislation see David F. Musto, *The American Disease: Origins of Narcotic Control* (New York: Oxford University Press, 1999).

9. Jay Stevens, *Storming Heaven: LSD and the American Dream* (New York: Grove, 1987), 306.

10. Albert Hofmann quoted in Adam Bernstein, "Chemist Accidentally Discovered LSD," *Vancouver Sun*, 1 May 2008, A13.

11. Martin A. Lee & Bruce Shlain, *Acid Dreams. The Complete Social History of LSD: The CIA, the Sixties, and Beyond* (New York: Grove, 1985), 44–70.

12. Aldous Huxley, *The Doors of Perception* (New York: Perennial, 1970).

13. Sybille Bedford, *Aldous Huxley: A Biography* (New York: Knopf, 1974).

14. Timothy Leary, *The Politics of Ecstasy* (New York: Putnam, 1970), 7.

15. Nicholas Von Hoffman, *We Are the People Our Parents Warned Us Against* (Chicago: Quadrangle Books, 1968), 23. Albert Hofmann, in particular, was concerned about Leary's willingness to experiment with students to advance his case for an LSD-based lifestyle. See Colby Cosh, "Albert Hofmann's 'problem child,'" *National Post*, 2 May 2008, A10.

16. Ken Kesey's most celebrated works include *One Flew Over the Cuckoo's Nest* and *Sometimes a Great Notion*.

17. "Ken Kesey," in *The ABC-CLIO Companion to the 1960s Counterculture in America*, ed. Neil A. Hamilton (Santa Barbara CA: ABC-CLIO Press, 1997), 172.

18. Quoted in Stevens, *Storming Heaven*, 306.

19. The term acid rock was introduced by Tom Wolfe in *The Electric Kool-Aid Acid Test*.

20. ProgArchives.com, "Psychedelic/Space Rock: A Progressive Rock Sub-Genre," http://www.progarchives.com/subgenre.asp?style=15.

21. Craig Morrison, "The Folk Roots of San Francisco Psychedelic Music," http://www.craigmorrison.com/article.php3?id_article=31 (originally published as "Folk Revival Roots Still Evident in 1990s Recordings of San Francisco Psychedelic Veterans," *Journal of American Folklore* 114 [Fall 2001]: 478–88). The folk legacy of the San Francisco sound distinguished it from the harder-edged music of The Doors coming out of Los Angeles.

22. Ken Kesey quoted in Michael W. Doyle, "Debating the Counterculture: Ecstasy and Anxiety over the Hip Alternative," in *The Columbia Guide to America in the 1960s*, ed. David Farber and Beth Bailey (New York: Columbia University Press, 2001), 147.

23. Jerry Garcia quoted in Lee and Shlain, *Acid Dreams*, 143.

24. Jonathan Gould, *Can't Buy Me Love* (New York: Harmony Books, 2007), 349–66.

25. "B.C. Heroin Problem Worst in Canada," *Montreal Star*, 18 November 1971, 54.

26. "Today's Junkies Surprising," *Vancouver Sun*, 22 June 1969, 11; "Many Heroin Users Shown To Have Disrupted Lives," *Vancouver Sun*, no date.

27. Erica Dyck (author of a recent study of LSD experiments in Saskatchewan), interview by Lawrence Aronsen, 10 September 2008.

28. Evelyn Benson, "Hollywood Sanatorium," *The News* (New Westminster), 8 April 1992, 1.

29. Ross Crockford, "B.C.'s Acid Flashback," *Vancouver Sun*, 8 December 2001, D3. The hospital files are still classified, but LSD was administered to over 1,100 patients from 1957 to 1975.

30. "Stimulant, Sedative Drugs Bigger Threat Than Heroin," *Vancouver Sun*, 28 May 1969, 13.

31. "Coffee Burns Holes in Genes," *Georgia Straight*, 17 May 1968, 1.

32. Glen C. Altschuler, *All Shook Up: How Rock 'N' Roll Changed America* (New York: Oxford University Press, 2003), 67–68.

33. Quoted in David Spaner, "Next Thing I Knew, I Was Biting the Cop's Arm," *Province*, 19 August 2007, B3.

34. Red Robinson, interview by Lawrence Aronsen, 20 October 2008. See also Red Robinson, "Red's Rock," in *The Greater Vancouver Book*, ed. Chuck Davis (Vancouver: Linkman Press, 1997), 680–81.

35. CFUN, "DIAL 1410," 4 November 1961, 1.

36. Martin Melhuish, *Oh What a Feeling: A Vital History of Canadian Music* (Kingston ON: Quarry, 1996), 68.

37. Gould, *Can't Buy Me Love*, 182–86.

38. "Four Working Lads from Liverpool," *Pacific Tribune*, 28 August 1964, 9.

39. Paul McCartney quoted in Ian MacDonald, *Revolution in the Head* (London: Fourth Estate, 1994), 112.

40. John Mackie, "B.C.—A Pot-Friendly, Pot-Profitable *Province*," *Vancouver Sun*, 20 January 2003; available on the Cannabis News website, www.cannabisnews.com/news/15/thread15232.shtml.

41. Norman O. Brown, *Life against Death: The Psychoanalytical Meaning of History* (Middletown, CT: Wesleyan University Press, 1959).

42. Dan McLeod, "We Are All God, You Are All God," *Georgia Straight*, 12 January 1968, 1.

43. "LSD Offers a Quick Trip to Oblivion," *Vancouver Sun*, 22 March 1967, 21.

44. Ivan Avakumovic (chair of UBC's political science department during the 1960s), interview by Lawrence Aronsen, 15 August 2008.

45. Fred Curtin, "Quick Trip with LSD Leads to Psychiatrist," *Province*, 10 April 1967, 5.

46. "Suicides Rise With Use of LSD, Says Psychiatrist," *Vancouver Sun*, 3 March 1967, 5.

47. "LSD Made Woman's Son 'A Helpless Vegetable,'" *Vancouver Sun*, 8 April 1967, 16.

48. "LSD Use Grows in B.C.," *Vancouver Sun*, 5 March 1967, 21.

49. Ibid.

50. "LSD Usage Send 14 to Doctor," *Vancouver Sun*, 18 March 1967, 11; "Government to Draft LSD Informers," *Vancouver Sun*, 21 March 1967, 1.

51. "Government to Draft LSD Informers."

52. "LSD in Schools Alarms Police," *Vancouver Sun*, 4 March 1967, 1.

53. Ibid.

54. "City Opens War on Marijuana, LSD," *Vancouver Sun*, 7 March 1967, 1; "Rid City of LSD—Mayor," *Vancouver Sun*, 8 March 1967, 1.

55. "Face Rotten World, LSD Users Told," *Vancouver Sun*, 23 March 1967, 8.

56. Merrilee Robson, "Straight Survives Decade," *The Ubyssey*, 16 September 1977, *Page Friday* 3.

57. "T.V. Rays Cause Brain Damage," *Georgia Straight*, 11 August 1967, 1.

58. "To Get out of Our Minds and into Our Senses," *Georgia Straight*, 12 January 1968, 3.

59. "Almasy: The Fearless Freak," *Georgia Straight*, 18 April 1969, 10.

60. Ibid., 9.

61. Ibid., 10.

62. Johanna Chelmis quoted on the Retinal Circus Nightclub Psychedelic Handbills website, www.rickmcgrath.com/retinal_circus.html.

63. "Fred Latremouille on Music," *Georgia Straight*, 24 November 1967, 13.

64. The Dead were the first acid rock band to travel outside the United States.

65. David Lemieux, "July 30 – August 5 [2007]," in the Tapers Section on the Grateful Dead website, http://www.dead.net/features/tapers-section/july-30-august-5.

66. The concept of "creative destruction" was first described by Joseph Schumpeter in *Capitalism, Socialism, and Democracy* (New York: Harper and Row, 1942).

67. Neal Hall, "Soundtrack of 67," *Vancouver Sun*, 17 July 2007, B3.

68. Ibid.

69. Neal Hall, "When Vancouver Rock Radio Bubbled Up from the Underground," *Vancouver Sun*, 8 August 2007, B1.

70. Stephen Brown, "Radio Free Vancouver," *Georgia Straight*, 15 October 1969, 15.

71. Robson, "Straight Survives Decade."

72. "United Empire Loyalists," at the Canadian 60s Garage Bands website, www.mindspring.com/~felinefrenzy/UEL.html.

73. "Cawsey's Club's," *The Ubyssey*, 10 January 1969, 6.

74. Bruce Baugh, "Bands Flourish in Golden Age," *The Ubyssey* 16 September 1977, *Page Friday* 5.

75. Bob Cummings, "Circus Re-Classification Routine Harassment," *Georgia Straight*, 1 March 1968, 3.

76. Bo Hansen, "Church High on LSD Take-off," *The Ubyssey* 25 November 1966, 3.

77. "The Acid Dream Is Over," *Georgia Straight*, 23 April 1971, 1.

78. Ibid.

79. Narcotic Addiction Foundation of British Columbia, *Summary Report on Tobacco, Alcohol, and*

Marijuana (Vancouver: Author, 1971).

80. "Psychedelia Fades Away," Ubyssey, 16 September 1977, *Page Friday* 11.

81. "Cocaine Use Up in High Schools," *Vancouver Sun*, 4 December 1978, 1.

82. "Diggers Put Down Haight," *Georgia Straight*, 5 May 1967, 3.

83. See *CLAM Newsletter*, October 1970, UBC Special Collections.

84. "Death Drugs," *Young Blood* (Winter 1971), 12.

85. Bill Storey, "The Unmaking of the Counter Culture," *Georgia Straight*, 12 October 1971, 19.

86. Some examples of local activist bands included Travelling River Band, Burner Boys, and Uncle Slug.

87. "Uncle Slug Unloads," *Georgia Straight*, 4 November 1970, 11.

88. Ibid.

89. "CKLG Radio For Which People?" *Georgia Straight*, 20 April 1971, 7.

90. "Don't Knock the Cock," *Georgia Straight*, 18 May 1971, 6.

91. The Stones wrote "Street Fighting Man" after riots in Paris during the summer of 1968.

92. Michael Barnholden, "The Gastown Riot 1971 and The Rolling Stones Riot 1972," *West Coast Line* (Fall 2005): 160–70.

93. Rick McGrath, "More of a Bridge," *Georgia Straight*, 24 August 1971, 11.

94. This point is developed in Peter Dogget, *There's a Riot Going On: Revolutionaries, Rock Stars, and the Rise and Fall of the '60s* (New York: Canongate, 2007), 219–25.

95. Storey, "The Unmaking of the Counter Culture."

96. Charles Campbell, "Drug Messiah Proves Poorer Comic Than Pop Philosopher," *The Ubyssey*, 19 September 1980, *Page Friday* 6.

97. "Timothy Leary Redefines His Own Unreality," *The Ubyssey*, 19 September 1980, *Page Friday* 7.

98. Karl Burau, "Fitness" (letter to the editor), *The Ubyssey*, 18 October 1968, 5.

Chapter 5: Taking It to the Streets

1. Abbie Hoffman, *Revolution for the Hell of It* (New York: Dial Press, 1970), 18.

2. The descriptive "pig" was usually applied specifically to the police but was occasionally used in reference to the United States. Abbie Hoffman explained that he used the term "pig" because "on TV we can't call them cocksuckers." See "Steal This Issue: Abbie Hoffman interview," *The Ubyssey*, 24 September 1982, 1.

3. "Yippies," in Neil A. Hamilton, ed., *The ABC-CLIO Companion to the 1960s Counterculture in America* (Santa Barbara, CA: ABC-CLIO Press, 1997), 339–41.

4. Dominique Clement, "Rights in the Age of Protest: A History of the Human Rights and Civil Liberties Movement in Canada, 1962–1982" (Ph.D. diss., Memorial University, 2005), 210.

5. At times the distinction between Yippies and the Vancouver Liberation Front was blurred. For example, both groups were involved in publishing newsletters and organizing theatrical events such as the May 1970 Blaine invasion.

6. In San Francisco and New York City alone, 400,000 demonstrators marched in the anti-war protests in 1967 that drew activists from both the peace movement and the counterculture. The largest demonstration before then had drawn 16,000 at the University of Michigan in 1965.

7. Charles DeBenedetti and Charles Chatfield, *An American Ordeal: The Antiwar Movement of the Vietnam Era* (Syracuse, NY: Syracuse University Press, 1990), 231–33.

8. Abbie Hoffman, *Soon To Be a Major Motion Picture* (New York: Perigee Books, 1980), 127.

9. William L. O'Neil, *The New Left: A History* (Wheeling, IL: Harlan Davidson Press, 2001), 49.

10. Hoffman, *Revolution for the Hell of It*, 16.

11. Quoted in Todd Gitlin, *The Sixties: Years of Hope, Days of Rage* (New York: Bantam Books, 1987), 233.

12. This vision is portrayed in Abbie Hoffman, *Woodstock Nation* (New York: Vintage, 1969).

13. For a summary of Hoffman's critique of the student New Left see "Abbie Hoffman Quits the Movement," *Georgia Straight*, 3 September 1971, 10–11.

14. Hoffman, *Soon To Be a Major Motion Picture*, 126.

15. Gitlin, *The Sixties*, 234.

16. Abbie Hoffman quoted in Milton Viorst, *Fire in the Streets: America in the 1960s* (New York: Simon and Schuster, 1979), 430.

17. David Farber, *Chicago '68* (Chicago: University of Chicago Press, 1988).

18. See Abbie Hoffman's account in *Soon To Be a Major Motion Picture*.

19. Mark Kurlansky, *1968: The Year that Rocked the World* (New York: Random House, 2005), 284–85.

20. Marty Jezer, *Abbie Hoffman: American Rebel* (Piscataway, NJ: Rutgers University Press, 1992), 220–21.

21. In 1979, Hoffman was approached by three advertising companies impressed with his "mediagenic revolutionary" image. One company even wanted to market a windup Abbie doll. Jezer, *Abbie Hoffman*, 214.

22. Gitlin, *The Sixties*, 417.

23. "The City Government," *Georgia Straight*, 22 March 1968, 1.

24. T.A. Myers, "This Little Piggy Went to the Club," *UBC Reports*, October 1968, 4–5.

25. "Protest Planned?" *The Ubyssey*, 25 October 1968, 3.
26. "Raucous Ruckus Rouses Faculty Club," *The Ubyssey*, 25 October 1968, 3.
27. Ibid.
28. "If Reactionary Malcolm Was Prez," *The Ubyssey*, 25 October 1968, 2.
29. "Vancouver Street Theatre," *Georgia Straight*, 27 May 1969, 3.
30. "Death of the Yippie," *Georgia Straight*, 13 February 1969, 1.
31. Cover image, *Georgia Straight*, 2 September 1969, 1.
32. "*Georgia Straight* Presents Benefit: John Sinclair Self-Defense Fund," *Georgia Straight*, 21 January 1970, p. 10. The Seeds of Time and High-Flying Bird played at the event.
33. Julian Benedict, "Radical Yellow: Exploring Vancouver's Guerilla Journal," *West Coast Line* 49 (Fall 2007), 1-3.
34. Red Lion Publishing, "Vancouver Yippie," http://vcmtalk.com/vancouver_yippie.
35. Yippies were particularly indifferent to exhortations to read Lenin as a revolutionary guide or to accept party discipline, as suggested by Elizabeth Hill, "Young Communist League Works for Socialism," *Pacific Tribune*, 3 April 1970, 10. As a result, the BC Communist Party denounced counterculture behaviour as adolescent and childish, and the Yippie protest at the Bay as counterproductive. See "Protest Police Riot Gear," *Pacific Tribune*, 29 May 1970, 1.
36. Red Lion Publishing, "Vancouver Yippie."
37. Benedict, "Radical Yellow," 4-19.
38. Youth International Party, news release, 8 May 1970.
39. Ibid.
40. "Sip-In Escalates," *The Peak*, 13 May 1971, 1.
41. Robert Sarti, "Yippies Behind Rash of Street Action Here," *Vancouver Sun*, 27 June 1970, 1.
42. Benedict, "Radical Yellow," 7.
43. "Blaine Townspeople Force Back Invading Canadians," *Seattle Times*, 10 May 1970, 1.
44. "Government Orders Invasion Report," *Bend (OR) Bulletin*, 13 May 1970, 12, http://news.google.com/newspapers?nid=1243&dat=19700513&id=wJUSAAAAIBAJ&sjid=E_cDAAAAIBAJ&pg=6236,4891528.
45. Malcolm Bell, *The Turkey Shoot: Tracking the Attica Cover-up* (New York: Grove, 1985), 6-9; "A Year Ago at Attica," *Time*, 25 October 1972, 1-3.
46. "Yippies Plan War Paint for Oakalla Be-Out," *Vancouver Sun*, 9 July 1970, 62.
47. "Yippie! Shakes Oakalla," *Georgia Straight*, 15 July 1970, 3.
48. Ad for Uncle Slug, *Georgia Straight*, 25 November 1970, 20.

49. The author recalls an upper-level sociology course at SFU in which students were asked to prepare a shoplifting manual appropriately titled "Expropriating the Hudson's Bay Company."
50. "Free Vancouver," *Georgia Straight*, 22 July 1970, 11-13.
51. Roger Marshall, "We Deserve Everything Yippie Chief Tells Students," *Vancouver Province*, 23 October 1968, 2.
52. Unnamed article, *Georgia Straight*, 17 June 1970, 9.
53. This is the opinion of the author, a Yippie fellow traveller in 1970.
54. "Riot-Equipped Police Scatter Gastown Pot Protesters," *Vancouver Sun*, 9 August 1971, 9.
55. The Le Dain Commission Report, *The Non-Medical Use of Drugs: Interim Report of the Canadian Government Commission of Inquiry* (Ottawa: Information Canada, 1972).
56. Lorraine Shore, "Mayor Fears Gastown Riot If Drug Crackdown Tried," *Vancouver Sun*, 22 July 1971, 3.
57. Michael Barnholden, "The Gastown Riot 1971 and the Rolling Stones Riot 1972," *West Coast Line* 39, 2 (Fall 2005): 165–66.
58. Yippie news release, 18 April 1970, Ken Lester collection.
59. "Dohm Cites Excessive Police Force," *Vancouver Province*, 8 October 1971, 8.
60. "Grasstown Smoke-In & Street Jamboree," *Georgia Straight*, 6 August 1971, 3.
61. "Crowds Chant: Legalize Dope," *Vancouver Province*, 8 August 1971, 1.
62. BC Commission of Inquiry, *Report on the Gastown Inquiry*, 7.
63. "Crowd Manipulation Alleged," *Vancouver Province*, 22 September 1971, 31.
64. "After a Wild City Night," *Vancouver Province*, 8 August 1971, 1.
65. For an overview of the Gastown riot see, Michael Barnholden, *Reading the Riot Act* (Vancouver: Anvil, 2005).
66. Ibid., 59–73, 97–99.
67. British Columbia, *Commission of Inquiry into the Gastown Riot* (Dohm Commission), *Report on the Gastown Inquiry* (Victoria: Author, 1972). One police officer commented to the media that although Lester and Sommer were not involved in any illegal acts, they were nonetheless engaged in provocative behavior that could be interpreted as incitement ("Police name pair as Gastown inciters," *Vancouver Sun*, 22 September 1971, 7).
68. Clement, "Rights in the Age of Protest," 210–11.
69. Ibid. The author sought to get the police to open their files while researching this book, but the documents remain closed to further inquiry. Lawrence Aronsen email to media@vpd.ca, 11 October

2008.

70. "Gastown Party Fantastic," *Vancouver Sun*, 16 August 1971, 1.

71. "Gastown Set for Party," *Vancouver Sun*, 14 August 1971, 2.

72. "Gastown Plot Charged," *Vancouver Sun*, 1 October 1971, 2. The article identified four groups at the Gastown riot; innocent bystanders, professional agitators, non-violent hippies, and "tough kids not necessarily longhairs." The latter were quick to resort to violence and "did not need any incitement."

73. "Citizen Takes on 4 Seasons Giant," *Vancouver Sun*, 29 May 1971, 16.

74. "Four Seasons Fact Sheet," *Georgia Straight*, 21 May 1971, 4.

75. Ibid.

76. "Stanley Park Party/Do It!" *Georgia Straight*, 13 June 1970, 1.

77. "People's Park" in Neil Hamilton, ed., *The ABC-Clio Companion to the 1960s Counterculture in America* (Santa Barbara: ABC-CLIO Press, 1997), 242–43.

78. "Instant Park Made at Project Site," *Vancouver Sun*, 31 May 1971, 2.

79. Ibid.

80. Ken Spotswood, "From Park of Hope to a Grubby Campsite," *Vancouver Sun*, 23 September 1971, 18.

81. Ibid. 1.

82. Michael Finlay, "Hippie Wedding Rather Casual," *Vancouver Sun*, 20 August 1971, 13.

83. "All Seasons Park Campers Get Message to Cool It," *Vancouver Sun*, 30 July 1971, 27.

84. "Mayor's Plan Fools Hippies," *Vancouver Sun*, 18 August 1971, 35.

85. Ibid.

86. "Whatever Happened to the All Seasons Park?" *Vancouver Sun*, 11 August 1971, 47.

87. Alex Young, "Rathie Threatens Squatters," *Vancouver Sun*, 19 April 1972, 23.

88. "Shantytown Walls Tumble Down," *Vancouver Province*, 21 April 1972, 29.

89. "Squatter Park Squalor Rapped," *Vancouver Province*, 20 April 1972, 21.

90. "Mud City Falls, Squatters Quit Last Stronghold," *Vancouver Province*, 22 April 1972, 44.

91. "Four Seasons Firm Backs Out," *Vancouver Sun*, 22 August 1972, 1.

92. "Citizen Takes on 4 Seasons," *Vancouver Sun*, 29 May 1971, 16.

93. Red Lion Publishing, "Vancouver Yippie."

94. Benedict, "Radical Yellow," 11–12.

95. Ken Lester, interview by Lawrence Aronsen, 12 November 2007.

96. "People's Park" in Hamilton, 242–43.

97. Robert Sarti, "Yippies Behind Rash Of Street Actions Here."

98. Ken Lester, interview by Lawrence Aronsen, 7 November 2007.

99. "Gastown Riot—Stan Douglas—A Night To Remember (or forget)," *Globe and Mail*, 30 October 2008, 1.

100. Ibid.

Chapter 6: 'Peaceniks' and Protest

1. "Community Demo for Vancouver," *Georgia Straight*, 2 November 1971, 3.

2. Frank Zelko, "Making Greenpeace: The Development of Direct Action Environmentalism in British Columbia," BC Studies 142–43 (Autumn 2004): 197–239.

3. The term "peaceniks" was originally used to describe pro-Soviet supporters in the 1950s and was popularly used in the media to describe anti-war activists until about 1966.

4. Charles DeBenedetti and Charles Chatfield, *An American Ordeal: The Antiwar Movement of the Vietnam Era* (Syracuse, NY: Syracuse University Press, 1990), 238–52, 387–90.

5. Christopher Andrew and Vasili Mitrokhin, *The Mitrokhin Archive and the Secret History of the KGB* (New York: Basic Books, 1999), 287–93; John Earl Haynes, Harvey Klehr, and Alexander Vassiliev, *Spies: The Rise and Fall of the KGB in America* (New Haven, CT: Yale University Press, 2009), 431–548.

6. Milton Katz, *Ban the Bomb: A History of SANE, 1957–1985* (New York: Praeger, 1986).

7. "Vote NO Nuclear Weapons in Canada," *The Ubyssey*, 12 February 1963, 4.

8. Todd Gitlin, *The Sixties: Years of Hope, Days of Rage* (New York: Bantam Books, 1987), 179–80.

9. Ibid., 209–10.

10. Adam Garfinkle, *Telltale Hearts: The Origins and Impact of the Vietnam Antiwar Movement* (New York: St. Martin's Press, 1997).

11. Pew Research Center for the People and the Press, "Generations Divide over Military Action in Iraq," *A Pew Research Center Note*, 17 October 2002, www.people-press.org/commentary/?analysisid=57.

12. At the time, the public was generally unaware of how devastating the Tet offensive was for the communists. See Michael Maclear, *The Ten Thousand Day War, Vietnam: 1945–1975* (Toronto: Avon Books, 1981), 219–23.

13. Maurice Isserman and Michael Kazin, *America Divided: The Civil War of the 1960s* (New York: Oxford University Press, 2000), 230–36.

14. Ibid., 231–32.

15. "B.C. Peace Groups Step Up Activity on Petition," *Pacific Tribune*, 1 September 1961, 3.

16. "No Nuclear Arms Parade in City Draws Big Turnout," *Pacific Tribune*, 7 April 1961, 3.

17. "East Berlin Action Blocks West German Warmongers," *Pacific Tribune*, 1 September 1961,

3; "26,000 in BC Sign against Nuclear Arms for Canada," *Pacific Tribune*, 16 June 1961, 3.

18. Dorothy Thompson, "No Connection," *The Ubyssey*, 3 October 1961, 2.

19. "Is RCMP out to Get CUCND Members?" *The Ubyssey*, 21 February 1962, 4. See also Steve Hewitt, *Spying 101* (Toronto: University of Toronto Press, 2002), 70–71, 120–22.

20. "Ban the Bomb," *The Ubyssey*, 22 September 1961, 2.

21. "Ban-Bombers to Protest," *The Ubyssey*, 3 November 1961, 1. One recalls, for example, Nikita Khrushchev's warnings in 1956 about "rocket bombing" London and Paris during the Suez Crisis.

22. "Ban-the-Bombers Hit by Rain and Luth," *The Ubyssey*, 10 November 1961, 1.

23. "Letters: On the Cuban Missile Crisis," *The Ubyssey*, 30 October 1962, 3.

24. "March against A-Arms Saturday," *Pacific Tribune*, 29 March 1963, 3.

25. "Campus Goes against A-Arms (sort of)," *The Ubyssey* 14 February 1963, 1. Nationally, 57 percent of Canadians supported the deployment of nuclear-tipped BOMARCs. See also Robert Bothwell, *Alliance and Illusion: Canada and the World* (Vancouver: UBC Press, 2007), 218–19.

26. Bryan Palmer, *Canada's 1960s: The Ironies of Identity in a Rebellious Era* (Toronto: University of Toronto Press, 2009), 258–59.

27. James Pitsula, *New World Dawning: The Sixties at Regina Campus* (Regina: University of Regina Press, 2008), 37–38.

28. "We're Being Watched," *The Ubyssey*, 18 January 1963, 1. See also Hewitt, *Spying 101*.

29. "SUPA Gone," *The Ubyssey*, 28 September 1967, 5.

30. Mike Morris, "British Columbia's Vietnam War" (honours thesis, history department, University of British Columbia, 2008), 18–19.

31. *Pacific Tribune*, 11 April 1965, 1. The UBC petition also received minor coverage in the *Vancouver Sun*, 6 April 1965, 2.

32. "Berkeley Bunch Calls Viet Beef," *The Ubyssey*, 28 September 1965, 2.

33. "2000 Peaceful Protesters March against Vietnam War," *Vancouver Province*, 23 October 1967, 2.

34. "Campus Reds and Radicals Take Over Teach-In at U.B.C.," *Vancouver Province*, 12 October 1965, 12.

35. "What Is VDD?" Box 2, Vancouver Vietnam Action Committee papers, UBC Special Collections (hereafter VVAC papers).

36. "Trade Unions and the War in Vietnam," 19 March 1967, Box 3, VVAC papers.

37. "Vancouver Joins World Wide Protest," *Pacific Tribune*, 22 October 1965, 1.

38. "Labour Backs NDP Stand against Ruling Class," *Pacific Tribune*, 18 June 1965, 3.

39. "NDP Asks Withdrawal," *Vancouver Sun*, 16 April 1966, 2.

40. VVDC to North Vancouver NDP constituency, 14 November 1966, Box 1, VVAC papers.

41. "Church Urges PM Seek Viet Peace," *Vancouver Province*, 1 June 1965, 21.

42. United Church memo, 6 July 1966, Box 1, VVAC papers.

43. "Babes in Arms Join City Peace Parade," *Vancouver Province*, 28 March 1966, 2.

44. "What Is a Marshal?" No date, Box 5, VVAC papers.

45. Ibid.

46. "National Student Days of Protest," Box 2, VVAC papers.

47. "VC Backers Mess Discussion," *The Ubyssey*, 10 November 1966, 1.

48. Daphne Morrison, "The Rituals of Rallies," *Vancouver Sun*, 2 November 1970, 40.

49. Ibid.

50. Doug Owram, *Born at the Right Time: A History of the Baby Boom Generation* (Toronto: University of Toronto Press, 1996), 221–22.

51. Morrison, "The Rituals of Rallies," 40.

52. The author recalls obtaining at least two phone numbers as a first step in the advance of social justice.

53. Paul Hollander, *Anti-Americanism* (London: Transaction, 1995), 411–19.

54. Vietnam Day Committee, Minutes, 14 February 1967, Box 1, VVAC papers.

55. VVDC to Spring Mobilization Committee, 9 January 1967, VVAC papers. See also "Influx 67," *Pacific Tribune*, 7 April 1967, 3.

56. "Newsletter," October 1967, Box 3, VVAC papers.

57. Press release, 18 February 1966, Box 1, VVAC papers.

58. Meeting, 6 July 1966, Box 1, VVAC papers.

59. Memo, 14 April 1966, VVAC papers.

60. "Bulletin of the Student Association to End the War in Vietnam," 29 April 1967, Box 2, VVAC papers.

61. "Call for Immediate Withdrawal of U.S. Troops," 3 April 1967, Box 2, VVAC papers.

62. "Report," 26 October 1966, Box 1, VVAC papers.

63. VVDC to Collins, 28 March 1967, VVAC papers.

64. Tommy Douglas quoted in "Editorial," *Pacific Tribune*, 21 April 1967, 12.

65. "Vietnam Hots Up Legislature," *Vancouver Sun*, 25 March 1967, 12

66. James K. Nesbitt column, *Vancouver Sun*, 27 March 1967, 10.

67. "Americans Desert Now," *Georgia Straight*, 11 August 1967, 1.

68. Morris, "British Columbia's Vietnam War,"

47–48.

69. In preparation for the spring 1968 demonstration, 2,500 leaflets were distributed to Surrey, a bedroom community 30 kilometres from downtown.

70. Vietnam Action Committee, Minutes, 17 October 1968, Box 1, VVAC papers.

71. "Vancouver Suggested for Peace Talks," *Vancouver Sun*, 25 April 1968, 55.

72. "Candidate Scolds Vietnam Protesters," *Vancouver Sun*, 14 June 1965, 15.

73. Morris, "British Columbia's Vietnam War," 50.

74. Turgeon to Watson, 15 October 1968, Box 3, VVAC papers.

75. "Yankee Refugee," 1 March 1968, Box 3, VVDC Papers.

76. "Mobilization on Vietnam," 3 April 1969, Box 3, VVAC Papers.

77. Robert Sarti, "Cold War Splits Protesters," *Vancouver Sun*, 3 April 1969, 7.

78. "Vietnam Sparks Rival Rallies, with US a Friend or Ogre," *Vancouver Province*, 7 April 1969, 2.

79. "Two Marches Better than One," *Georgia Straight*, 3 April 1969.

80. "Obscenities Hurled," *Vancouver Sun*, 9 August 1969, 5.

81. "How Does the Vietnam War Affect the People of Vancouver?" Box 4, VVAC papers.

82. "Report to NDP," 28 February 1970, Box 1, VVAC papers.

83. "Civic Election To Be Focus of Mass Anti-war March October 31," Box 4, VVAC Papers.

84. "Behind Viet War Protest," *Vancouver Province*, 16 October 1969, 37.

85. Ibid.

86. "3,000 Hold Peaceful Protest," *Vancouver Province*, 17 November 1969, 2.

87. Morris, "British Columbia's Vietnam War," 79.

88. Ibid., 81.

89. "Peace Rally Lands Up at City Hall," *Vancouver Sun*, 27 May 1970, 31.

90. Robert Sarti, "East and West Get Together," *Vancouver Sun*, 1 June 1970, 17.

91. Ibid.

92. Sandy Kass, "Viet Nam Protest to be Allowed," *The Ubyssey*, 30 October 1970, 1.

93. Press release, 28 October 1970, Box 4, VVAC papers.

94. "The First Question: Why Amchitka?" *The Ubyssey*, 28 September 1971, 1.

95. "They Did It in the Road," *The Ubyssey*, 3 October 1969, 1.

96. "Alaska Mothers' Campaign Against Cannikin," 15 August 1971, Box 5, VVAC papers.

97. Zelko, "Making Greenpeace," 234.

98. Ibid.

99. Ibid., 233.

100. Jim Bohlen, *Making Waves: The Origins and Future of Greenpeace* (Montreal: Black Rose Books, 2001), 30-31.

101. Berton Woodward, "Amchitka Protesters Ready as Crucial Hour Draws Near," *The Ubyssey*, 2 November 1971, 1.

102. Owram, *Born At the Right Time*, 212.

103. "Student Protest," *Vancouver Province*, 7 October 1971, 1.

104. Sandy Kass and Vaughn Palmer, "Classes Yield to Streets," *The Ubyssey*, 7 October 1971, 1.

105. Ibid.

106. Sylvia Hawreliak, "Amchitka: Victory for God," *Georgia Straight*, 11 November 1971, 15.

107. "Action Proposal for the VACT Conference," 1 November 1971, Box 5, VVAC papers.

108. "Beakaway Group Invades Post Office," *The Ubyssey*, 4 November 1971, 1.

109. "Protest Parade All Right—If," *Vancouver Sun*, 6 November 1971, 3.

110. "War-cause Wage Freeze and Inflation," 19 January 1972, Box 5, VVAC papers.

111. "Historical Information," Box 1, VVAC papers.

112. "Peace Group Seeks Union Support," *Vancouver Sun*, 26 February 1973, 5.

113. "Freedom's Price," Box 4, VVAC papers.

114. This was especially true for UBC organizers. See, for example, "Peaceful Resistance Urged," *The Ubyssey*, 23 September 1971, 1–2.

115. "Views Differ on Vietnam," *Vancouver Sun*, 23 March 1968, 16.

116. Bothwell, Alliance and Illusion, 312–31.

117. See, for example, Robin Mathews, "Opinion: On Draft Dodging and U.S. Imperialism in Canada," *Canadian Dimension* 6 (February/March 1970): 10–11.

118. "2,500 in Canada to Dodge Draft," *Vancouver Sun*, 30 March 1967, 5.

119. Bob Hunter interview, *Georgia Straight*, 4 November 1971, 2.

Conclusion: Who Owns Sixties Vancouver?

1. Pat Johnson, "Call of Wild Spreads Its Infection," *Vancouver Province*, 24 January 1972, 21–22.

2. The absence of a historical consensus about the 1960s is discussed in Rick Perlstein, "Who Owns the Sixties?" Lingua Franca (May/June 1996): 1–9.

3. David Morton, "Youth Revolution Bites Dust," *Ubyssey*, 16 September 1977, Page Friday 7.

4. This point has been made by some American writers. See, for example, Myron Magnet, *The Dream and the Nightmare: The Sixties Legacy to the Underclass* (New York: William Morrow, 1993), 8–9.

5. Marcel Danesi, *Forever Young: The "Teen-Aging" of Modern Culture* (Toronto: University of Toronto Press, 2006).

6. "Phat," *Georgia Straight*, 20 January 1972, 10.

7. "UVic Historian Argues That This Country

Became More Peaceful," *Globe and Mail*, 2 June 2007, A3.

8. Becki Ross, "Good Girls Gone Bad or Fiscal Godsend," *Globe and Mail*, 24 July 2009, 3.

9. Eric Damer and Herbert Rosengarten, *UBC: The First 100 Years: A commemoration* (Vancouver: University of British Columbia, 2009), 261–62.

10. Jeannine Mitchell, "At UBC, Recycling Means Education," *Georgia Straight*, 20 January 1970, 12.

11. "Women's Lib Busted," *Georgia Straight*, 14 May 1971, 5.

12. Frances Wasserlein, "An Arrow Aimed at the Heart" (master's thesis, Department of History, Simon Fraser University, 1990).

13. Women's Action Group of UBC and Shelagh Day, *Report on the Status of Women at UBC* (Vancouver: UBC, 1973).

14. Wendy Charr, "I Ain't Gonna Drink Beer at Nelson's No More," *Georgia Straight*, 21 May 1971, 2.

15. Sylvia Hawreliak, "Greenpeace 3 to Sail," *Georgia Straight*, 12 April 1972, 3.

16. David McTaggart, "Round One in My Battle Against France," *Vancouver Sun*, 28 June 1975, 6.

17. Brian Fortune, "Media Mellows Greenpeace," *Terminal City Express*, 23 February 1973, 5.

18. Bob Hunter quoted in "Where Are They Now?" *Vancouver Sun*, 21 July 2001, E6.

BIBLIOGRAPHY

Books

Allyn, David. *Make Love, Not War: The Sexual Revolution, An Unfettered History.* Boston, 2000.

Collier, Peter and David Horowitz. *Destructive Generation: Second Thoughts About the Sixties.* New York, 1969.

Draves, Bill. *The Free University: A Model for Lifelong Learning.* Chicago, 1980.

Farber, David and Beth Bailey. *The Columbia Guide to America in the 1960s.* New York, 2001.

Gitlin, Tod. *The Sixties: Years of Hope, Days of Rage.* New York 1993.

Hamilton, A. Neil. *The ABC-CLIO Companion to the 1960s Counterculture in America.* Santa Barbara, 1997.

Herring, George. *America's Longest War: The United States in Vietnam, 1950–1975.* New York, 1996.

Hewitt, Steve. *Spying 101: The RCMP's Secret Activities at Canadian Universities, 1917–1997.* Toronto, 2002.

Hoffman, Abbie. *Revolution for the Hell of It.* New York, 1968.

Jezer, Marty. *Abbie Hoffman, American Rebel.* New Brunswick, NJ, 1992.

Johnston, Hugh. *Radical Campus: Making Simon Fraser University.* Vancouver, 2005.

Lee, A. Martin and Bruce Shlain. *Acid Dreams: The Complete Social History of LSD: The CIA, the Sixties, and Beyond.* New York, 1992.

Matusow, Allen. *The Unraveling of America: A History of Liberalism in the 1960s New York.* New York, 1984.

Mietkiewicz, Henry and Bob Mackowycz. *Dream Tower: The Life and Legacy of Rochdale College.* Toronto, 1988.

Miller, T. Douglas. *On Our Own: Americans in the Sixties.* Lexington, KY, 1996.

O'Neill, L. William. *The New Left: A History.* Wheeling, IL, 2001.

Owram, Doug. *Born at the Right Time: A History of the Baby Boom Generation.* Toronto, 1996.

Palmer, Bryran. *Canada's 1960s: The Ironies of Identity in a Rebellious Era.* Toronto, 2009.

Pitsula, James. *New World Dawning: The Sixties at Regina Campus.* Regina, 2008.

Reich, Charles. *The Greening of America.* New York, 1971.

Robinson, Red. *Rockbound Rock'n'Roll Encounters.* Surrey, BC, 1983.

Rosengarten, Herbert. *UBC: The First 100 Years: A Commemoration.* Vancouver, 2008.

Rubin, Jerry. *Do It! Scenarios of the Revolution.* New York, 1970.

Shorter, Edward. *Written in the Flesh: A History of Desire.* Toronto, 2005.

Wolfe, Tom. *The Electric Kool-Aid Acid Test.* New York, 1968.

Articles

Barnholden, Michael. "The Gastown Riot of 1971 and the Rolling Stones Riot of 1972." *West Coast Line* 47

(2005), 164–169.
Benedict, Julian. "Radical Yellow: Exploring Vancouver's 'Guerilla' Newspaper, The Yellow Journal." *West Coast Line* 51 (2007), 38–56.
Hennell, Valerie. "The Love Generation." *Vancouver Life* (September 1967), 23–24.
Loo, Tina. "Flower Children in Lotusland." *The Beaver* 78 (1998), 36–42.
Morris, Mike. "British Columbia's Vietnam War." Honours essay, history department, University of British Columbia, April 2008.
Perlstein, Rick. "Who Owns the Sixties?" *Lingua Franca* 6 (May–June 1996), 3–14.
Petnigny, Alan. "Illegitimacy, Postwar Psychology, and the Reperiodization of the Sexual Revolution." *Journal of Social History* (Fall 2004), 63–79.
Powe Jr., L.A. "The Georgia Straight and Freedom of Expression in Canada." *Canadian Bar Review* XLVIII (September 1970), 410–438.
Wayman, Tom. "LSD: Gate Opener to Heaven or Hell?" *Vancouver Life* (September 1966), 36–41.
Zelko, Frank. "Making Greenpeace: The Development of Direct Action Environmentalism in British Columbia." *BC Studies* 142–143 (2004), 197–239.

Newspapers and Archives

The Georgia Straight
The Pacific Tribune
The Peak
The Province
Terminal City Express
Time Magazine
The Ubyssey
The Vancouver Sun
Yellow Journal

Simon Fraser University Archives
SFU Library Editorial Cartoon Collection
UBC Rare Books and Special Collections (Berkeley Poster Collection; Georgia Straight Collection; The Fisherman Publication Society Collection)
Vancouver Vietnam Action Committee Fonds
Vancouver City Archives (Mayor's Office Fonds; "Sub-Committee of the Special Committee of Council: The Hippie Situation 8 July 1968")
Ken Lester Collection
Official Vancouver Free University Calendars, 1969–1974.
CBC Digital Archvies

Interviews

John Baillie, 1 December 2006
Tom Campbell, 10 October 2006
Warren Coughlin, 15 October 2007
Erica Dyck, 10 September 2008
Rick Enns, 18 August 2009
Ken Lester 17 October 2006
Bob Masse, 26 August 2007
Roger Mattiussi, 11 November 2006
John Tanner, 15 August 2009
Daniel Wood, 12 November 2006

INDEX

Page numbers in italics refer to pictures.

acid rock. *See* music
activist groups, 108
    See also Diggers, Yippies
All Seasons Park occupation. *See* Four Seasons Park occupation
Amchitka nuclear test, 159–63
anti-war activism, 4, *6*, 136–41, 141–44, 148, 151, 155, 156, 157–59
    See also activist groups; Vietnam War
Almasy, "Zipp" Peter, 80–81, 94
Afterthought dance hall, 20, 25, 98, 99
"Age of Aquarius". *See* anti–war activism, counterculture

baby boomers, 5, 12, 14, 38, 51–53, 60, 64, 88, 91, 95, 107, 135
Baceda, Danny, 64
Baillie, John, 39
Baillie, Margaret, 39
beatniks, 12–14, 17, 57, 88
Beatles, The, 4, *58*, 61, 84, 86, 89, 90
beats. *See* beatniks
Be-In. *See* Human Be-In
birth control, 52, 55, 57, *60*, 62, 64, 67
Blaine invasion, 117–18, *119*, *120*, *123*
Bohlen, Jim, 43
Bremer, John, 46
Brown, Helen Gurley, 55
Brown, Norman O., 69–70, 91

Café Kobenhavn, 68
Campbell, Mayor Tom "Terrific", 6, *23*, 167
    hippies, 22, 24, 25–26, 30
    sexual revolution, 59, 60
    drugs and music, 80, 93–94, 99
    Yippies, 115, 121, 123, 128
    anti-war activism, 153, 157
CFUN, 3, 4, 88, 96, 97
Chong, Tommy, 89
City Lights bookstore, 12
CKLG-FM, 97, 99
CKVN, 97, *98*
    See also CFUN
Cocke, Dennis, 4, 175n1, 181n36
Cocke, Yvonne, 4
Cool-Aid House, 26, *27*, 30, 119
Committee for Sane Nuclear Policy, 136–38
Coordinating Committee. *See* Vancouver Vietnam Day Committee
Commercial Drive, 3, 5, 33, 45, 48, 103, 159
Communist Party of British Columbia, 14, 15, 90, 103, *137*, 141, 143, 145, 150, 163, 164
Communist Party of Canada, 41, *140*
Communist Party of the United States, 136
counterculture
    and Vancouver anti-war movement, 151
    beginning, 11
    characteristics, 30
    figures, 6
    fragmentation into subgroups, 46
    historical markers, 4

influence of Californian culture on, 7
lifestyle, 70
and mainstream culture, 11
See also drugs; environmentalism; feminism; hippies; sexual revolution; vegetarianism
counter-universities. *See* Vancouver Free University; free universities (USA)
CPBC. *See* Communist Party of British Columbia
CPUSA. *See* Communist Party of the United States
Crumb, R., *50*, 51
Cuban Missile Crisis, 7, 143
Cummings, Bob, 69, 99

Dante's Inferno, 98
Day, Korky, *69*
Dellinger, David, 149
Diggers, 7, 12, 13, 100, 108, 120, 178n85
Drive, the. *See* Commercial Drive
Dohm Commission, 123
Douglas, Stan, 5, 132
Douglas, Tommy, 150
draft dodgers, 149–51, 153, 164
drugs, 86–94
 alcohol, 88
 and music, 3, 7, 86–104
 east vs. west side usage, 18
 enforcement, 23, 25
 Methedrine/speed, 15, *92*
 mainstream fears/misconceptions, 23, 25
 mushrooms, 88
 usage demographics, 19
 in USA, 80–86
 See also LSD; marijuana.
Dylan, Bob, 90

Empire Stadium, *58*, 61, 88, 89
environmentalism, 8, 30, 156–65, 170, 172

Feminine Mystique, The, 46
feminism, 46–47, *47*, 62–64, 66, 69, 71, 74, 102, 112, 170–71
Filippone, Ross, 67
Fisk, John, 17, 158
flower power, 109, 124
Foikis, Joachim "Kim", 6, 8, 114, *115*
Four Seasons Park occupation, 4, 124–30, *126*, *129*
Fourth Avenue. *See* West 4th Avenue
Francis, Daniel, 67
Free Love Society, 62
Free Store, 119
Free U. *See* Vancouver Free University
free universities (USA), 34–38
 See also Vancouver Free University

Freud, Sigmund, 69
Friedan, Betty, 46, 48
Front de libération du Québec, 158

Garcia, Jerry, 84
Gastown, 5, *90*, 99, 171
Gastown Riot, 4, 11, 31, 94, 100–101, *106*, 120–24, 108, 179n31, 187n72
gay rights, 46, *75*
Georgia Straight, 6–7, *28*, 70, 94, 172
 anti–war movement, 151, 153
 drugs, 80, 81, 87, 94, 100
 "in your face" journalism, 70–71
 legal action vs., 26, *56*, 71
 sex, 21, *50*, *52*, *56*, *66*, *68*, 69, 70–71, 73
 promotes events, 21
 and Mayor Tom Campbell, 26
 and political fundraisers 115, 119
 See also Almasy, Peter "Zipp"; Crumb, R.; Cummings, Bob; Holmes, Rand; McLeod, Dan
Ginsberg, Allen, 12, 14, 92, 100
Grasstown Smoke-In. *See* Gastown Riot
Grateful Dead, 20, 80, 84, 96, *97*, 98, 122
Greater Vancouver Youth Communication Centre. *See* Cool-Aid
Greenpeace, 43, *130*, 160, *162*, 163, 165, 172–173
guerilla theatre. *See* street theatre

Haight–Ashbury district, 7, 12, 13, 18, 79, 176n23, 178n85
Hendrix, Jimi, 86, 89, 97
Hippie Daze festival, 7, 30, 104, 131, 178n83
hippies, 8, 15–16, 17–21
 capitalist, 17
 drugs, 22–23
 emergence, 17–18
 and free love, 69–71
 decline, 26–29
 legacy, 29–31
 mainstream response, 21–29
 origin of term, 12–13
 social problems, 25
 in USA, 11–13
 See also drugs; music; sexual revolution; Vancouver Free University
hitchhiking, *24*, 64
Hoffman, Abbie, 4, 108–112
Hofmann, Albert, 82
Hollywood Hospital, 82
Holmes, Rand, 94, 134
Hook, Frank, 67
Horizon Book Store, 24
Hubbard, Al, 87
Human Be-In, 11, *13*, 18, 20, 21, 26, 29, *90*, *95*, *109*, 113

Hunter, Bob, 23, 165, 172
Huxley, Aldous, 83

International Café, 14

Jefferson Airplane, 80, 84, 98, 101
Joy of Sex, The, 52
Joplin, Janis, 86, 96

Kerouac, Jack, 12
Kesey, Ken, 83, 84
Kidd, Harold, 23, 26
Kinsey, Alfred, 61
Kitsilano, 3, 6, 14, *15*, 19, 22
Krebs, Alan, 37

Latremouille, Fred, 95, *98*
Leary, Timothy, 83, 91, 92
Led Zeppelin, *102*
Le Dain Commission, 121
Lester, Ken, 122, 131, 179n31
Linnell, Marianne, 25
longhairs. *See* hippies
LSD, 16, 18, 19, 21, 22
   CIA experiments, 82–83
   deaths, 93
   history, 82
   for treatment, 87
   in psychedelic era, 91–94, 100

marijuana, 19, 23, 82, 88, 91–92
Masse, Bob, 20, 32, 97, 99, 103–104
Mattiussi, Roger, 44
materialism, 54
McLeod, Dan, 17, *28*, 70, 91, *94*
Miller, Henry, 51, *54*
Mulligan, Terry David, 97, 98
Munro, Alice, 13
music, *19*, 20, *58*, 84, 95–100
   See also Beatles, the; CFUN; CKVN; Grateful Dead; Hendrix, Jimi; Jefferson Airplane; Robinson, Red

Naam, The, 6, 20
Narcotics Addiction Foundation, 93, 100
Narcotics Contol Act, 122
Native rights, 8, 170, 171–72
NDP. *See* New Democratic Party
New Democratic Party)
   and All-Seasons Park, 127
   and anti-war movement, 145–46, 150, 153, 154, 163
   appeal to baby boomers, 60, 115, 181n36
   in government, 47, 115, 163
   and education, 47, 49
   and sexual revolution, 60, 61
   and Yippies, 118

nightclubs, 5, 64–66, 67–69
Nixon, Richard, 112, 113, 114, *135*, 140, 157, 164.
   See also Amchitka nuclear test; anti-war activism; Vietnam War

Oil Can Harry's, *65*
   See also nightclubs
One Flew Over the Cuckoo's Nest, 83
"Operation Dustpan", 121
Owram, Doug, 53

Pacific Tribune, 14, 90, 141, 144
peace movement in Vancouver. *See* anti-war activism
peaceniks, 136, 187n3
Peak, The, 40
Pender Auditorium, 98
Penthouse, The (club), 67
Phase 4 Coffee House, 24
Philliponi, Joe, 67
Phillips, Art, 123, 129, 158
Playboy, 44, 55, 57, 59
lifestyle, 55, 64–65, 69, 74
pornography, 61
Presley, Elvis, 80, 88
prostitution, 58, 67
Province, The, 23, 94, 152, 161
psychedelic era. *See* music, drugs
psychedelic music. *See* music
Psychedelic Shop, 24

Rags and Riches (shop), 24
Rankin, Harry, 6, *16*, 17, 25, 26, 30, 94, 127, 130, 153
Rathie, Bill, 129
Reich, Wilhelm, 45
Retinal Circus, 5, 99, 101, 112
Revolution for the Hell of It, 117
Robinson, Red, 88, 96, 97
Robson Street, 4, 14
Rochdale College, 39
rock music. *See* music
Rolling Stones, 86, *101*, 103
Ross, Becki, 68
Rubin, Jerry, 110, 113, *114*,120

San Francisco. *See* Haight–Ashbury; hippies; Trips Festival
SANE. *See* Committee for Sane Nuclear Policy
Sex and the Single Girl, 55
sexual revolution, 51–53, 57–60, 71–72, 74–76, 169
   academic view of, 53, 54, 57, 74, 76
   and beatniks, 12, 57
   and censorship, 51, 59–61

and commoditization of sex, 54–55, 57, 64, 70–72
effect on the family, 167–68
female, 55, 57, 64, 66–68, 73, 75
and gay sex, 57, 72–73, 76
and hippies, 20–21, 29, 57, 69–72, 75
male, 21, 64–65, 69, 71, 73–74, 75
pre-revolution, 57
and prostitution, 58, 67–68
and rock music, 86, 89–90
on UBC campus, 61–64, 74
in USA 53–57, 74
and Vancouver Free University, 43–45
See also birth control; feminism; nightclubs; *Playboy*; sexually transmitted diseases; Ultra Love
sexually transmitted diseases, 58–59, 76
Shanghai Junk (club), 68
Shayne, J.B., 97, *98*
Smith, Adam, 41
Smith, Robert, 91–92
Smith, Robin, 64
Spring Mobilization Committee. *See* Vancouver Vietnam Day Committee
street theatre, 108–111
See also Diggers; Yippies
strip clubs. *See* nightclubs
Students for a Democratic Society, 138, 139
"Summer of Love", 1967, 4, *10*, 96
surrealpolitik. *See* street theatre
Suzuki, David, 88
Sweeney, Edward, 25

Tanner, "Long John", 3, *4*, 96, 97, *168*
Thomas, Hilda, 154, 156
Tiny Tots Together, *42*, 45–48, *48*
Trips Festival, 79–80, 84, 92, 95
Tropic of Cancer, 51, *54*, 63
Trower, Peter, 91
Trudeau, Pierre, *47*, 57, 135, 154, *156*, 163, 164

UBC. *See* University of British Columbia
UBC Faculty Club, 113
UBCNDC. *See* University of British Columbia Nuclear Disarmament Club
Ubyssey, The
  Amchitka tests, 159
  drugs, 100
  sex, 63, 66
  Yippies, 114
Ultra Love (shop), 5, *71*, 71–74
United States
  anti–war activism, 136–141
  drugs, 80–86
  free university, 34–38
  hippies, 11–13
  music, 84–85

sex, 53–57
Yippies, 108–112
University of British Columbia
  anti-war activism, 142
  drugs, 91–92, 93, 100, 104
  free university, 40, 48
  hippies, 31
  music, 98
  sex, 52, *60*, 61–64, 74
  Yippies, 112–14, 120, 142–44, 144–51, 156, 160
  See also Ubyssey, The
University of British Columbia Nuclear Disarmament Club, 142

Vancouver
  anti-war activism, 141–65
  drugs, 86–88, 91–94
  free university, 39–49
  hippies, 15–21
  music, 95–103, 88–90
  sex, 57–76
  Yippies, 112–32
Vancouver East Cultural Centre, 5, *35*
Vancouver Free University, 6, *32*, 33–34, 39–46
  enrolment, *36*, *38*, 41, *45*, 48
  location, 6, 34, 35, 40, 46
  vision, 34
  origins, 39–41
  See also free universities (USA); Tiny Tots Together
Vancouver Inner City Service Project, 39
Vancouver Liberation Front, 108, 117, 185n5
Vancouver Police Department, 22, *117*, 125
Vancouver Sun, 23, 44, 94, 152, 170
Vancouver Vietnam Day Committee, 145, 152, 153, 156, 158, 163
vegetarianism, 20, 31
VFU. *See* Vancouver Free University
Victory Square, *137*
Vietnam Action Committee, 145, *147*
  See also Vancouver Vietnam Day Committee; Vietnam War
Vietnam War, 138–41, *143*, 144–51
Vogel, Hank, *155*, 158
VPD. *See* Vancouver Police Department
VVDC. *See* Vancouver Vietnam Day Committee

Watson, Neil, 71, 72
Willmott, William, 144, 146
West 4th Avenue, 3, 6, 18, 19, 20, 21, 24, 30, 94, 98, 104, 132, 176n32
Wilson, Halford, 157
Woodstock Nation, *110*
Woodward's redevelopment, 131–32
Wreck Beach, 21, 70, 75

Index

Yellow Journal, The, 38, 40, 116, 130–131
Yellow Submarine (shop), *90*
Yippies, 8, 29, 112–130
    and activism, 114–20, *148*
    characteristics, 120
    comparison to other movements, 112, 185n5
    goals, 107
    origins, 108
    personalities, 122
    strategies, 116
    in USA, 108–112, 131
    See also Four Seasons Park occupation; Gastown Riot; Rubin, Jerry; *The Yellow Journal*
Youth International Party. *See* Yippies.
Zanzibar (club), 68